MIKE MEYERS' CERTIFICATION
Passport ⋆

MCSE Windows® 2000
Network Infrastructure Administration

EXAM
70-216

RORY McCaw

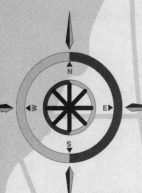

 OSBORNE

New York • Chicago • San Francisco
Lisbon • London • Madrid • Mexico City
Milan • New Delhi • San Juan
Seoul • Singapore • Sydney • Toronto

McGraw-Hill/Osborne
2600 Tenth Street
Berkeley, California 94710
U.S.A.

To arrange bulk purchase discounts for sales promotions, premiums, or fund-raisers, please contact McGraw-Hill/Osborne at the above address. For information on translations or book distributors outside the U.S.A., please see the International Contact Information page immediately following the index of this book.

Mike Meyers' MCSE Windows 2000 Network Infrastructure Administration Certification Passport

1 2 3 4 5 6 7 8 9 0 DOC DOC 0 1 9 8 7 6 5 4 3 2 1

Book p/n 0-07-219591-6 and CD p/n 0-07-219590-8
parts of
ISBN 0-07-219568-1

Publisher	**Acquisitions Coordinator**	**Indexer**
Brandon A. Nordin	Jessica Wilson	Irv Hershman
Vice President & Associate Publisher	**Technical Editor**	**Design and Production**
Scott Rogers	Mike Lagase	epic
	Copy Editors	**Illustrators**
Acquisitions Editor	Bart Reed, Carl Wikander	Michael Mueller, Lyssa
Nancy Maragioglio		Sieben-Wald
	Proofreader	
Project Editor	Carroll Proffitt	**Cover Series Design**
Katie Conley		Ted Holladay

This book was composed with QuarkXPress™.

About the Author

Rory McCaw is an independent certified technical trainer with more than five years of experience in information technology and the author of numerous technical books. Rory's interest in writing led him to courseware development where he has designed courses focused on different Microsoft technologies. Rory holds numerous designations, including the MCSE, MCT, and CTT. An experienced speaker, Rory developed and delivered presentations for Microsoft at Comdex and designs custom courses to meet the needs of his growing list of corporate clients.

For the last three years, Rory has been providing technical instruction to IT professionals and consulting for large organizations on enterprise implementations of IIS and active directory. Prior to training, Rory filled the role of systems administrator for an Internet startup after graduating from University with a B.A. in Business Administration and a major in Management Information Systems.

Rory's excellent student evaluations speak for themselves about the quality of training that he provides.

"No improvement required! Excellent presentation intermixed with candid moments. Set atmosphere comfortably!"
—*Chris Andrews, Oracle Instructor*

"The instructor was very good and I would change nothing about his technique. His ability to teach and get his point across is excellent. I would recommend him to all my co-workers."
—*Chuck Johnson, Silicon Graphics*

"Rory was excellent, very knowledgeable, and a great teacher!"
—*Patrick Cheung, Ministry of the Environment*

"I just wanted to say that I thoroughly enjoyed myself at the course last week, largely due to the quality of the instruction. I must tell you that Rory McCaw is one of the best instructors I have EVER had the pleasure to learn from. I tried to emphasize that on the course-end questionnaire but I don't think that it was enough. Quality of instruction is tantamount to success in our field, and to find someone who can not only deliver the knowledge but to do it with flair, wisdom, and without arrogance is something I've not seen for a long time."
—*Michael Jeggo, EDS Innovations*

About the Tech Editor

Mike Lagase is currently a support engineer working at Microsoft supporting their web server products and related technologies. He has been in the IT business for approximately ten years and has strong experience in the network infrastructure and implementation of large heterogeneous networks. Prior to Microsoft, he had implemented a worldwide messaging system that was converted over from a cc:Mail environment to a complete Microsoft Exchange solution using VPN, RAS, and ISDN on Windows NT technology. His passion for technology stems from his desire to understand the intricacies of how everything is put together and how to overcome almost any obstacle. Mike has a family of three, including his wife Jackie and their two daughters Olivia and Sayer.

Dedication

I would like to dedicate this book to all of the families that have lost both friends and family members in the World Trade Center and Pentagon tragedies on September 11, 2001. Family and friends are there in good times and bad. This tragic event caused people all around the world to remember just how fragile human life is. My heart goes out to all the people affected by this horrific event.

God bless freedom, democracy, and the sanctity of human life around the world!

Acknowledgments

I would like to thank a number of people responsible for the success of this project. First, thanks must go to Nancy Maragioglio, Senior Acquisitions Editor at Osborne, who is an absolute joy to work with. Your friendly and sincere way and funny jokes in those crunch times and late nights spent writing to meet the tight deadlines are very much appreciated. I would also like to thank all of the other folks at McGraw-Hill/Osborne, who are often behind the scenes, from my perspective, like Gareth Hanock and Jessica Wilson and all the others whose contributions made this book possible. A special thanks also to Mike Meyers, for without Mike's insight and success, this series may not have materialized. I hope the fish are biting for you these "nights" Mike!

I would also like to thank my wife Dina who is wonderful and so very supportive of my interest in writing—even when it means "our" weekends and nights are consumed. The writing of this book really helped to show Dina's supportive nature as our honeymoon fell in the middle of the production schedule, making the meeting of deadlines that much more difficult. Dina, you mean the world to me and every book that I write should really list you as a co-author because it is your support and loving glances that get me back on track when writers block sets in.

Lastly, I would like to thank the many people I call students, with whom I have had the opportunity to share my knowledge of Microsoft products. Often it is your thought provoking questions and interest in learning that provide me with inspiration.

Contents

II Windows 2000 PKI and IPSec
Network Infrastructure

4 Certificate Services and
Public Key Infrastructure

Check-In

May I See Your Passport?

What do you mean you don't have a passport? Why, it's sitting right in your hands, even as you read! This book is your passport to a very special place. You're about to begin a journey, my friend, a journey towards that magical place called CERTI-FICATION! You don't need a ticket, you don't need a suitcase—just snuggle up and read this passport—it's all you need to get there. Are you ready? Let's Go!

Your Travel Agent—Mike Meyers

Hello! My name's Mike Meyers. I've written a number of popular certification books and I'm the President of Total Seminars, LLC. On any given day, you'll find me replacing a hard drive, setting up a Web site, or writing code. I love every aspect of this book you hold in your hands. It's part of a powerful new book series called the *Mike Meyers' Certification Passports*. Every book in this series combines easy readability with a condensed format. In other words, the kind of book I always wanted when I went for my certifications. Putting this much information in an accessible format is an enormous challenge, but I think we have achieved our goal and I am confident you'll agree.

I designed this series to do one thing and only one thing—to get you the only information you need to achieve your certification. You won't find any fluff in here—the author Rory McCaw packed every page with nothing but the real nitty gritty of the certification exam. Every page is packed with 100% pure concentrate of certification knowledge! But we didn't forget to make the book readable. I hope you enjoy the casual, friendly style—I want you to feel as though the author is speaking to you, discussing the certification, not just spewing facts at you.

My personal e-mail address is mikem@totalsem.com and Rory McCaw's personal e-mail address is rorym@istar.ca. Please feel free to contact either of us directly if you have any questions, complaints, or compliments.

Your Destination—Implementing and Administering a Microsoft Windows 2000 Network Infrastructure

This book is your passport to the Implementing and Administering a Microsoft Windows 2000 Network Infrastructure exam (70-216), which is one of the four core Windows 2000 MCSE exams required in your pursuit of the coveted Microsoft Windows 2000 MCSE certification. The Network Infrastructure exam tests your skills and knowledge of some of the most complex network infrastructure issues involved in the implementation and administration of a Windows 2000 Network. You'll learn about networking services like DHCP, DNS, and WINS. Then we'll turn our attention to security components like certificate services, PKI, and IPSec. Lastly, we'll visit the remote-access infrastructure implemented through the Routing and Remote Access Server service, including IP routing and Internet sharing features like Internet Connection Sharing and Network Address Translation, just to name a few of the major points. The Implementing and Administering a Windows 2000 Network Infrastructure exam is generally said to be the toughest of the four Windows 2000 MCSE core exams, but with your passport, you'll be well prepared for this exam and can let it act as a stepping stone to your certification.

The Windows NT 4.0 MCSE certification has enjoyed tremendous industry support, but the Windows 2000/XP MCSE certification will without a doubt be an even more sought after certification.

Your Guide—Rory McCaw

Look out folks! Your guide, the author of this book, is none other than Mr. Rory McCaw. If by some chance you don't know Rory or haven't had the opportunity to hear him speak, let me tell you—Rory is the author of multiple titles on the topic of Windows 2000 and is a sought after Microsoft Certified Trainer. You may have seen and heard Rory speak at Comdex, where he developed and presented seminars on the features of Windows 2000 for Microsoft. When not writing or speaking, Rory's hard at work teaching Microsoft curriculum throughout North America at a number of Certified Technical Education Centers (CTECs). Rory operates his own consulting company out of the Toronto area, and in his personal time can be found gracefully carving turns on ski slopes throughout the world. Whether speaking in front of a group or writing a book, Rory's presentation style glows with personality. You'll feel his infectious enjoyment of Windows 2000 and appreciate his marvelous ability to explain technical concepts in laymen's terms. Get ready for nothing less than a literary breath of fresh air!

Why the Travel Theme?

One of my favorite topics is the parallel of gaining a certification to taking a trip. All of the elements are the same: preparation, an itinerary, a route—even mishaps along the way. Let me show you how it all works.

This book is divided into eight chapters. Each chapter begins with an itinerary, which provides objectives covered in each chapter and an ETA to give you an idea of the time involved in learning the skills in that chapter. Each chapter is broken down by real exam objectives—either those officially stated by the certifying body or, if the vendor doesn't provide these, our expert take on the best way to approach the topics. Also, each chapter contains a number of helpful items to bring out points of interest:

Exam Tip

Points out critical topics you're likely to see on the actual exam.

Travel Assistance

Provides you with additional sources, such as books and Web sites to give you more information.

Local Lingo

Describes special terms in detail in a way you can easily understand.

Travel Advisory

Warns you of common pitfalls, misconceptions, and downright physical peril!

The end of the chapter gives you two handy tools. The Checkpoint reviews each objective covered in the chapter with a synopsis—a great way to quickly review. Plus, you'll find end-of-chapter questions to test your newly acquired skills.

But the fun doesn't stop there! After you've read the book, pull out the CD and take advantage of the free practice questions! Use the full practice exam to hone your skills and keep the book handy to check answers.

If you want even more practice, log on to www.Osborne.com/Passport where, for a nominal fee, you'll get additional high-quality practice questions.

When you're passing the practice questions, you're ready to take the exam—go get certified!

The End of the Trail

The IT industry changes and grows constantly—and so should you. Finishing one certification is just a step in the ongoing process of gaining more and more certifications to match your constantly changing and growing skills. Read the Career Flight Path at the end of the book to see where this certification fits into your personal certification goals. Remember, in the IT business, if you're not moving forward, you are way behind!

Good luck on your certification! Stay in touch!

Mike Meyers
Series Editor
Mike Meyers' Certification Passport

PART

I

Windows 2000
Network Services

DHCP
Network
Infrastructure

	NEWBIE	SOME EXPERIENCE	EXPERT
ETA	7–10 hours	3–7 hours	1–3 hours

3

Your journey of studying for and passing the Implementing and Administering a Windows 2000 Network Infrastructure exam (70-216) begins with the network services in Windows 2000, including Dynamic Host Configuration Protocol (DHCP), Domain Name System (DNS), and Windows Internet Naming Service (WINS). In order to pass the exam, Microsoft expects you to have a good understanding of the roles that each of these services play in a network, to be familiar with their new features, to know how to configure and maintain them, and to troubleshoot their common problems. If you are not comfortable with basic concepts for one or more of these network services, you should probably start your exam preparation by setting up a computer with Windows 2000 Server and installing each of these three network services to gain the hands-on experience that is necessary to pass any of the core Windows 2000 MCSE exams.

Objective 1.01

Install, Configure, and Troubleshoot DHCP

Dynamic Host Configuration Protocol, more commonly referred to as DHCP, is the first network service that we will explore. DHCP plays a significant role in most networks, automatically assigning Internet Protocol (IP) addresses, as well as other critical IP configuration settings, to client computers from a system running the DHCP server service. Before we jump into the installation, configuration, and troubleshooting of the DHCP service, it's important that you understand the basics of DHCP.

DHCP Basics

Computers are configured with an IP address and other configuration settings in one of two ways: statically or dynamically. Static configuration requires that an administrator manually configure the IP address and additional configuration settings. This chapter's focus is on the dynamic assignment of IP addresses via the DHCP service. The client's Internet Protocol settings determine whether or not it is statically or dynamically configured. Choosing the Obtain An IP Address Automatically setting, shown in the Internet Protocol (TCP/IP) properties dialog box in Figure 1-1, configures the client to obtain an IP address automatically.

Unlike static configurations, which never change (unless they are changed manually), dynamically assigned information can change from time to time with no ill effect to the computer.

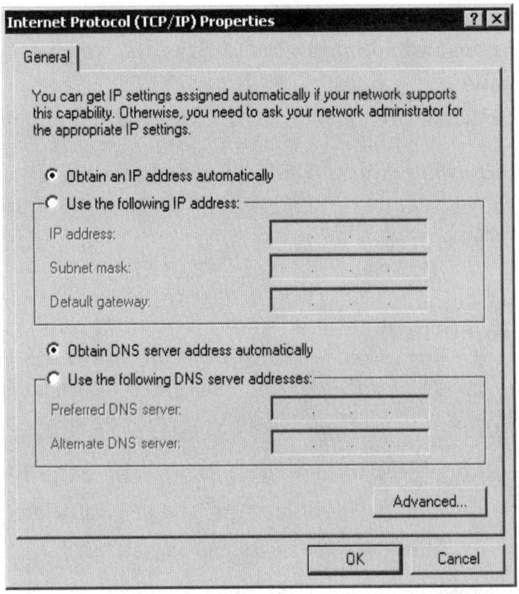

Internet Protocol (TCP/IP) Properties   ? ☒

General |

You can get IP settings assigned automatically if your network supports
this capability. Otherwise, you need to ask your network administrator for
the appropriate IP settings.

◉ Obtain an IP address automatically

○ Use the following IP address:

IP address:

Subnet mask:

Default gateway:

◉ Obtain DNS server address automatically

○ Use the following DNS server addresses:

Preferred DNS server:

Alternate DNS server:

Advanced...

OK   Cancel

FIGURE 1-1   Client DHCP configuration

Static or manual configuration requires a great deal of administrative effort
and has significant drawbacks in larger networks. First and foremost, you will have
to configure each computer on your network with a static IP address, a subnet,
and gateway information. Can you imagine the time required to do this? With
hundreds or thousands of computers on a network, it would be a full-time job!
Not to mention that, if your typing is anything like mine, typos in this information would lead to network problems, disgruntled users, and more headaches.
There are, however, good reasons to use static or manual configuration on some
computers on your network. Static configurations are ideal for computers whose
IP addresses you never want to change. Servers running network services such as
DHCP, DNS, and WINS are the types of computers that not only require static IP
addresses but also benefit by having an IP address that never changes (without
human intervention).

The dynamic assignment of IP addresses via the DHCP service has a number
of benefits. Reductions in the amount of administration are achieved by

- Drastically reducing the amount of time required to assign IP address
  and configuration information
- Reducing the number of typos, which also reduces the amount of time
  spent troubleshooting network connectivity problems

- Simplifying the distribution of additional configuration information
- Reducing ongoing administration such as the changing of IP address configurations
- Reducing the time required to make future configuration changes

As you can see, using a mix of DHCP-assigned and static IP addresses is definitely the way to go! Now that you are sold on the benefits of using DHCP, let's take a look at the lease process.

Travel Assistance

For more information on the DHCP service, there are a number of resources available. For a fairly dry read, reference RFCs 2131 and 2132 found at http://rfc.net. Microsoft also has a white paper on DHCP titled "Dynamic Host Configuration Protocol for Windows 2000 Server (dhcp.doc)." This can be found at http://www.microsoft.com/windows2000/techinfo/howitworks/communications/nameadrmgmt/dhcp.asp.

The DHCP service in Windows 2000 has been enhanced dramatically from its implementation in Windows NT 4.0. The DHCP service in Windows 2000 can be integrated with DNS to act as a DNS proxy and update DNS information on behalf of computers running down-level Windows operating systems. DHCP is also tightly integrated with the Routing and Remote Access Service (RRAS) and can be used to lease out IP addresses to remote access clients. This RRAS integration can also be seen in the configuration of DHCP relay agents, which is also incorporated into RRAS.

On the client side, a new default feature known as Automatic Private IP Addressing (APIPA) enables DHCP clients to automatically configure themselves with an IP address on the 169.254.0.0 network if they are unable to find a DHCP server during the lease process. APIPA then continues to broadcast for a valid DHCP-leased IP address every five minutes on behalf of the client.

DHCP Lease Process

In order for a computer configured as a DHCP client to obtain an IP address from a DHCP server, the client must initiate the IP address lease process. The DHCP lease process is very similar to the lease process that you would initiate to lease an apartment. The DHCP lease process, in its simplest form, is a four-step process, as displayed in the next illustration and described in the text that follows.

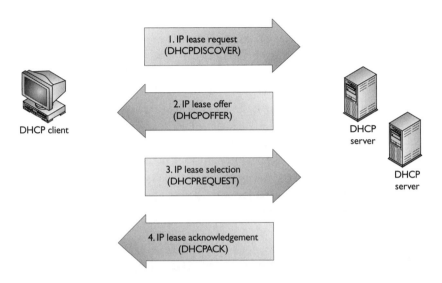

1. **IP lease request (DHCPDISCOVER)**   This step is similar to the first step a person takes when he is hunting for an apartment: the potential lessee identifies available apartments and calls to inquire about availability. In the case of the DHCP client, the computer looking for an IP address broadcasts out a request known as a DHCPDISCOVER message. The intent of this message is to discover a DHCP server with an available IP address. The potential lessee in this case is the DHCP client, and it is the DHCP client service that broadcasts out the DHCPDISCOVER message. As this communication is a broadcast, its distribution is limited to its own subnet.

2. **IP lease offer (DHCPOFFER)**   The second step in the "apartment hunting process" occurs on the DHCP server(s). All DHCP servers that receive the call from the prospective lessee—or in DHCP terms, receive the DHCPDIS-COVER message—and that have an available IP address to lease out will respond via broadcast to the IP lease request with an IP lease offer.

3. **IP lease selection (DHCPREQUEST)**   Unlike the apartment hunting process, where multiple offers can be compared before accepting the one that best suits you, the first DHCPOFFER message received by the requesting client computer is accepted, leading to the third step, known as the IP lease selection or DHCPREQUEST message. The DHCP client broadcasts its DHCPREQUEST, which is a message that serves two primary functions: First,

all other DHCP servers that made an offer withdraw their offers to make those IP addresses available to other clients requesting an IP. Second, the DHCP server whose offer was accepted gathers and prepares to send the last of the messages to confirm the IP lease. This last communication sent from the DHCP server to the client is known as the IP lease acknowledgement.

4. **IP lease acknowledgement (DHCPACK)**   The fourth and last step in the apartment hunting process is getting confirmation from the landlord that your references checked out and that you have been accepted. At that point the landlord informs you of the lease start and end dates and other important information. In the DHCP lease process, the IP lease acknowledgement (DHCPACK) is a broadcast that the DHCP server sends to the requesting computer to acknowledge the successful lease of the IP. The DHCPACK message contains the IP address being leased and all other configuration information, such as DNS server locations, gateways or router addresses, WINS server locations, and more.

DHCP Lease Renewal Process

Once a computer has received an IP address through the DHCP lease process described above, it must be renewed from time to time much like a real estate lease. If you don't renew your real estate lease, you could get evicted. In the context of computers, eviction is equated with the loss of your IP address, and without an IP address, the computer will no longer be able to communicate on the network with other computers. The length of time after which the lease must be renewed is one of the many DHCP properties that you, the administrator, are able to configure.

The configuration of the lease renewal period is something that you determine based on the number of available IP addresses and the number of computers requesting IP addresses.

| **Travel Assistance** |
| Keep the lease time shorter when the number of computers requiring IP addresses is close to the amount of available IP addresses. |

Automatic Lease Renewal

Like a real estate lease of an apartment, an IP lease is set for a specific period of time, and during this time the computer that receives the IP address is the exclusive owner of that IP address, even if the computer is not physically connected to the network or powered on during a portion of the lease period. Think of it as if you were to lease an apartment for a year and go away for a month of vacation: the apartment is still yours during the month that you are away. The same is true for the leased IP. The computer's IP lease remains for the original length of the lease.

The DHCP service is configured to automatically renew its lease at various intervals, starting at 50 percent of the original lease time. At 50 percent of the original IP address lease period, the computer's DHCP client service tries to renew its lease with the DHCP server that originally leased the IP. If this effort fails, the computer tries again at regular intervals until it is successful or until its lease expires.

Manual Lease Renewal

The Windows 2000 DHCP client service also supports the ability to manually release or renew a DHCP lease. To release a DHCP lease at the client, type the following command from the command prompt:

```
Ipconfig /release
```

Once a DHCP lease is released, that client will not have any IP information until it renews the DHCP lease. To renew a DHCP lease at the client computer, type the following command from a command prompt:

```
Ipconfig /renew
```

Most techs find that the IPCONFIG /RENEW option is more useful than the IPCONFIG /RELEASE—but you will need to know both of these for the test!

Exam Tip

Be familiar with the ipconfig command and switches for the exam. For more information on all of the switches, type **ipconfig /?** at the command prompt.

APIPA Assignment

Back in the days of Windows NT, a DHCP client that couldn't find a DHCP server was, well, not going to be on the network. One of the new default features of the

Windows 2000 DHCP client service is APIPA. Should a Windows 2000 DHCP client computer not receive an IP address from a DHCP server or not be able to renew its existing IP address, it will, by default, automatically configure itself with an IP address on the 169.254.0.0/16 network. Unfortunately, unless the other network clients are configured with an IP address on the same network, the DHCP client will not be able to communicate on the network. Knowing this, the DHCP client server continues to broadcast for an available DHCP server at five-minute intervals. Microsoft's idea behind automatic private IP addressing was to give a DHCP client a chance to be on the network even if a DHCP server wasn't available. In reality, this rarely works, but it does have a big benefit: it's a darn easy way to see if your DHCP client is accessing a DHCP server. Just check the IP address using the ipconfig command!

APIPA is a great feature for small, non-routed networks in which users don't want to bother with IP address configuration. There is no graphical user interface (GUI) administration tool, however, that allows you to disable APIPA; it must be disabled by following the steps shown next and editing the registry with one of the available registry editing tools, such as Regedit or Regedt32.

1. From the Start menu, select Run, type **regedt32** and click OK.
2. In Regedt32, select the HKLM window.
3. Browse to the key HKLM\System\CurrentControlSet\Services\Tcpip\Parameters\Interfaces\AdapterGUID.
4. Change the value IPAutoConfigurationEnabled to REG_DWORD data type with a data value of 0, where, for each network adapter installed on the computer for which you wish to disable APIPA, AdapterGUID is the globally unique identifier (GUID).

Exam Tip

When troubleshooting DHCP problems at the client, if the ipconfig /all command returns an IP address on the 169.254.0.0/16 network, check to ensure that the DHCP server is online and has available IP addresses. Also check that other clients are able to connect with the DHCP server and lease an IP. The automatically assigned IP address on the 169.254.0.0/16 network will not give the client computer any network connectivity unless other computers are on the same subnet.

Now that we have a solid understanding of the DHCP service basics, we are ready to continue our journey with a look at the requirements for installation and how to install the DHCP service on a computer running Windows 2000 Server.

Install the DHCP Server Service

The DHCP service, like all other services, is installed through the Add/Remove Windows Components section of the Add/Remove Programs in the Control Panel. The DHCP service can be installed and configured on both a Windows 2000 member server or a domain controller. To install the DHCP service, you must be a member of the local administrator's group. One of the nice improvements that you will notice after installing the DHCP service is that Windows 2000 does not require a reboot, unlike its earlier counterpart (Windows NT).

The requirements for installing and configuring the DHCP server service on a computer running Windows 2000 Server or Advanced Server are a computer configured with a static IP address, a subnet mask, and an optional default gateway address.

Exam Tip

The computer on which you are installing the DHCP service must be configured with a static IP address and subnet mask.

The only client-side configuration required is to configure each client to automatically obtain an IP address from a DHCP server. In order to configure a client with this setting, the operating system on the client computer must support the DHCP service. The following clients all support the DHCP service:

- Windows 2000 Server, Advanced Server, and Professional
- Windows NT Server or Workstation 3.51 or later
- Windows 95, 98, ME
- Windows 3.11 running TCP/IP 32
- MS-DOS with Microsoft Network Client 3.0
- LAN Manager 2.2c
- Numerous non-Microsoft operating systems

Objective 1.03

Create and Manage DHCP Scopes, Super Scopes, and Multicast Scopes

A DHCP scope is a range of valid IP addresses and related configuration settings that the DHCP server can use to issue IP address leases to DHCP clients. To go back to the real estate analogy, a DHCP scope is similar to the listing of apartments available for lease. Once the DHCP service is installed and, if required, authorized within the active directory domain, the next steps are to configure the scopes, super scopes, and multicast scopes; activate them; and set client reservations. Each scope on a DHCP server represents all or part of the available IP addresses on a single segment.

Exam Tip

A scope can include only a single subnet.

Creating Scopes

Exam Tip

A minimum of one scope must exist and be activated in order to lease out IP addresses.

To create a new scope, right-click the name of the DHCP server and select New Scope from the context menu. (In Figure 1-4, the name of the server on which you would right-click is lexus.mcsejobs.net.) Doing this will launch the New Scope Wizard, which will walk you through the configuration process. The information that you supply when creating the new scope will determine the properties of the scope. This information includes the following:

- Name of the scope
- Starting and ending IP address
- Any exclusion ranges within the starting and ending IP address range
- The lease duration

Travel Assistance

The Netsh command is a command line tool that can be used to configure and administer the DHCP service. Search for "Use DHCP Command-line Tools" in Windows 2000 Help for more information.

Scope Options

Scope options enable you to configure properties that the client will receive with the lease of their IP address. Examples of scope options are the addresses of DNS or WINS servers and addresses of routers. There are numerous scope options available for configuration. Scope options are configured by expanding the scope, right-clicking Scope Options, and selecting Configure Options. There are two tabs—General and Advanced—in the Scope Options dialog box, as shown in Figure 1-2. The General tab enables you to select and configure options such as router or gateway addresses and DNS and WINS server addresses, and it allows

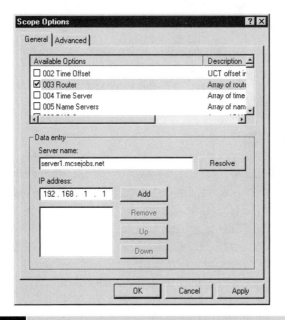

FIGURE 1-2   Configuring the router scope option

you to set the WINS server node type. The advantage of configuring the different scope options is that the information you select and configure will be supplied to all DHCP clients with their IP address lease. By configuring DHCP to provide this type of information, you simplify administration and reduce the likelihood of errors generated from incorrect information manually entered on each client.

In the Advanced tab of the Scope Options dialog box, two additional options known as *option classes* exist, both of which are new to Windows 2000. The two option classes are the Vendor and User classes. Option classes can be used to provide unique configuration settings to specific types of clients.

Vendor-defined classes identify the operating system vendor of the DHCP client. This class option enables you to configure vendor-defined options that are assigned to clients based on their operating system. For example, if your network has a number of computers running Windows 98, the Windows 98 vendor class option can be selected and configured with the option to release the client's IP address on shut down. This vendor class option would then apply to all DHCP client computers running Windows 98 on the network.

User-defined classes identify DHCP clients by their types. Supported client types include

- The Boot Protocol (BOOTP) class
- The RRAS class
- The default-user class

The BOOTP class can be used to assign common configuration options to diskless workstations such as Net PCs. The user-defined RRAS class enables you to assign common configuration options to computers that are accessing your network remotely through an RRAS server.

Exam Tip

TCP/IP properties configured on the client computer always take precedence over any information provided by a DHCP server. Server options apply to all DHCP clients, and scope options only apply to DHCP clients that have leased an IP address from that specific scope.

Scope options can be defined at three different levels:

- Server level
- Scope level
- Class level

Scope options defined at the server level apply to all scope options defined on that server. Defining scope options at the server level simplifies administration by enabling you to configure and maintain the options in only a single location. The scope options defined at the server level are inherited by all scopes on that server and will apply to all scopes unless options defined at the scope or class level differ. The scope options are applied in the order shown in the above list, starting with the server level options, but if there are any conflicts between settings at different levels, the scope options applied last always take precedence.

Scope options defined at the scope level only apply to that single scope. Scope options applied to a specific user-defined or vendor-defined class only apply to clients within that class. An example of this might be a vender-defined class for computers running Windows 98 that are configured to release their IP address on shutdown. This scope option defined in the Windows 98 vendor class would apply only to computers running Windows 98 that have obtained their IP address from the scope in which the vendor-defined option is configured.

Client Reservations

A scope can be configured with DHCP client reservations so that the DHCP server will always provide the same IP address to a particular client. This is configured by expanding the scope, right-clicking Reservations, and selecting New Reservation. The information required when creating a new reservation can be seen in Figure 1-3 and includes the name client's computer's name as the Reservation Name, the IP Address you wish to reserve, the client's Media Access

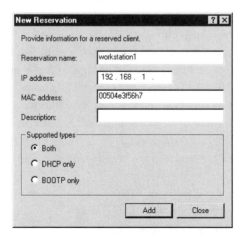

FIGURE 1-3   Configuring a DHCP client reservation

Control (MAC) Address, and an optional Description. It is the MAC address of the network adapter that is used to identify the requesting client and ensure that the client receives the reserved IP address.

Finding the MAC address for a client can be accomplished a number of ways. One way to get the MAC address of a remote client computer is to install the Windows 2000 Resource Kit on your computer and use the Getmac utility. An easier way, however, that does not require the Windows 2000 Resource Kit is to use the command line utilities included with the Windows 2000 operating system. The following steps walk you through using the included tools to identify and resolve the MAC address.

1. Open a Command Prompt by clicking Start, Run, typing **cmd**, and clicking OK.
2. At the Command Prompt, *ping* the name or IP address of the computer for which you wish to identify the MAC address (for example, **ping 192.168.1.1**).
3. At the Command Prompt, type the command **arp–a**. In the resulting list, note the Physical Address (MAC) next to the IP address of the remote client computer.

Activating Scopes

Once you have created the scope and configured its options, it must be activated in order to lease out IP addresses. Activating the scope can be done via the New Scope Wizard or manually by right-clicking the new scope and selecting Activate. You will notice that when a scope is not activated, it appears similar to an unauthorized DHCP server, with a red arrow next to it pointing down. When the scope is activated (again appearing similar to an authorized DHCP server), the arrow turns green and points upward indicating that it is activated.

In order to activate a scope, you must be logged on as a member of either the Administrators, DHCP Admins, or Server Operators groups to have the required permissions. Only members of the Enterprise Admins group are permitted to authorize the DHCP server.

Exam Tip	
DHCP scopes must be activated, and DHCP servers in an active directory domain must be authorized.	

Super Scopes

A super scope is a group of two or more scopes that can be manually combined to enable you to administer multiple scopes as a single unit. Super scopes enable you to accomplish the following:

- Add additional hosts
- Replace existing address ranges with new address ranges without affecting the DHCP service for the client's computer
- Combine IP addresses in noncontiguous ranges into a single scope

Multicast Scopes

Multicasting is primarily used for audio and video conferencing. Multicasting enables a single packet of TCP/IP data to be broadcast to a group of computers at the same time, reducing the amount of traffic on the network.

Multicast scopes can be configured on the DHCP server to enable client applications, such as video conferencing, to take advantage of them. Multicast IP addresses must fall within the range of valid multicast addresses 224.0.0.0 to 239.255.255.255.

A client application's requests for a multicast address does not affect any of the client's other IP addresses leased from the DHCP server. It is possible to have both a leased IP for network connectivity and a leased multicast IP for applications that require multicasting.

Travel Assistance
For more information on multicast addresses, look to Request for Comments (RFC) 1112, 2236, and 2730 at http://rfc.net.

Troubleshooting DHCP

The DHCP service is not a difficult service to troubleshoot and is not prone to problems. The first place to begin your troubleshooting efforts is in the system log in Event Viewer. The DHCP service writes any and all information and warning or error messages to the system log, enabling you to begin to understand what may be causing the problem. With DHCP related problems, ask yourself the following questions to try and eliminate possible causes:

- Is the DHCP service operating in an active directory domain environment? If yes, has the service been authorized?
- Are all DHCP clients on the network experiencing problems with the service? If yes, has the scope been authorized? Is the DHCP server online? Are all hardware devices such as hubs, routers, and switches that separate the clients from the DHCP server online and functioning?
- Is the scope configured properly?
- Are DHCP relay agents located on the proper subnets if your routers are configured to not enable BOOTP forwarding?
- Is it a problem with the DHCP database?

Once you have identified what is causing the problem, you can begin to take steps to correct the problem. If the problem is related to the DHCP database, a utility named jetpack can be used to help you to correct the problem.

The DHCP service stores the DHCP database in the systemroot\system32\ dhcp directory. The DHCP service automatically backs up this database to the systemroot\system32\dhcp\backup\jet\new directory. The DHCP service also performs a consistency check of its database at startup and periodically thereafter to detect and correct any problems, but sometimes, even with these measures, the database can become corrupt.

The jetpack utility is included with Windows 2000 Server to help correct a corrupt DHCP database or to manually compact the DHCP database. To run jetpack, follow these steps:

1. Stop the DHCP service.
2. Open the Command Prompt and navigate to the systemroot\system32\dhcp directory.
3. Type **jetpack dhcp.mdb jetold**, where "jetold" is the name of a temporary database location that is used during the repair. Press Enter.
4. Start the DHCP service.

Configuring DHCP in a Routed Environment

The configuration of DHCP in a routed environment is more complicated. As we discovered earlier in this chapter, DHCP relies on clients making broadcasts to find a DHCP server. Broadcasting works just dandy on a network until a broadcast packet encounters a router. Routers are designed to contain broadcast traffic within a given subnet and typically are not configured to forward broadcast messages to other subnets, thereby making a real problem for DHCP in a routed environment. Fortunately, there are three ways to configure DHCP to work in a routed network infrastructure. The first is to include at least one DHCP server on each subnet. This is not the recommended solution, as it significantly increases the amount of administration and the cost required for the server hardware and licenses.

The second option is to configure an RFC 1542 (remember this!) compliant router to forward BOOTP messages between subnets. This solution is preferred to the first one, but it can complicate router configuration.

Exam Tip

RFC 1542 is important to remember because routers configured to the standard set out in the RFC are capable of forwarding DHCP broadcasts on UDP ports 67 and 68. This is one option in the configuration of DHCP in a routed environment.

Local Lingo

RFC 1542   A router that is RFC 1542 compliant is capable of forwarding BOOTP messages between network segments.

The third way is to configure a DHCP relay agent on each subnet. The DHCP relay agent listens on its own subnet for DHCPDISCOVER messages and forwards them on to a DHCP server, as shown in the illustration on the following page. This enables a single DHCP server to lease IP addresses to clients on multiple subnets through the DHCP relay agent.

Exam Tip

If a DHCP server does not exist on the subnet that a DHCP client computer is broadcasting on, a special Windows 2000 computer called a "DHCP relay agent" is required. The function of the DHCP relay agent is to forward the (DHCPDISCOVER) message to an available DHCP server, negotiate the IP lease on behalf of the client, and, when the negotiations are complete, forward the DHCPACK to the requesting client.

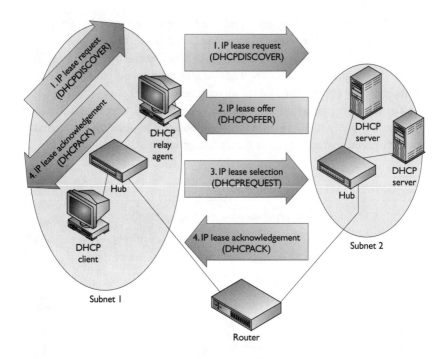

Installing a DHCP Relay Agent

The installation of a DHCP relay agent is done with the RRAS Microsoft Management Console (MMC) snap-in following these configuration steps:

1. Open RRAS.
2. Expand the Server icon, and click IP Routing.
3. Right-click General and select New Routing Protocol.
4. In the New Routing Protocol dialog box, click DHCP Relay Agent and click OK.
5. Right-click DHCP Relay Agent, select Properties, and, in the Server Address box, type the IP address of a DHCP server. Click Add.

That's it—you have set up a DHCP relay agent! If only everything in the Windows 2000 world was so easy!

RRAS, as we will discuss in Chapters 6 and 8, can also be configured to lease out an IP address itself or to take advantage of an existing DHCP server on the network. If you have configured your RRAS server to obtain IP addresses through DHCP, the RRAS service will obtain a block of ten IP addresses, plus one for itself for a total of eleven, to make available to remote access clients. Once the block of ten IP addresses has been leased out, the RRAS server contacts the DHCP server to obtain another block of ten. The remote access clients never communicate directly with the DHCP server; rather, all communication with DHCP is handled by RRAS. The RRAS by default will not forward any additional scope information such as the address of DNS or WINS servers. For this information to be forwarded, a DHCP relay agent must be configured. RRAS clients automatically drop their lease when they disconnect, making the IP address they were using available to other remote access clients.

Authorize a DHCP Server in Active Directory

In an active directory domain environment, one additional DHCP server configuration step is required. In order for the DHCP service to function properly and lease out IP addresses in an active directory environment, it must be authorized in the Active Directory. The Windows 2000 DHCP service is configured to query the Active Directory for a list of authorized DHCP servers when it initializes. If it finds that it is not on the authorized list, the DHCP service does not initialize and, therefore, is not available to lease out IP addresses. This automatic detection has been introduced to enable the detection of rogue Windows 2000 DHCP servers, but it does not detect any other DHCP server implementations, such as a UNIX DHCP server or a Windows NT 4.0 DHCP server.

Exam Tip

Only Windows 2000 DHCP servers require authorization in the active directory.

When you open the MMC to administer your DHCP server for the first time, you will notice a red arrow immediately to the left of the computer name and pointing down, as shown in Figure 1-4. This red arrow indicates that the DHCP service on this computer is not authorized, as does the Not Authorized message that you can also see in Figure 1-4. To authorize the service, you have a couple of options.

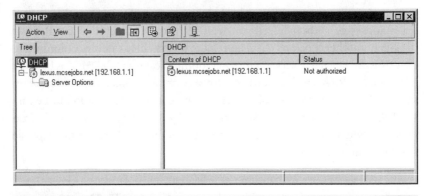

FIGURE 1-4   The DHCP server MMC

Exam Tip

Only members of the Enterprise Admins group are permitted to authorize DHCP servers.

The first option is to authorize it individually by right-clicking the computer name lexus.mcsejobs.net and selecting Authorize. The second option enables you to authorize multiple servers at the same time. This can be done by right-clicking DHCP in the DHCP MMC and selecting Manage Authorized Servers, which will bring up the Manage Authorized Servers dialog box displayed in Figure 1-5. In this box, select the computers that you would like to authorize and click the Authorize

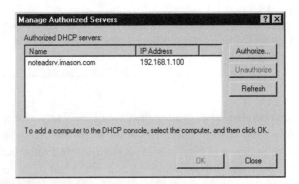

FIGURE 1-5   Authorizing multiple DHCP servers

button on the right of the dialog box. You can also see that this dialog box enables you to unauthorize servers as well, should you need to do that.

Once the DHCP server is authorized, the red arrow pointing down should change to a green arrow pointing up.

 # Configure DHCP for DNS Integration

The DNS dynamic update protocol is a new feature that is supported only on computers running versions of the Windows 2000 operating system. This support for DDNS by computers running Windows 2000 allows those computers to dynamically update their host address record information on a Windows 2000 DNS server that contains a zone database file configured for dynamic updates. In other words, the DNS server must first be configured to accept dynamic updates before the client will be permitted to dynamically update their host resource record information. This is great if all of your computers run Windows 2000, but in most networks you will have a mix of other Microsoft operating systems as well. Any computers not running a Windows 2000 operating system will not support the new dynamic update protocol.

Thanks to the forethought of Microsoft's developers, this new feature in DNS—known as dynamic updates, or Dynamic DNS (DDNS)—can be integrated with the Windows 2000 DHCP service to assist computers running older Microsoft operating systems with DNS name registration. By default, computers running Windows 2000 that are configured to obtain an IP address from a DHCP server will update their own Host (A) resource records on the Windows 2000 DNS server. The Windows 2000 DHCP server updates the Pointer (PTR) record for the computer running Windows 2000. The DHCP server can also be configured to act as a DNS proxy on behalf of down-level clients that do not support the dynamic update protocol. As a DNS proxy, the DHCP server can be configured to update both the Host (A) and the Pointer (PTR) resource records on behalf of the down-level client as well as all Windows 2000 clients.

The Dynamic Update Process

When a DHCP server assigns an IP address to a Windows 2000-based DHCP client, the following process occurs as a result of the dynamic update process:

Exam Tip

The default setting for a Windows 2000 DHCP server that has been authorized in Active Directory is to dynamically update all PTR resource records for Windows 2000 Professional clients. The options to automatically update DHCP client requests and the sub-option to Update DNS only if client requests are both selected. In other words, by default, the Windows 2000 DHCP server will update the DNS information only for DHCP clients that request that their DNS information be updated. No down-level clients will have their DNS information updated, as they will not request that it be updated.

1. The client broadcasts a request for an IP address to all DHCP servers on its segment and includes in the request the client's Fully Qualified Domain Name (FQDN).
2. All DHCP servers that receive the request and that have an available IP address to lease broadcast an IP lease offer to the client.
3. The first IP address offer that the client receives is the one that it accepts. The client broadcasts its acceptance of the IP address so that not only the DHCP server that extended the offer is aware but all other DHCP servers that extended offers can withdraw their offers and make those IP addresses available to other DHCP clients.
4. The DHCP server returns a DHCP acknowledgement message to the client granting an IP address lease and sending along with the lease any additional server and scope-configured options and user and/or vendor option class-configured options.
5. The DHCP server returns a DHCP acknowledgement message to the client granting an IP address lease.
6. The DHCP client then sends its Host (A) record to the Windows 2000 DNS server in the form of a DNS update message for the forward lookup zone on the Windows 2000 DNS server. Alternatively, the Windows 2000 DHCP server can be configured to send the updates on behalf of the client, as shown in Figure 1-6.
7. The Windows 2000 DHCP server sends an update to the Windows 2000 DNS server on behalf of the client to update the client's reverse lookup record, its Pointer resource record (PTR). The FQDN that the DHCP server received in the first step of this process is used in this operation.

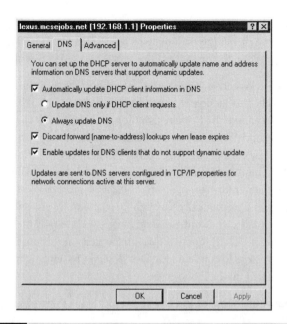

FIGURE 1-6 Configuring the DHCP server to send all dynamic updates on the client's behalf

---

Exam Tip

Only Windows 2000 clients support dynamic updates. To allow other Microsoft operating systems to take advantage of dynamic updates, configure the DHCP server to update the DNS records on the DNS server.

If the Windows 2000-based DHCP client is statically configured, the process changes slightly from that described above. The following process occurs when the DHCP client is statically configured with an IP address.

1. The client initializes and broadcasts its statically configured IP address, allowing for any potential conflicts to be identified. If no conflicts are found, the client configures itself with the static IP address.

2. The client's DHCP client service, which is running by default on all computers running Windows 2000, sends the client's Host (A) record to the DNS server as a DNS update for the forward lookup zone on the DNS server.

3. The DHCP server sends an update to the DNS server on behalf of the client to update the client's reverse lookup record (PTR). The FQDN that the DHCP server received in the first step of this process is used in this operation.

To allow both Windows 2000 clients that support dynamic update and down-level Windows clients that do not to use dynamic update, the DHCP service must be configured to handle the name registration on behalf of all clients. The extension of dynamic updates to down-level clients that do not support it on their own can be achieved by configuring a Windows 2000 DHCP server to automatically update DHCP client information in DNS. In order for the DHCP service to update DHCP client information, down-level clients must be configured to obtain their IP addresses automatically through DHCP, and a Windows 2000 DHCP server must be installed and configured on the network, as only the Windows 2000 implementation of DHCP supports this functionality at this time.

Follow these steps to configure the DHCP server to send all dynamic updates on the client's behalf to the DNS server:

1. Right-click the name of the DHCP server (lexus.mcsejobs.net) and select Properties.
2. In the Properties dialog box, select the DNS tab.
3. Place a check mark in the box to the left of the following:

- Automatically update DHCP client information in DNS
- Always update DNS
- Discard forward lookups when lease expires
- Enable updates for DNS clients that do not support dynamic update

Travel Assistance

To become more familiar with the implementation and function of DHCP servers, see the Microsoft white paper "Dynamic Host Configuration Protocol for Windows 2000 Server," available from www.microsoft.com\Windows2000, or read Module 2 in the Microsoft certified course 2153, "Implementing a Microsoft Windows 2000 Network Infrastructure." (However, the elements of DHCP that you need to know for the exam are covered in this book.) You can also learn more about DNS dynamic update by watching the online support webcast titled "How Windows 2000 Dynamic DNS Updates Work" at http://support.microsoft.com/servicedesks/Webcasts/WC050301/ wcblurb050301.asp.

Manage and Monitor DHCP

The ability to manage and monitor the DHCP service has been improved in Windows 2000. The DHCP service is configured to record both startup and shutdown events as well as critical errors in the system log. Common tools such as Performance Monitor and Task Manager can be used to help troubleshoot problems with the DHCP service. The DHCP service also has its own logging functionality that can be enabled by following these steps:

1. Open the DHCP snap-in, right-click the server that you want to configure logging for, and select Properties.
2. On the General tab of the Properties dialog box, click Enable DHCP Audit Logging.

The default size of the DHCP log file is 7MB, but this can be increased by editing the registry.

The System Monitor tool included with Windows 2000 can also be used to measure and monitor DHCP server performance by adding in counters such as Packets Received/sec. Slow response times can also be identified using counters, such as Packets Expired/sec, in System Monitor.

Exam Tip

Familiarize yourself with the DHCP counters available to monitor performance in System Monitor, as you may be required to select specific counters to solve performance-related problems.

Moving a DHCP Database Between Servers

Part of your management of the DHCP service will inevitably lead you to move a DHCP database from one server to another. The DHCP snap-in provided in Windows 2000 is not an all-encompassing administrative tool when it comes to the DHCP service. One of its limitations is that it does not include the functionality to allow you to move a DHCP database from one server to another server.

This section of the chapter will outline the steps involved in performing this administrative task from two perspectives. First, we will look at how to transfer a DHCP database from a computer running Windows NT 4.0 to a computer running Windows 2000, and second we will look at the process of transferring a DHCP database from a computer running Windows 2000 to another computer running Windows 2000.

Travel Advisory

You will not be required to know this for the exam, but in your daily administration of DHCP you might find the knowledge base article "Q130642 — How to move a DHCP database to another Windows NT server" quite useful.

The transfer of a DHCP database from one server to another can also be accomplished using a new tool called DHCPExIm.exe that is included in Supplement 1 of the Windows 2000 Resource Kit. The DHCP Export Import tool allows you to move any combination of scopes between Microsoft DHCP servers. Moving all your scopes with the DHCP Export Import tool is equivalent to moving the database. The DHCP Export Import tool is not listed in the alphabetical listing of tools, but instructions on using it can be found in the readme file.

Transferring a DHCP Database from Windows NT 4.0 (Source) to Windows 2000 (Destination)

To move a DHCP database from a Windows NT 4.0 Server to a Windows 2000 Server, follow the detailed steps that follow.

Note that these steps assume that the destination Windows 2000 Server does not have the DHCP service installed. If the DHCP service is installed on the Windows 2000 destination server, stop the service. Also note that this transfer method will not migrate the following DHCP server settings:

- APIProtocolSupport
- DatabaseCleanupInterval
- DatabaseLoggingFlag
- DetectConflictRetries
- DatabasePath

These settings can be changed after the migration by using the DHCP snap-in and editing the DHCP server Properties.

1. Create a backup of your Windows NT 4.0 source server.
2. On the Windows NT 4.0 Server, click Start, Settings, and Control Panel, then double-click Services. In the Services box, select Microsoft DHCP Server and click Startup and choose Disable under Startup type.
3. Open a Command Prompt and type the command **net stop dhcpserver** and press Enter.
4. Click Start, Run and type **regedt32**, then click OK.
5. In RegEdit32, view the HKEY_LOCAL_MACHINE\SYSTEM\CurrentControl Set\Services\DHCPServer\Configuration registry key.
6. Select the Configuration Key, then select Save Key from the Registry menu and save the key as c:\config.key.
7. On the Windows 2000 Server to which you want to transfer the DHCP server, install DHCP by clicking Start, Settings, Control Panel, and double-clicking Add/Remove Programs. Select the Add/Remove Windows Components button and double-click Networking Services (the words, not the check box). Place a check mark in the check box next to Dynamic Host Configuration Protocol (DHCP).
8. Open a Command Prompt on the Windows 2000 Server and enter the command **net stop dhcpserver** to stop the DHCP server service.
9. Copy the Config.key file to the Windows 2000 destination server from the Windows NT 4.0 Server and save the file as c:\Config.key.
10. Click Start, Run and type **regedt32** and click OK.
11. Use Regedt32 to view the HKEY_LOCAL_MACHINE\SOFTWARE\Microsoft\ DhcpServer\Configuration registry key. Select the configuration key and click Restore on the Registry menu. Select the file c:\config.key and click Yes when you are prompted to restore over the existing key.
12. Delete all of the files and folders in the %systemroot%\system32\dhcp directory on the Windows 2000 Server and copy the DHCP database file dhcp.mdb from the source computer to the destination computer.
13. At the Command Prompt, type the command **net start dhcpserver**. Starting the DHCP server should result in the following error message: "System error 20036 has occurred. The system cannot find message text for message number 0x4e44 in the message file for BASE." This is to be expected.
14. You may also receive the following error message: "Jet Conversion Process. The conversion was not successful! The conversion tool could not locate a file called edb500.dll which is required for the conversion. This file should be present on your Windows NT 5.0 CD-ROM. Please copy it to your

SystemRoot\\System32 directory (it may need to be uncompressed) and re-start." This message corresponds with an EventID 1008 in the Application Log; copy the Edb500.dl_ file from the Windows 2000 CD-ROM, and expand it in the System32 folder. Then repeat step 12, and 13 until you no longer receive the error message.

15. Check the Application log in the Event Viewer for additional messages. The EventID 1000 message indicates that the database has been converted successfully.

16. Open the DHCP snap-in on the Windows 2000 Server destination computer and right-click the DHCP server and select Reconcile All Scopes. In the Reconcile All Scopes dialog box, click the Verify button.

The last step applies only if the Windows 2000 DHCP server is a member of an active directory domain. If it is a member of an active directory domain, the server must be authorized.

Transferring a DHCP Database from a Windows 2000 (Source) to Windows 2000 (Destination) Server

To move a DHCP database from one Windows 2000 server to another Windows 2000 Server, follow the steps below.

This method does not migrate any of the following DHCP server settings:

- APIProtocolSupport
- DatabaseCleanupInterval
- DatabaseLoggingFlag
- DetectConflictRetries
- RestoreFlag
- DatabasePath
- BackupDatabasePath
- DatabaseName
- BackupInterval

These settings can be easily changed by using the DHCP snap-in after the migration is complete.

1. Create a backup of your working configuration.
2. Stop the DHCP server service on the Windows 2000 destination computer.
3. On the Windows 2000 Server source computer, click Start, Programs, Administrative Tools, then select Services. In the Services box, select Microsoft DHCP Server, click Startup, and choose Disable under Startup type.

4. Open a Command Prompt and type the command **net stop dhcpserver** and press Enter.

5. Click Start, Run and type **regedt32** and click OK.

6. In RegEdt32, view the HKEY_LOCAL_MACHINE\SOFTWARE\Microsoft\ DhcpServer\Configuration registry key.

7. Select the Configuration Key and select Save Key from the Registry menu and save the key as c:\config.key.

8. On the Windows 2000 destination Server to which you want to transfer the DHCP server database, open a Command Prompt and type **net stop dhcpserver.**

9. Copy the Config.key file to the Windows 2000 destination server from the Windows 2000 source Server and save the file as c:\Config.key.

10. Click on Start, Run and type **regedt32** and click OK.

11. Use Regedt32 to view the HKEY_LOCAL_MACHINE\SOFTWARE\Microsoft\ DhcpServer\Configuration registry key. Select the configuration key and click Restore on the Registry menu. Select the file c:\config.key and click Yes when you are prompted to restore over the existing key.

12. Delete all of the files and folders in the %systemroot%\system32\dhcp directory on the Windows 2000 destination Server and copy the DHCP database file dhcp.mdb from the source computer to the destination computer.

13. At the Command Prompt, type the command **net start dhcpserver.** You should receive the following message: "The DHCP Server service was started successfully."

14. Open the DHCP snap-in on the Windows 2000 Server destination computer and right-click the DHCP server and select Reconcile All Scopes. In the Reconcile All Scopes dialog box, click the Verify button.

The last step applies only if the Windows 2000 DHCP server is a member of an active directory domain. If it is a member of an active directory domain, the server must be authorized.

CHECKPOINT

✔ **Objective 1.01: Install, Configure, and Troubleshoot DHCP**   The DHCP service is installed through the Add/Remove Windows Components section of Add/Remove Programs in Control Panel. APIPA is a default setting in Windows 2000 used to assign IP addresses to clients on the 169.254.0.0/16 network. APIPA can be disabled only by editing the registry.

✔ **Objective 1.02: Install the DHCP Server Service**   To install the DHCP service, you must be a member of the Administrator's group. Once the service is installed, the scope you create must be activated. The server will also require authorization if the DHCP server is installed in an active directory domain.

✔ **Objective 1.03: Create and Manage DHCP Scopes, Super Scopes, and Multicast Scopes**   Scope options can be defined at three levels: the DHCP server, each individual scope, and the class level. Server-level options are inherited by all other levels unless an option at a lower level conflicts. In the case of a conflict, the lower-level scope option becomes the effective option. The class-level options are broken into two types: user defined or vendor defined. A minimum of one activated DHCP scope is required to lease out IP addresses. Each scope can include only a single subnet. Keep your IP lease times shorter when the number of computers requiring IP addresses is close to the amount of available IP addresses. Client reservations can be configured in DHCP to enable a client with a specific MAC address to receive a reserved IP address. DHCP relay agents can be used to configure DHCP in a routed environment where the routers on the network are not RFC 1542 compliant. DHCP relay agents are configured using the RRAS snap-in.

✔ **Objective 1.04: Authorize a DHCP Server in Active Directory**   Windows 2000 DHCP servers that operate in an active directory domain must be authorized with the active directory. Only members of the Enterprise Admins group can authorize a DHCP server. DHCP scopes must be activated before they can lease out IP addresses. Only active directory aware servers require authorization.

✔ **Objective 1.05: Configure DHCP for DNS Integration**   Windows 2000 clients register their A resource records with DNS servers configured for dynamic updates by default, and the DHCP server registers the client's PTR record. DHCP servers can be configured to register both the A and PTR records for both Windows 2000 and non-Windows 2000 clients, enabling support for DDNS to be provided to down-level clients. Only Windows 2000 clients support dynamic updates. Use the ipconfig command with the /renew switch to force a renewal of a client's IP address, and use the /registerdns switch to update the client's DNS information on a DNS server configured to use dynamic updates.

✔ **Objective 1.06: Manage and Monitor DHCP**   Event messages for the DHCP service are logged in the System event log. Additional DHCP logging can be enabled via the DHCP snap-in. The jetpack utility can be used to compact the DHCP database. Use ipconfig command with the /all switch to list the IP configuration of all network adapters in your computer. The Netsh command line utility can be used to administer DHCP.

REVIEW QUESTIONS

1. A DHCP server appears to be having problems leasing IP addresses to client computers on its own subnet. Which of the following will enable you to manually terminate the existing lease at the Command Prompt?

   A. Ipconfig /all
   B. Ipconfig /terminate
   C. Ipconfig /release
   D. Dcpromo

2. You are troubleshooting DHCP problems at a client computer. When you open the Command Prompt and type the command ipconfig /all, an automatically assigned IP address is returned. Which of the following could be the IP address that was returned?

   A. 172.16.35.64
   B. 192.168.1.1
   C. 129.145.34.62
   D. 169.254.1.60

3. Which of the following are required for proper configuration of the DHCP service? (Choose all that apply.)

   A. Static DNS information
   B. Static IP address
   C. Default gateway
   D. Subnet mask

4. Which group or groups must you be a member of in order to install and configure the DHCP service on a member server running Windows 2000 Server?

   A. Power Users
   B. Administrators
   C. DHCP Admins
   D. Schema Admins

5. You have just completed the installation of the DHCP service on a member server in your active directory domain. As you test the service to ensure that it is working properly, you find that you are unable to lease an IP address. You check and confirm that the DHCP server is on the same subnet of the client requesting the IP and that other clients on the same subnet are also unable to lease IP addresses. Which of the following steps must you perform to correct the problem?

A. Activate the scope on the DHCP server.
B. Authorize the scope on the DHCP server.
C. Activate the DHCP server.
D. Authorize the DHCP server.

6. You have just completed the installation of the DHCP server service on a member server in your domain. You then successfully authorize the service with the active directory. What is the last configuration step required to enable DHCP clients to begin leasing IP addresses?

A. Create and activate a scope.
B. Create a client reservation.
C. Create and authorize a scope.
D. Reboot the server to complete the installation.

7. Once you have created a DHCP scope, which of the following is the only scope property that cannot be changed?

A. Starting IP address
B. Ending IP address
C. Subnet mask
D. Lease duration

8. You have configured a DHCP server with a single scope. The IP range for the DHCP server is 192.168.1.1 to 192.168.1.254. You have also defined a number of scope options, including two DNS servers with IP addresses of 192.168.1.250 and 24.63.78.145. You set the lease duration to six days and configured an exclusion range of 192.168.1.248 to 192.168.1.254. You are about to test the DHCP configuration that is configured to obtain an IP address automatically and that has a static DNS entry of 192.168.1.251. After obtaining an IP address from the DHCP server, you run the ipconfig /all command. What DNS addresses will be included in the results generated by the ipconfig /all command?

    A. 192.168.1.251

    B. 192.168.1.250 and 24.63.78.145

    C. 192.168.1.251, 192.168.1.250, and 24.63.78.145

    D. 24.63.78.145

9. You have just completed the installation of a new Windows 2000 DHCP server in your active directory domain. You have created a scope and activated it. You have also authorized the DHCP server and tested the server with both a computer running Windows 2000 Professional and a computer running Windows 98. When you check to confirm that dynamic updates are working correctly, only the Windows 2000 Professional client Host record exists in DNS. What can you do to solve this problem?

    A. At the computer running Windows 98, open a Command Prompt and type ipconfig /registerdns.

    B. At the DHCP server, open a Command Prompt and type ipconfig /registerdns.

    C. In the DHCP snap-in, select the DNS tab of the DHCP server's property dialog box and select Enable updates for DNS clients Install the Windows 2000 Directory Service Client on the Windows 98 computers.

10. In which event log would you find startup and shutdown events for the DHCP service?

    A. System

    B. Application

    C. Directory Service

    D. Security

REVIEW ANSWERS

1. **C** The command ipconfig /release would enable you to terminate an existing IP lease.

2. **D** An automatically assigned IP address will fall into the 169.254.x.y network.

3. **B** **D** To install and configure the DHCP service on a computer, the computer should be configured with both a static IP address and subnet mask. A default gateway is entirely optional.

4. **B** **C** Both the administrator's group on the local member server and the DHCP Admins group in a domain have the rights and permissions to install and configure the DHCP server service.

5. **D** In order for the DHCP server to lease out IP addresses in a Windows 2000 active directory domain, it must be authorized in the active directory.

6. **A** The last remaining step after installing and authorizing the DHCP service is to create and activate a scope.

7. **C** The only scope property that cannot be changed once the scope is created is the subnet mask.

8. **A** The only DNS address that will appear in the list is the IP 192.168.1.251 because the TCP/IP properties configured on the client always take precedence over any information provided by a DHCP server.

9. **C** Only Windows 2000 clients and servers support dynamic updates. To enable support for down-level Microsoft client operating systems, the DNS properties of the DHCP server must be changed to enable Enable Updates For DNS Clients That Do Not Support Dynamic Updates.

10. **A** Startup and shutdown messages can be found in the System log.

DNS Network Infrastructure

	NEWBIE	SOME EXPERIENCE	EXPERT
ETA	10–15 hours	6–10 hours	2–6 hours

Extensive knowledge of the features and configuration of the Domain Name Service (DNS) is necessary both for the exam and for your daily administrative responsibilities. DNS is the primary means of name resolution in a Windows 2000 Network and the key to the successful installation and ongoing functionality of the Active Directory service.

The popularity of the Internet and the economic focus on globalization has forced our networks into a state of constant change, whether that change be expansion, contraction, or integration. The DNS plays a significant role in your network, in Active Directory design, and in implementation. Understanding the installation and configuration process of DNS and the security configuration options available is required.

We will begin our journey with a look at the fundamentals of DNS, which include the query process, installation options, zone types, dynamic updates, and design fundamentals. Once we have learned how to configure the service, we will explore how to manage and monitor DNS. A solid understanding of DNS and its many new features is necessary for success on the Implementing and Administering a Microsoft Windows 2000 Network Infrastructure exam. The DNS component of the exam is one of the larger components, and it also tends to be a focus on the majority of other Windows 2000 exams. This chapter will provide you with the information necessary to prepare for the exams.

Install, Configure, and Troubleshoot DNS

Objective 2.01

D NS is the key to name resolution and Active Directory functionality in Windows 2000. Because of Windows 2000's reliance on DNS, Microsoft focuses heavily on DNS in this and other Windows 2000 certification exams. In other words, you must know DNS!

To provide you with a solid understanding of DNS, we will begin our journey with an overview of DNS. Think of this as basic training for DNS.

Overview of DNS

DNS is a network service that was designed to simplify and streamline name resolution of Transmission Control Protocol/Internet Protocol (TCP/IP) addresses to Fully Qualified Domain Names (FQDNs) of computers on your network. Prior to DNS, the resolution of host names to Internet Protocol (IP) addresses was achieved through the use of a centrally stored and administered file known as the *hosts file*. When changes to clients of the network occurred, this hosts file was maintained and modified by one or more DNS administrators. For example, when a new client computer was installed and initialized on the network, the computer's FQDN to IP address mapping would be added to the hosts file. You can imagine the work that was involved in a large corporate network where changes occurred frequently. Add to that the additional workload resulting from users working with notebooks that are sometimes connected to the network and other times disconnected, and the use of Dynamic Host Configuration Protocol (DHCP), which can result in a computer receiving a different IP address upon renewal, all of which further complicates the maintenance requirements of the host's file. Trying to stay on top on these constant changes became very difficult.

Local Lingo

FQDN   An FQDN (Fully Qualified Domain Name) represents a computer's location in the domain relative to other objects. The FQDN of a computer begins with its computer name (also known as the host name) and has its DNS namespace appended to it. A computer called "wks" in the sales.mcsejobs.net domain would have a FQDN of wks.sales. mcsejobs.net.

Even with its drawbacks, the hosts file is still used today. It is used in conjunction with DNS as a way to help optimize DNS name resolution. In Windows 2000, the hosts file can be found in the %systemroot%\system32\drivers\etc directory. The hosts file is a flat file that can be manually configured to include the name to IP address mappings of computers on your network. An example of a mapping found in a host file is shown below. Here, the computer wks in the domain mcsejobs.net is mapped to the IP address 192.168.1.40:

```
192.168.1.40      wks.mcsejobs.net
```

The big disadvantage of the hosts file is that updating the file is a manual process that can require a significant amount of time when dealing with a large number of computers, and this process is prone to human error. The big advantage is that it is still available for use as a backup in case DNS fails or in situations where it may be more efficient than DNS.

One example of using a host file to increase name resolution efficiency is in an organization configured with DNS servers and an Active Directory domain environment where Windows 2000 domain controllers must be able to find and locate DNS servers in order for Active Directory to function correctly. In this type of environment, the hosts file on each of the domain controllers can be configured with the FQDN to IP address mappings of all of the DNS servers in the domain as a backup should DNS name resolution fail.

Another example of a hosts file being more efficient than DNS is in an Active Directory domain that has a large head office and small branch offices. If only a few computers are located in each branch office, and they are all configured with static IP addresses, budgets may prevent you from adding a DNS server in each branch. The connection link between the head office and the branches might also be slow, and connectivity requirements to the head office may be rare. In this type of environment, a hosts file could be used at each branch to facilitate name resolution within the branch.

Thankfully, DNS provides us with a dynamic and more efficient way to resolve host names in larger networks. DNS is based on a hierarchical, scalable, and distributed database architecture that enables different DNS servers to maintain the resource records for hosts within the zone that the DNS server has authority over.

DNS Basics

DNS is a distributed database system that provides host name resolution in an IP network. Its hierarchical structured namespace consists of a root domain, represented by a ".", and top-level domains such as .com (commercial enterprises), .edu (educational institutions), and .ca (Canada). Each of these top-level domains is capable of having multiple levels of subdomains, such as microsoft.com, mit.edu, and on.ca, which can include one or more administrative zones. The zone file is used to store the resource records for computers and services within one or more domains and represents a contiguous portion of the namespace over which a DNS server (also known as a name server) has authority to provide name resolution. There are generally two types of zones: primary and secondary; however, the Windows 2000 DNS implementation includes a third type of zone known as the Active Directory integrated zone. These three zone types can be configured as either forward lookup or reverse lookup zones.

Forward lookup zones provide resolution of host names to IP addresses. Reverse lookup zones provide the reverse type of resolution, resolving IP addresses to host names.

Most implementations of DNS have one large drawback: they offer no fault tolerance but have a single point of failure. The single point of failure is the name server hosting the primary zone, because it is only the primary zone that is both readable and writable. This means that if the name server hosting the primary zone goes down or offline, no changes can be made to the zone file.

Secondary zones can be configured to distribute name resolution load across multiple servers, but again, the copy of the zone database file on a secondary server is read only. The secondary zone file contents are simply a copy of the primary zone database file that the DNS server hosting the secondary zone receives through a process known as *zone transfer*.

A zone transfer occurs when the name server configured with the primary zone sends an update notification to all secondary servers for the zone. This tells the secondary servers to contact the name server with the primary zone and transfer over either the entire database, in the case of a full zone transfer, or just the changes since the last transfer, in the case of an incremental zone transfer. Windows 2000 supports two types of zone transfers: full (AXFR) and incremental (IXFR). In a full zone transfer, the entire contents of the zone database file is transferred from the DNS server hosting the primary zone to the DNS server hosting the secondary zone. In an incremental zone transfer, only the changes made to the primary zone database file since the last transfer are sent to the name server hosting the secondary zone.

The third type of zone that is exclusive to Windows 2000 DNS is the Active Directory integrated zone. When a zone is configured as an Active Directory integrated zone, the zone database file is copied into the Active Directory database as an object and deleted from its original location in the %systemroot%\system32\dns directory. This results in a couple of immediate improvements. First, zone transfers are no longer required, as the zone database object in the Active Directory will now replicate to all domain controllers in the domain with Active Directory replication. Second, you no longer have a single point of failure, as all domain controllers now contain a readable and writable copy of the zone database object. There is one caveat, however, only domain controllers configured with DNS can response to DNS queries.

Exam Tip

An Active Directory integrated zone is not replicated to other Windows 2000 domains during Active Directory replication, only within its own domain. The Active Directory integrated zone object can be extended to other domains by creating standard secondary zones on a DNS server in the other domains.

Now that you have an understanding of the hierarchical structure of DNS and where DNS zone files containing resource records are located, let's begin our exploration of the DNS query process.

DNS Name Resolution

To better understand the DNS name resolution process, think of DNS as being similar to multiple generations in a family that all have the same last name. In a single family, you could have a son, a father, and a grandfather. The origin of this particular family would date back to the root of the family, which in this example would be the grandfather. In DNS, the root of the DNS structure is represented by a period (.), which is known as the root. Everything starts from the root, and as the grandparents have children, those children inherit the last name of the grandparents. In DNS, the first generation is represented by top-level domain names. These top-level domain names are used to represent organizational types such as .org, .com, .ed, and .ca, which are the suffixes for nonprofit organizations, for-profit organizations, educational institutions, and countries, which in this example is Canada, respectively. Continuing with the example of Canada (.ca), it can be further subdivided into provinces, each represented by unique domain names such as .on, .bc, and .mb for the provinces of Ontario, British Columbia, and Manitoba, respectively. The FQDN, however, is a combination of all of the individual domain names appended together with a period separating them. An example of this is on.ca, where "on" represents the province of Ontario, which is found in its parent domain .ca, which in turn represents Canada. And .ca is found within ".", which represents the root of all domains. You're probably asking yourself what the family structure has to do with this. Well, we are getting to that as it has to do with how name to IP addresses are resolved in DNS.

The following illustration shows the hierarchy of two families that were spawned from Adam and Eve with different family names: Magwood and McCaw, respectively. For simplicity, each family consists of a grandfather, a son, and a grandson. In DNS, the name resolution process is based on a hierarchical structure that is much the same as the hierarchical structure of a family. In a family, if the grandson had a query to resolve, he could ask his father, who would respond with the correct answer if he knew it; however, if the father didn't know the correct answer, the father could ask his father, the grandfather. If the grandfather knows the answer to the grandson's query, he would then give the answer to the father, who in turn would give the answer to the grandson.

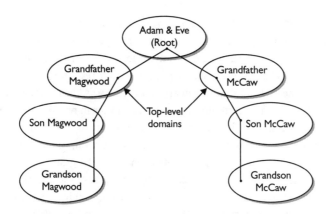

DNS is a distributed database system that depends on DNS servers, which contain databases of resource records for their portion of the DNS namespace. Using the generation example above, three individual domains exist for each family. In the McCaw family, the root domain is named .mccaw and is represented by the grandfather. The second-level domain is known as .son and is a child of the .mccaw domain. The third domain is a child to the .son domain and is known as the .grandson domain. When the DNS servers in the .grandson.son.mccaw domain cannot resolve a host or computer name to an IP address, they query a DNS server in their parent domain, .son.mccaw. If no mapping exists in this domain, a DNS server in the .mccaw domain is queried for an answer. This entire DNS name resolution process is made up of two types of queries: iterative and recursive.

The Iterative Query The iterative query is a query made by a DNS client to a DNS server in which the DNS server returns the best answer that it can provide. In other words, the DNS server checks its name cache and its zone database file for the name to IP address mapping of the computer the DNS client is querying for, and if it has it, the resolved name is returned. If the DNS server is unable to resolve the name, it responds to the client with a pointer to a server that would better be able to provide an answer.

The Recursive Query The recursive query provides the full answer to the name resolution request. This full answer will be one of two responses: either the name cannot be resolved or the name can, in which case the reply includes the IP that maps to that name.

The DNS Query Process   Both the iterative and recursive queries play a role in the DNS query process. Client computers typically send recursive queries to DNS servers, which in turn send iterative queries to other DNS servers to find an answer for the client and return the name to IP address mapping to the client, in response to the original recursive query. In other words, the recursive query sent to the DNS server that is configured on your computer may take a little longer to respond because it is querying other DNS servers for an answer. It must receive an answer before it can respond to you. Going back to the example we used earlier of the three generations in a family, the query sent from the grandson to his father would be a recursive query. The father, should he not have the answer, would use an iterative query to the grandfather. The father would receive the correct answer from the grandfather in response to the iterative query and pass that answer along to the grandson, fulfilling the original recursive query.

To drive home the query process, let's use an example of name resolution for a user connected to the Internet at home. The home user is connected to the Internet through an ISP, which leases the home user an IP address, subnet mask, gateway, and DNS server information, such as the following:

- IP address: 24.167.32.143
- Subnet mask: 255.255.255.0
- Default gateway: 24.167.32.1
- Primary DNS server: 24.3.56.2

The client is connected, opens up their web browser, and types in the URL **quote.yahoo.com**. The following resolution process, which is also depicted in the following illustration, will take place:

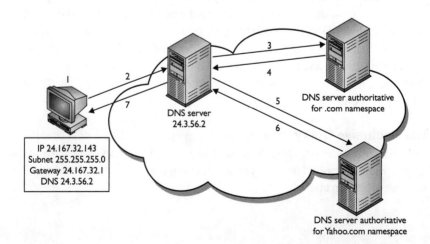

Local Lingo

name server   A name server is a computer running Windows 2000 server with DNS installed and configured with a DNS zone.

1. The client checks their name cache to see if this URL has been resolved recently and if it knows the name to IP address mapping, which in this case it doesn't.

Exam Tip

DNS name servers keep all query answers in their name cache for 5 minutes by default, which helps to reduce network traffic.

2. The client sends a recursive query to resolve quote.yahoo.com to its primary DNS server at 24.3.56.2.
3. The DNS server checks its database and cache and is unable to resolve the query. The DNS server then sends an iterative query to a DNS server that has authority for the .com namespace.
4. The .com DNS server responds to the DNS server at 24.3.56.2 with the IP address of the DNS server that has authority for the yahoo.com namespace.
5. The DNS server at 24.3.56.2 sends another iterative query to the DNS server with authority for the yahoo.com namespace asking for the name to IP address mapping of quote.yahoo.com.
6. The DNS server with authority for the yahoo.com namespace responds to the DNS server at 24.3.56.2 with the IP address of quote.yahoo.com.
7. The DNS server at 24.3.56.2 then responds to the DNS client at 24.167.32.143 with the IP address of quote.yahoo.com.

Exam Tip

Become very familiar with the query process and the sequence of host name resolution. Remember that a DNS server that receives a recursive query must respond with a definitive answer, and a DNS server that receives an iterative query can simply return a referral answer.

With solid understanding of DNS fundamentals under our belts, we will continue our journey into the world of DNS with a look at the installation process.

Objective 2.02

Install the DNS Server Service

L ike all network services in Windows 2000, DNS is installed from the Add/Remove Windows Components section of Add/Remove Programs in Control Panel, but before you jump in and try to install it, make sure that you meet all of the requirements:

- The DNS server must have a static IP address.
- You must be logged on as a user that is a member of either the administrators, domain administrators, or enterprise administrators group.
- The DNS must support service (SRV) resource records.

Active Directory relies on DNS for name and service resolution. The DNS implementation that you decide to use, however, does not have to be the Windows 2000 DNS. Both Windows NT 4.0 with SP4 or higher or any Berkeley Internet Name Domain software (BIND) implementation greater than version 8.2.1 are capable of supporting the Active Directory.

Exam Tip

The use of the Windows 2000 DNS is not mandatory. Any DNS implementation that supports Service Location Resource Records (SRV) is capable of supporting the name service for Windows 2000 based computers.

Local Lingo

resource records   All records in DNS are referred to as resource records. Resource records come in a number of different types. One of those types is service resource records. Each type of resource record has an associated abbreviation. The abbreviation for the service resource record is (SRV), short for service. Another example of a type of resource record is the host resource record. The abbreviation for the host resource record is (A), short for address. DNS resource records for mail servers use the abbreviation (MX), short for mail exchange. Reverse lookup resource records use the abbreviation (PTR), short for pointer.

The key DNS feature that the Active Directory service requires is the use of service (SRV) resource records. Service resource records provide resolution of host names to IP addresses for computers running Active Directory aware services. Examples of required Active Directory aware services include the Kerberos service and the Lightweight Directory Access Protocol (LDAP) service. Kerberos replaces NTLM authentication in Windows 2000 as the primary means of authentication. All Windows 2000 domain controllers run the Kerberos Key Distribution Center (KDC) service which provides for Kerberos authentication. LDAP is used to enable Active Directory domain users to query the Active Directory database and locate objects and object attributes such as shared folders, users, and computers.

Two additional DNS features that help to simplify administration but are not required for the Active Directory are the dynamic DNS update protocol (DDNS) and incremental zone transfers (IXFR).

DDNS enables the dynamic registration of resource and service records within DNS by client computers that run operating systems such as Windows 2000 that support the dynamic update protocol. DDNS can also interoperate with DHCP to register non-DDNS client computers.

Incremental zone transfers enable bandwidth conservation by only requiring the changes made to the zone database file to be transferred.

Once DNS is installed, it must be configured through the DNS snap-in found in Start, Programs, Administrative Tools. The DNS snap-in, like most Microsoft Management Console (MMC) snap-ins, can be used to administer the DNS on the local computer or on remote DNS name servers. The first step in the configuration process is the creation of a new zone, which we will explore next.

Objective 2.03 Configure Zones

As mentioned in the section "DNS Basics," there are three zone types in Windows 2000 to choose from:

- Standard primary zone
- Standard secondary zone
- Active Directory integrated zone

Standard Primary Zone

A standard primary zone contains a readable and writable copy of the zone database file. The zone database file is a simple text file that is stored in the %systemroot%\system32\dns folder. A read-only copy of the zone database file is sent out to DNS servers configured with standard secondary zones through a process known as a zone transfer. If you are familiar with Windows NT 4.0 domain environments, think of a primary zone as very similar to a Primary Domain Controller (PDC). Only the PDC could update the Security Account Manager (SAM) domain database in a Windows NT 4.0 domain, as it was the only domain controller with a writeable copy of the database. Backup Domain Controllers (BDC) can be likened to standard secondary zones as we will see next.

Standard Secondary Zone

The standard secondary zone contains a read-only copy of the zone database file. Any changes to the zone are made at the standard primary zone. The key benefit of standard secondary zones is that they enable name resolution workloads to be distributed among multiple DNS servers. This is very similar to the idea of a BDC in a Windows NT 4.0 domain, as BDCs also only contained a read-only copy of the domain database.

Active Directory Integrated Zone

The Active Directory integrated zone stores the zone information as an object in the Active Directory as opposed to a text file. When a zone type is changed to an Active Directory integrated zone, its zone file in %systemroot%\system32\dns is copied into the Active Directory as an object and then deleted from the original directory. As an object in the Active Directory, it is replicated to all other domain controllers in the domain during Active Directory replication, therefore eliminating the single point of failure that exists in traditional DNS implementations.

Exam Tip

Active Directory must be installed and available for the creation of Active Directory integrated zones. Active Directory integrated zones can only be created on Windows 2000 domain controllers, as member servers do not contain a copy of the Active Directory database.

Choosing a Zone Type

The choice of which of the three zone types to create first is not difficult. Your only choice is to create a standard primary zone. The reason for this is simple: a standard secondary zone cannot be created without the existence of a standard primary zone, and an Active Directory integrated zone requires the Active Directory to be installed. Assuming that the reason we are installing and configuring DNS is to later install the Active Directory, the option to create an Active Directory integrated zone will not yet exist. The second choice that must be made is the type of lookup zone you wish to create.

The three zone types can all be configured as either forward or reverse lookup zones. The most common lookup type is the forward lookup. Forward lookup zones enable for the resolution of host names to IP addresses. Their popularity stems from the fact that most people find it much easier to remember names such as Microsoft.com, Yahoo.com, or Toronto.com than they do remembering IP addresses. Because of this, every time someone enters a URL into a web browser, DNS must resolve that name to an IP address in order for a connection to be established, because the connection is made to the IP address and a specific port at that IP address, as opposed to the host name.

The second type of lookup is the reverse lookup in which a request is made to resolve an IP address to a host name. This type of resolution is often popular in security configuration settings for web or mail servers, as it enables you to ascertain whether the connecting user is trying to spoof the server they are connecting to. When a connection is received by a web server, only the IP address of the requester is known. Reverse resolution may be configured in the web servers security to identify the domain from which the IP address belongs in an effort to block out specific domains and prevent them from connecting to the web server.

Create a Standard Primary Zone

To create a standard primary, forward lookup zone, follow these steps:

1. Open the DNS snap-in and expand the name of the DNS server.
2. Right-click the Forward Lookup Zones folder, and from the context menu select New Zone.
3. The New Zone Wizard will appear. Click Next.
4. Select Standard Primary in the Zone Type dialog box, and click Next.
5. Type the name of the zone in the text box. This is generally the name of the domain, such as mcsejobs.net. Click Next, and click Next again.
6. Click Finish, and the new zone should appear.

Change Zone Types

In Windows 2000 DNS, you are able to change a zone from one type to another using the DNS snap-in. This enables you the flexibility of creating a standard primary zone and standard secondary zones to support the original installation of

Active Directory and then change the zone types to Active Directory integrated zones once the Active Directory is installed. Change the zone types by following these steps:

1. Right-click the name of the zone that you wish to change zone types for, and select Properties from the context menu. This will bring up the Zone Properties dialog box shown in Figure 2-1.
2. Click the Change button on the General tab, and select the type of zone you wish to change to. Click OK twice to close the dialog boxes.

Objective 2.04

Manually Create DNS Resource Records

Now that you know how to create a zone and you understand the various zone types, it is important to understand how to manually create resource records within the zone. The manual creation of resource records is required for clients who don't support DDNS or for DDNS zones that are not configured for dynamic updates.

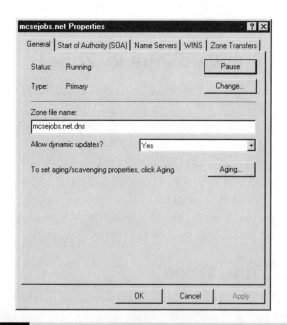

mcsejobs.net Properties

General | Start of Authority (SOA) | Name Servers | WINS | Zone Transfers |

Status: Running	Pause
Type: Primary	Change...

Zone file name:

mcsejobs.net.dns

Allow dynamic updates?   Yes

To set aging/scavenging properties, click Aging.   Aging...

OK   Cancel   Apply

FIGURE 2-1   The Zone Properties dialog box

Resource records represent host name to IP mappings in the case of a host A record and IP address to host name mappings in the case of a pointer PTR record. Resource records also exist for a number of other types of resources such as a DNS name server NS or mail server MX. The following is an example of a host name record in a forward lookup DNS zone:

```
server1v    A    192.168.1.15
```

In the previous example, server1 is the host name, A identifies the type of resource record as a host record, and 192.168.1.15 is the IP address associated with the host server1. These individual records can be created manually as shown in Figure 2-2 by following these steps:

1. Right-click the name of your forward lookup zone and select New Host from the context menu.
2. In the New Host dialog box, enter the host name in the text box under Name and enter the IP address of the host.
3. Click Add Host, OK, and Done.

Conventional DNS uses single master replication to send a copy of the zone database file stored on the name server configured with the primary zone to name servers configured with standard secondary zones. All changes, updates, or deletions are made to a primary zone database file, as it is the only readable and writeable copy. These changes are then replicated, through a process known as a zone transfer, to all other DNS servers with secondary zone files.

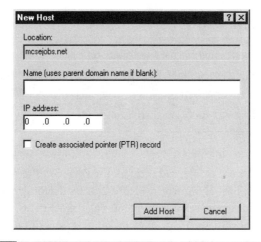

FIGURE 2-2   Manually creating DNS resource records

Zone Transfers

The Windows 2000 implementation of DNS supports two types of zone transfers:

- Full zone transfer (AXFR)
- ncremental zone transfer (IXFR)

In a full zone transfer, the entire contents of the zone database file is transferred to all DNS name servers hosting standard secondary zones. Full zone transfers increase bandwidth consumption and should be avoided across slow network connections.

Incremental zone transfers are the preferred choice for updating secondary zones as only the changes that have occurred since the last update are transferred.

The benefits of the Active Directory integrated zone are noteworthy and include the following:

- Multimaster replication, which eliminates the single point of failure customary in conventional DNS implementations
- Fault tolerance, as all domain controllers contain a copy of the zone database object
- Single replication topology, making configuration of zone transfers unnecessary
- Secure dynamic updates are supported, enabling only clients with accounts in the Active Directory to be able to dynamically update their A records

Exam Tip

The standard primary and standard secondary zone types are common among all DNS implementations. The Active Directory integrated zone is unique to Windows 2000 DNS and is only available if DNS is installed on a Windows 2000 domain controller.

Zone transfers are configured through the Zone Transfers tab in the Zone Properties dialog box, as shown in Figure 2-3. By default, zone transfers are enabled to be made to any DNS server requesting them, but two alternate choices are available to increase security. Allowing zone transfers To Any Server would enable anyone with access to your network to configure a standard secondary zone and, through a zone transfer, receive all of the computer names and their respective

IP addresses. The second choice available is to allow zone transfers Only to Servers Listed On The Name Servers Tab. This in turn requires that you configure the Name Servers tab to include the FQDNs and IP addresses of all of the DNS servers that you want to enable zone transfers to. The third configuration option is to enable zone transfers Only To The Following Servers and to type the IP addresses of those specific servers.

Local Lingo

zone transfer A zone transfer is the process of transferring zone database files from one DNS server to another. Zone transfers can be incremental or complete. The primary DNS server keeps the only read and write copy of the zone database file.

Configuring notification can be accomplished by clicking the Notify button on the Zone Transfers tab. The default setting is to automatically notify all of the servers listed on the Name Servers tab, but a second option of notifying only those servers that you specify by IP address is also available. This enables you to ensure that your zone databases are not transferred to any servers that you are unaware of.

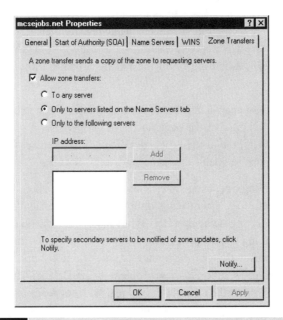

FIGURE 2-3   Configuring zone transfers

Windows 2000 Server supports both types of zone transfers: full and incremental. Down-level Windows operating systems such as Windows NT 4.0 do not support incremental zone transfers, requiring that DNS implementations that use both Windows NT 4.0 and Windows 2000 be configured to use only full zone transfers.

Exam Tip

A Windows NT 4.0 DNS server configured with a secondary zone cannot ask for an incremental zone transfer. A Windows NT 4.0 DNS server configured with a primary zone cannot transfer partial information.

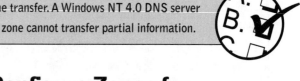

Objective 2.05

Configure Zones for Dynamic Updates

Unlike Windows Internet Naming Service (WINS), where clients automatically register their name mappings with a WINS server, conventional DNS requires that all client mappings be entered manually. The DNS implementation in Windows 2000 changes this with its support of DDNS. All computers running Windows 2000 are configured to automatically register their A resource records with their primary DNS server, assuming the zone is configured to support dynamic updates. Configuring a zone for dynamic updates is as simple as following these steps:

1. Open the DNS snap-in and select the zone that you wish to enable dynamic updates for, right-click the zone, and select Properties.
2. On the General tab of the Properties dialog box, select Yes from the drop-down box next to Enable Dynamic Updates? Click OK.

Clients running operating systems such as Windows 2000, which support DNS, are only able to register their A resource records; the client's PTR resource records can only be registered by a DHCP server, not the individual client. Down-level clients running Windows operating systems other than Windows 2000 also run into problems with dynamic updates, as they do not support the dynamic update protocol. The solution to these problems lies in DHCP. DHCP can be configured to interact with the DNS server and register resource records on behalf of all clients, not just those clients that support DDNS. This forcible registration ensures that all the clients on the network are registered in DNS and are able to be resolved by other clients on the network. To configure DHCP to forcibly register all clients with DNS, follow these steps in the dialog box shown in Figure 2-4:

1. Open the DHCP snap-in, right-click the name of the DHCP server, and select Properties.
2. Select the DNS tab in the DHCP server Properties dialog box and place a check mark in the box next to Automatically Update DHCP Client Information In DNS. Choose the second radio button next to Always Update DNS.
3. Ensure there is a check mark in the box next to Enable Updates For DNS Clients That Do Not Support Dynamic Updates. Click OK.

The Dynamic Update Process

The dynamic update process works differently depending on the choices that you make when configuring dynamic updates in the DHCP snap-in. To better understand how the dynamic update protocol works, let's first take a look at the default configuration.

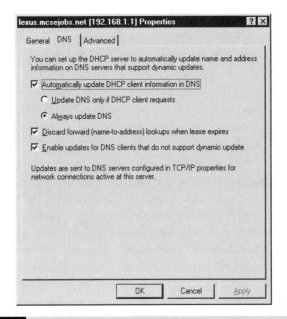

FIGURE 2-4 Configuring DNS dynamic updates in DHCP

Exam Tip

Only Windows 2000 clients support dynamic updates. To enable other Microsoft operating systems to take advantage of dynamic updates, configure the DHCP server to update the DNS records on the DNS server.

By default, Windows 2000 clients are automatically configured to perform dynamic updates even when they are configured with a static IP address. Regardless of whether a Windows 2000 client is configured statically or dynamically, the client sends a DNS update request to the DNS server for its own forward lookup record: its A resource record. The Windows 2000 client's reverse lookup record, its PTR resource record, is registered dynamically by the DHCP server when the option Automatically Update DHCP Client Information In DNS is selected, which it is by default.

Exam Tip

Static DNS servers are not able to interact with DHCP servers and support dynamic updates. Microsoft recommends that Windows 2000 DNS servers be used and configured for optimal DDNS support.

If you configure DHCP to forcibly register all clients' DNS records, including down-level clients that do not support dynamic update, the automatic registration process is different and requires that the clients have their IP address automatically assigned through DHCP. The first step in the dynamic update process is for the client to initiate a DHCP request. If the client is a Windows 2000 client, this request includes the FQDN; however, if the client is running a previous Windows operating system, the FQDN is not included in this request. Second, all DHCP servers that receive the request and have IP addresses available for lease, respond to the client with an offer of an IP address. The first response received by the client is the one the client chooses. The client then broadcasts its acceptance. The broadcast serves two purposes. First, it allows all other DHCP servers whose offers were not accepted to withdraw their offers making those IP addresses available to other clients. Second, it informs the DHCP server whose request was accepted and allows that server to send an acknowledgement and additional scope information with the lease IP address. The acknowledgement message sent from the DHCP server to the client, grants the lease of the IP address and provides other information like the lease expiry and scope information. The next step in the dynamic update process can differ depending on the operating system that the client is running. If the client computer is running Windows 2000, the client updates its own A resource record and the DHCP server updates the Windows 2000 client's PTR record with the DNS server. If the client is a down-level Windows client, the DHCP server updates both the A and PTR records with the DNS server.

Another possibility exists where the client computer is running Windows 2000 and is configured with a static IP address. In this case, the client can forgo the steps discussed that dealt with obtaining an IP address from a DHCP server and proceed right to the dynamic update component. In this example, the Windows 2000 client's DHCP client service would attempt to update the client's "A" and "PTR" records with the DNS server. The DHCP client service is configured and running by default on every computer running Windows 2000 regardless of whether the client computer is configured as a DHCP client or not.

The integration of DNS with DHCP can be used to extend the dynamic update protocol functionality to down-level clients that do not support it directly. As we have discussed, DHCP can be configured to forcibly register the "A" and "PTR" records of all clients. Configuring DHCP to "Always update forward and reverse look-ups" results in a third possible scenario. The third scenario involves all clients being configured as DHCP clients and at initialization broadcasting out for an IP address lease. All DHCP servers with available IP addresses to lease, that receive the broadcast, respond with an IP address offer. The client computer accepts the first offer it receives by broadcasting its acceptance. All DHCP servers that made an offer that was not accepted withdraw their offers making those IP addresses available to other computers. The DHCP server whose offer was accepted, broadcasts an acknowledgement back to the client with the leased IP address, terms associated with the lease and additional scope information. The DHCP server then attempts to register the clients "A" and "PTR" resource records with the DNS server on behalf of the client.

One very important point to make when discussing the dynamic DNS update process is that the use of dynamic DNS does have the potential to "dirty" the DNS database over time. When I use the term dirty I mean that name registration records that are no longer in use have a greater potential of building up within the zone database file. The reason for this is that at the expiration of the IP address lease, only the computer that registered the records is allowed to request that the records be deleted. As we have seen from the different scenarios discussed above, that could be the DHCP client, the DHCP server or a combination of the two. To address this problem, the scavenging setting for the DNS zone file can be configured and enabled.

Exam Tip

Know how the default dynamic update process works and how other iterations of this feature work, as well as how to configure dynamic updates.

Windows 2000 clients are automatically configured to support dynamic updates. This can be confirmed by following these simple steps:

1. In Networking And Dial-up Connections, right-click the local area connection that you want to ensure is configured and select Properties.
2. In the Properties dialog box for the local area connection, select Internet Protocol (TCP/IP) and click Properties.
3. In the Internet Protocol (TCP/IP) Properties dialog box, click Advanced.
4. In the Advanced TCP/IP Settings dialog box, shown in Figure 2-5, select the DNS tab and verify that a check mark exists in the box next to Register This Connection's Addresses In DNS. Place a check mark in the box next to Use This Connection's DNS Suffix In DNS Registration only if the DNS suffix differs from the domain name. Click OK three times to close all open dialog boxes.

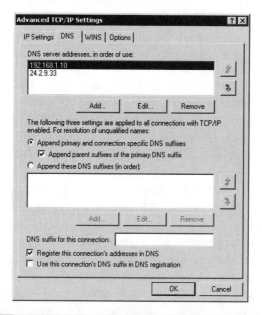

FIGURE 2-5   Confirming dynamic update support on a Windows 2000 client

Travel Assistance

For more information on the dynamic update protocol, check out the online webcast at http://support.microsoft.com/servicedesks/webcasts/wc050301/wcblurb050301.asp.

The Active Directory service in Windows 2000 does not require the support of dynamic updates; however, it is highly recommended that your DNS implementation support them. It is the dynamic update protocol that creates all of the required SRV records in DNS after the installation of the Active Directory. If you were to use an implementation of DNS that did not support dynamic updates, you would be responsible for the manual creation of the SRV records. All of the required SRV records that must exist for proper functionality in DNS are stored in a file named netlogon.dns in the path %systemroot%\system32\config.

Secure Dynamic Updates

Dynamic updates can also be made secure to enable only client computers with an account in the Active Directory or clients that originally updated their client record to register their resource records or update them again. There are two key benefits of secure dynamic updates:

- The ability to grant the permission to modify zones and resource records to specific users and groups
- The ability to protect zones and resource records against unauthorized modification

Configuring secure dynamic updates can be accomplished on the DNS server by selecting Only Secure Updates from the drop-down menu next to Allow dynamic Updates? on the General tab of the DNS servers Properties dialog box, shown in Figure 2-1.

Exam Tip

Only Active Directory–integrated zones can be configured for secure dynamic updates.

One problem might arise with the use of secure dynamic updates: Secure dynamic updates require that the owner of the resource record (the computer) be the only computer enabled to update that record. This becomes an issue when you have configured DHCP to perform the DNS updates on behalf of the client computer. To resolve this problem, the DHCP server computer account must be added to the DnsUpdateProxy group.

Exam Tip

To enable DHCP servers to update DNS when the zone is configured for secure dynamic updates, the DHCP servers must be added to the DnsUpdateProxy group.

Now that we have learned about the configuration of zone database files, it is time to turn our attention to the delegation of zones that enables us to divide DNS namespaces into smaller, more manageable pieces that can be administered by different administrators.

Objective 2.06   Implement a Delegated Zone for DNS

DNS divides namespaces into both domains and zones, which tends to confuse some people. The difference between a zone and a domain is subtle. Zones are used to store name information about one or more DNS domains or a contiguous portion of a DNS domain namespace. The DNS server, also known as a name server, that stores the zone information is said to have authority for that zone. In other words, if you have the keys to a safe that contains security deposit boxes, each with their own locks, you have authority over the contents of the safe but not necessarily the contents of each individual security deposit box. A zone is very similar to a safe, and some of the domain names in the zone may be delegated. These delegated zones would be represented by individual security deposit boxes which, with their own keys, you do not have authority over. In DNS, the name server in the root zone does not have authority over the names and data that have been delegated; that authority belongs to another name server. A zone file is simply a text file that contains the resource records used in the name resolution process. Let's revisit the example I used earlier in the chapter about the top level

.ca domain that included subdomains for each province (.bc, which is British Columbia; .mb, which is Manitoba; and .on, which is Ontario). The .ca domain contains all the data in .ca plus all the data in bc.ca, mb.ca, and on.ca, but the zone .ca contains only the data in the .ca domain. Authority for the bc.ca, mb.ca, and on.ca domains may be delegated to organizations in each of the individual provinces.

A zone can be delegated to accomplish a number of goals, including the following:

- The need to delegate management of a DNS domain to a specific individual or group of individuals
- The improvement of performance by distributing the load and maintenance of one large DNS database among multiple name servers
- The creation of a fault tolerant DNS environment by distributing one large DNS database among multiple name servers
- The need to enable for a host's organizational affiliation by inclusion in the appropriate domain

Delegation simply enables you to assign responsibility or authority for a portion of the DNS namespace to a separate entity or other zone. Delegation is represented by the Name Server (NS) resource record that specifies the delegated zone and the name server authoritative for that zone. Delegation is the primary mechanism that enables DNS to be a distributed, hierarchical namespace.

The Start of Authority (SOA) resource record, which exists in every zone file, is the first record created with the creation of the zone. The SOA resource record identifies the primary DNS name server for the zone and indicates which name server holds the read/write copy of the zone database file. Names within a zone can be delegated to other zones. Let's use the .ca domain as an example to drive home the concept of delegation and how to implement delegation.

Let's assume that you are the administrator of the .ca domain and the primary DNS zone is configured on a server named NS1CA. Servers named NS2CA, NS3CA, and NS4CA are all configured as secondary name servers in the .ca domain. To date, all administration of the .ca zone, which includes all of the provincial domains, has been handled in Ottawa, the nation's capital. Then, one day, the provinces ask to be given the authority over each of their own individual namespaces, and to support this change in authority, each province configures one name server with the primary DNS zone for its province, which is named NS1ON in the case of Ontario and NS1BC for British Columbia. Each province also configures four secondary servers. The delegation of the zones must now take place on NS1CA in Ottawa following these steps:

1. On NS1CA, in the DNS snap-in, right-click the .ca domain and select New Delegation from the context menu. This step will have to be repeated for each zone you wish to delegate, which in this case is for each province.
2. Click Next in the first dialog box of the New Delegation Wizard. In the second dialog box, enter the name of the domain to be delegated to a different zone. In our example, this would be .on for Ontario or .bc for British Columbia, and click Next.
3. Click Add to specify the server name and IP address of the DNS name server that you wish to host the delegated zone, then click Next and Finish.

Exam Tip

A DNS server can contain multiple zone database files, and a single zone can contain multiple domains.

A single DNS server is capable of hosting multiple zones and different zone types. For example, an ISP can operate one DNS server that contains hundreds of zones for different customers (for example, rory.com, jason.com, dina.com, and laura.com). That same DNS server could contain the primary zones for each of these domain names and also contain the secondary zones for domains named bill.com, terry.com, sue.com, and doug.com.

Now that we have an understanding of the role zones play in your DNS architecture, we will continue our DNS journey by looking at some of the different ways in which DNS can be implemented in an organization's network.

DNS Design Fundamentals

The proper DNS namespace design is fundamental to the successful deployment, maintenance, and growth of your Active Directory structure. Each Active Directory domain that you create requires a DNS domain for resolution of the computer names and services within that domain. In order to architect the most suitable DNS namespace for your organization, you must begin by evaluating your existing network and planning for the future. Some of the things that you should be considering during this planning period are your organization's existing connectivity to the Internet, anticipated network changes or expansions, and existing and future client base. The existing and future client base is important in helping you to assess how you must configure DNS for effective name resolution.

For example, if your client base will remain running Windows 98 for the next two years, the integration of WINS with DNS might be an option that you should consider. On the other hand, if your client base will be migrated to Windows 2000 relatively soon, the use of dynamic update will be supported at the client level, meaning that the integration of DNS and DHCP might not be required in the long term. For security reasons, the internal DNS zone information should be completely hidden from the Internet on the private DNS namespace. External resolution of the computers, such as your organization's web and mail servers that are exposed to the Internet directly, or in a DMZ, whose resource records are located on the public DNS name server, must also be considered when planning your DNS namespace. This section of the chapter will look at the different approaches available for the design of the private namespaces and the configuration of your DNS servers and zones.

The general approach to DNS configuration is to have both an internal and external DNS server. The purpose of the internal server is to maintain the records of both the external and internal computers and only replicate this information to other internal DNS servers. The external DNS server is designed to provide name resolution for only those computers exposed to the Internet. Before deciding on an appropriate design, the clients that require DNS resolution must also be factored in. There are four types of clients, distinguishable by their software proxy capability:

- Proxy unaware
- Supporting Local Address Table (LAT)
- Supporting name exclusion list
- Supporting proxy auto configuration file

If name resolution is required by either proxy unaware or LAT supporting clients, the internal namespace can't have a private root. The internal DNS server must be configured to forward unresolved queries to the Internet, and the internal namespaces created would be subdomains of the public namespace. An example of this is shown in the following illustration, where the internal clients support LAT but are proxy unaware. The organization's domain name is mcsejobs.net, but the internal DNS domain created to support the Active Directory and internal name resolution should be created as a subdomain, in this case, corp. This will enable internal clients to be configured as DNS clients of the internal DNS server, and when the internal DNS server can't resolve the name that the internal client is querying for, the resolution request will be forwarded to the external DNS server; therefore, it is not possible to configure a private root domain in this example. Doing so would prevent all external names from being resolved, as the internal clients would always contact their internal DNS server for resolution, and when the internal DNS server isn't able to resolve the name, it has nowhere to forward the query to for resolution.

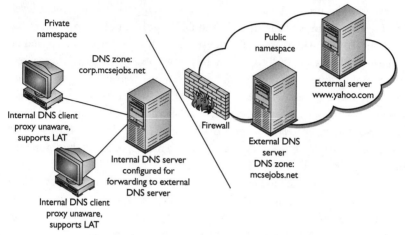

The situation becomes more complicated if the public and private name-spaces are the same, as depicted in the following illustration. In this illustration, mcsejobs.net is both the internal and external namespace. The complication here arises when an internal client needs to resolve the name of an external server (www.yahoo.com). In order for the client to be able to resolve the www.yahoo.com and contact www.yahoo.com, the client must support a Proxy Auto Configuration file. This would enable the client to identify www.yahoo.com as an external server and send the resolution request to the proxy server, which in turn would send it to the external DNS server authoritative for the yahoo.com domain.

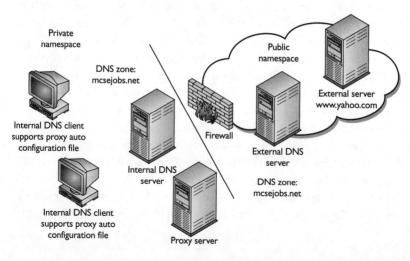

The other alternative in this situation is to clone external servers internally and copy external DNS records to the internal DNS server. This would enable the company's own external servers to be resolved from the internal DNS records and enable resolution requests for servers outside the namespace of the organization to be resolved through the proxy server to an external DNS server. This alternative might appear simple in this example, where only the external DNS server's records would have to be copied to the internal DNS server, but think about an example that contains multiple web and mail servers on the public network. Each one of the external servers would have to be cloned internally, and any administrative changes made to one would have to be made to the clone. The result would be an administrative nightmare, and in most cases, cost prohibitive.

Exam Tip

If your organization does not require external Internet name resolution, delete the entries in the cache.dns file on the DNS server and add in entries for your root servers.

Objective 2.07

Configure a Root Name Server

Another DNS namespace scenario that is available is the configuration of an internal root name server. The use of an internal DNS root name server is generally limited to organizations that are not connected to the Internet or are connected through a proxy server. The .local domain extension can be used when the company is not connected to the Internet. An example of this would be mcse-jobs.local. It's more likely that you will find the internal root name server created in environments where Internet access is provided through a proxy server and client computers are either configured with a Proxy Auto Configuration file or an LAT to help them determine where to send their name resolution requests.

Exam Tip

Only configure a root name server if your organization is not connected to the Internet or if it is connected to the Internet via a proxy server.

Environments in which a root name server is used and Internet access is required must have clients that are proxy aware and are able to tell whether the destination IP address that they are trying to communicate with is an internal or external address.

Objective 2.08 Configure a Caching-Only Server

The last type of DNS server that you should be aware of for the exam is the caching-only server. A caching-only server is a DNS server that is capable of resolving names for clients and then storing those results but do not contain any forward or reverse lookup zones. Where you tend to find caching-only servers deployed is in networks that are divided by slow network connections. Think of it as a mining company that has a head office in Calgary with a fast connection out to the Internet but slow connections to all of its remote mining sites. Placing a caching-only server at the remote mining sites would enable recursive queries to be sent from the caching-only server at the remote office to the DNS server at the head office in Calgary. The DNS server at the head office would then use the fast network connection to resolve the query and pass the resolved query back to the caching-only server, which would first store the information in its cache and then return the information to the client.

The benefit derived from a caching-only server is that it does not utilize bandwidth for zone transfers as it doesn't maintain any zone database files. Should its cache be large enough, all resolution attempts have the potential of being resolved locally, resulting in decreased resolution traffic over the slow wide area network (WAN) connection.

Configuring a caching-only server is as simple as installing DNS on a computer running Windows 2000 Server. No other configuration is required for a caching-only server; although, it is recommended that the server be set to perform recursive queries through the use of *forwarders*. Forwarding can be configured by following these steps:

1. Open the DNS snap-in and right-click the DNS server that you wish to configure forwarding on.
2. In the DNS Servers Properties dialog box, select the Forwarders tab and place a check mark in the box next to Enable Forwarders.
3. Enter the IP address of the server that you wish to forward resolution queries to in the IP Address box and click Add. When you are finished adding DNS server IP addresses, click OK.

Local Lingo

forwarders Forwarders are DNS servers that are specifically designated to receive resolution queries for the resolution of external
domain names and to forward those queries to external DNS servers.

Integrating with BIND

One additional scenario you may run into is a network that currently uses a BIND
implementation of DNS for name resolution. BIND versions 8.1.2 and greater can
support the Active Directory as they support SRV resource records; however,
BIND implementations cannot be integrated with WINS as WINS resource
records are not a standard record type.

If it is necessary or mandated that the existing BIND implementation remain
in place, the recommended solution is to create a subdomain hosted by Windows
2000 DNS servers and delegate control of the subdomain zone to the Window
2000 DNS servers. An example of this is shown in the following two illustrations.
The first illustration demonstrates the creation of the new subdomain, corp, and
the second illustration shows the corp subdomain after delegation, where the DNS
servers in the corp domain now have authority for that zone.

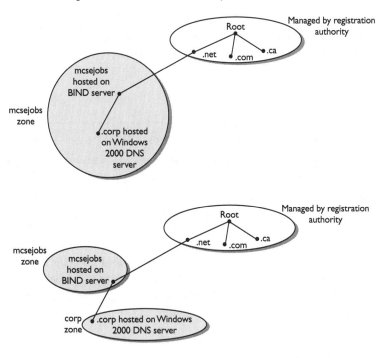

Exam Tip

To integrate Windows 2000 DNS into a network that currently uses and wants to maintain a BIND implementation, create a DNS subdomain within the company's existing namespace and delegate control of that new domain to a Windows 2000 DNS server. This configuration enables the subdomain to be configured with Active Directory integrated zones that have dynamic updates enabled.

Now that you are familiar with how to design DNS namespaces for different network infrastructures and how to install and configure a DNS server, we will continue with a look at how to manage, monitor, and test DNS to ensure continued functionality.

Objective 2.09   Manage and Monitor DNS

A number of tools are included in Windows 2000 to manage, test, and troubleshoot DNS. In this section, we will take a look at each of these tools and how they can be used to help you diagnose and solve DNS-related issues.

Exam Tip

To administer DNS on a Windows 2000 member server, you must be a member of the local administrators group. To administer DNS on a Windows 2000 domain controller, you must be a member of the DNS Admins, Domain Admins, or Enterprise Admins group.

The majority of your DNS administration will be done using the DNS snap-in found in the Administration Tools menu. The DNS snap-in can be configured to manage and monitor multiple DNS servers, enabling administration of local DNS zones as well as zones on remote DNS servers.

Dnscmd

Dnscmd is a command-line tool that can be used to administer DNS from both the command prompt and through scripted batch files. Knowing the exact switches and uses of dnscmd will not be a focus on the exam, but knowing what it can be used for may prove useful in your daily administration.

Travel Assistance

To find out more about the dnscmd tool, copy it from the Support\
Enterprise\Reskit folder on the Windows 2000 Server CD to the
hard drive and at the command prompt, type **dnscmd /?**.

The following abbreviated list of DNS administration tasks can be accomplished with the Dnscmd tool:

- List information about the server including its configuration settings, configuration flags, aging configuration, IP addresses, listening addresses, and forwarders
- Clear the DNS servers cache
- Identify information about a specific zone file
- Add, delete, pause, and resume a zone
- Force the refresh of a zone from the DNS master server
- Change the type of zone
- Add and delete records in a zone, root hints, or the cache

Event Logs

The event logs are always a good place to start your monitoring and troubleshooting efforts. One important note to make is that DNS has its own event log in Windows 2000 where DNS messages will be logged. Don't be fooled by looking in the system log and not finding any DNS messages!

Additional Tools

Additional monitoring and troubleshooting tools include Network Monitor and System Monitor. Network Monitor can be used to capture and view details of DNS packets sent to and from the DNS server. The numerous DNS counters in System Monitor can also be configured to monitor DNS and to ensure that certain performance metrics are being met.

Objective 2.10
Test the DNS Server Service

A number of tools are available to test the DNS to ensure that it is functioning correctly. The monitoring tab is a component of the DNS snap-in, that was intended to provide DNS service testing functionality but the reliability of this tool is not great. Beware, as it often produces incorrect results. This might be addressed in future service packs, but in the original release, it is unreliable. To monitor DNS using the DNS snap-in follow these steps:

1. In the DNS snap-in, right-click the name of the DNS server and select Properties.
2. Select the Monitoring tab in the DNS Server Properties dialog box, as shown in Figure 2-6.

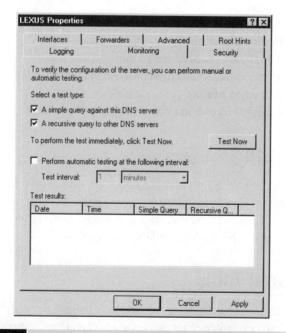

FIGURE 2-6   Testing DNS using the Monitoring tab

3. To test your forward lookup zone, place a check mark in the box next to A Simple Query Against This DNS Server. To test your reverse lookup zone, place a check mark in the box next to A Recursive Query To Other DNS Servers. Click Test Now.

In the Test Results box in the bottom portion of the monitoring tab, one of two results should appear: Pass or Fail. Pass indicates that the DNS you have tested is working fine, and fail indicates problems. The fail result, however, is where the tool tends to produce incorrect results, often stating that the service is failing when it appears to be working fine. These incorrect results tend to occur when using the Monitoring tab immediately after a zone has been added or removed. Sometimes closing and reopening the DNS snap-in fixes this problem. To get a better understanding of any problems with the service, I recommend you stick to using Nslookup, a command line utility that is much more reliable.

Nslookup

Nslookup is the default troubleshooting tool for all implementations of DNS. Nslookup functions in one of two modes: interactive or noninteractive. Interactive mode is intended to be used when you will be making multiple queries against the DNS server. Noninteractive mode is intended to be used when you simply require a single query. Next, we will look at some examples of the Nslookup command.

To query the DNS server server1.mcsejobs.net for a listing of all host A resource records, execute the command nslookup, then ls –t a <domain name> where ls instructs the DNS server to provide a list of a specific type –t of resource record A or host records and domain name is the domain that you want to query. The same command can be issued for different kinds of records by replacing the *a* in the above command with other record types such as PTR, MX, and CNAME.

Travel Advisory

You cannot run this query unless Allow Zone Transfers is checked on the zone transfer tab on the properties of the zone in question. You will receive a query refused error if zone transfers are not allowed which will prevent you from receiving a response from your nslookup query.

Nslookup can also be used to test the forward and reverse name resolution on a DNS server. To test forward lookup resolution in the mcsejobs.net domain, execute the command nslookup hostname.mcsejobs.net where hostname is the name of a valid host in the mcsejobs.net domain. The response to this query should be the IP address of the host. To test the reverse lookup resolution in the same domain, execute the command nslookup 192.168.1.4 where 192.168.1.4 is a valid IP address in the mcsejobs.net domain. The response to this query should be the FQDN of the host mapped to that IP address.

Exam Tip

For Nslookup to function correctly, a PTR resource record must exist for the server on which you perform the lookup. At startup, Nslookup performs a reverse lookup query on the IP address of the server that is running DNS and generates an error message if it is unable to resolve the address to a name.

It may be necessary from time to time to troubleshoot DNS from the client as well as the server. Name resolution problems are not limited to the DNS server. They can occur when a client's IP address changes and the name registration does not get updated; hence, the clients name is mapped to the incorrect IP address. The ipconfig command can be of great use when trying to resolve name resolution problems at the client. Two ipconfig commands have been specifically incorporated into Windows 2000 to assist with the troubleshooting process.

The first command is the ipconfig /registerdns command, which when executed on the client computer, instructs the client to forcibly register its FQDN with the DNS server, updating any previous information on the DNS server. This command can also be used to forcibly register the client if it is found that no resource records for the client exist on the DNS server. Should no client records exist, this could suggest a problem exists with the configuration of dynamic update for the zone.

The second command is the ipconfig /flushdns command, which when run on the client, deletes any name to IP or IP to name mappings in the client's local cache. Because the client will always look to its local cache first in the name resolution process, having a "polluted" cache or a cache with incorrect mappings can result in name resolution problems. Flushing the cache with the ipconfig /flushdns command deletes all of the entries in the cache, forcing the client to query a DNS server for the name resolution.

Objective 2.11 Configure a DNS Client

The last step in the configuration of DNS is the configuration of the clients. DNS clients can be configured with the address or addresses of one or more DNS servers either manually or automatically via the DHCP service. Manual configuration requires more administrative effort as the DNS addresses must be entered individually. As with any manual process, the chances of human error increase proportionally with the number of computers that require manual configuration. I am fairly confident that if I had to enter more than 25 static IP addresses on 25 different computers, I would probably incorrectly enter at least one. To manually configure a DNS client follow these steps:

1. Click Start, Settings, Network and Dial-up Connections, and right-click the local area connection that you wish to configure DNS on. Select Properties.
2. In the Properties dialog box, on the General tab, select TCP/IP Properties from the section titled Components Checked Are Used By This Connection, and click the Properties button.
3. In the bottom section of the TCP/IP Properties dialog box, select Use The Following DNS Server Addresses and enter the IP address of the DNS server you wish to configure as your primary and secondary DNS server.
4. Click OK twice to close all dialog boxes.

Exam Tip

Manually configured DNS information takes precedence over information that is obtained by a client through a DHCP server.

If a client computer's IP address changes its name mapping in the DNS, the zone database will have to be updated. This information can be forcibly updated by entering the following command:

```
Ipconfig /registerdns
```

If the IP address of a server changes and you have connected to that server recently, the local DNS cache on your client machine will contain the wrong name-mapping information. To delete the contents of the local DNS cache, use the following command:

```
Ipconfig /flushdns
```

The DNS replaces WINS as the primary name resolution service in Windows 2000. WINS, which we will explore further in Chapter 3, is no longer required for native Windows 2000 networks. Computers running Windows 2000 clients use DNS as their primary means of name resolution and service location, including locating domain controllers for logon. Computers running down-level Windows operating systems such as Windows 95, 98, NT 4.0, and so on, however, still use NetBIOS name resolution to locate domain controllers.

Travel Assistance

For more information on the DNS, see RFC 2136 or Microsoft's Windows 2000 DNS white paper located at http://www.microsoft.com/windows2000/ techinfo/howitworks/communications/nameadrmgmt/w2kdns.asp. Microsoft has a number of web seminars available on TechNet that cover numerous aspects of Windows 2000 DNS.

CHECKPOINT

✔ **Objective 2.01: Install, Configure, and Troubleshoot DNS** DNS is the primary means of name resolution in Windows 2000. Down-level Windows clients still use NetBIOS name resolution. DNS is a hierarchical namespace that is organized into domains, subdomains, and zones. The order in which DNS name resolution takes place is localhost, DNS client cache, DNS Server, NetBIOS Name Cache, WINS, Broadcast, Lmhosts file. The DNS client cache keeps all answers to DNS queries for five minutes by default, helping to reduce network traffic.

✔ **Objective 2.02: Install the DNS Server Service** DNS is installed through the Add/Remove Windows Component section in Add/Remove Programs in Control Panel. Each Active Directory domain requires a DNS domain but each DNS domain does not require an Active Directory domain. Active Directory is dependent of DNS for the resolution of host name and service resource records. The DNS implementation used to support the Active Directory must include support for SRV resource records. It is also recommended that it support the dynamic update protocol and incremental zone transfers, but these features are not requirements. If the dynamic update protocol is not supported, the SRV records must be manually created from the netlogon.dns file in the %systemroot%\system32\config directory.

✔ **Objective 2.03: Configure Zones** There are three types of zones: standard primary, standard secondary, and Active Directory integrated. Each zone type can be configured for forward or reverse lookups. A forward lookup zone, regardless of its type (primary, secondary, or Active Directory integrated) is used to resolve host names to IP addresses. A reverse lookup zone is used to resolve IP addresses to host names. A single DNS server can host multiple zones and different zone types. Conventional DNS that uses primary and secondary zones is limited by a single point of failure: the server hosting the standard primary zone. Active Directory integrated zones enable you to leverage multimaster replication, eliminating the single point of failure. Traditional DNS zones use zone transfers to send changes made to the primary DNS zone file to name servers configured with secondary zones. Windows 2000 supports two types of zone transfers: full (AXFR) and incremental (IXFR). Active Directory integrated zones require the Active Directory to be installed before they can be configured. Active Directory integrated zones replicate using Active Directory replication to all domain controllers in the domain. When a zone is changed to an Active Directory integrated zone, the original zone database file is copied into Active Directory as an object and deleted from its original location in the %systemroot%\system32\dns directory.

✔ **Objective 2.04: Manually Create DNS Resource Records** DNS resource records can be created manually using the DNS snap-in. SRV resource records also have to be created if the DNS installed to support Active Directory does not support dynamic updates. The SRV resource records in the netlogon.dns file are the records that are required to be created.

✔ **Objective 2.05: Configure Zones for Dynamic Updates** Only Windows 2000 clients support dynamic updates. The DHCP service can be configured to enable all clients–Windows 2000 and down-level Windows clients-to have their resource records automatically updated. Windows 2000 clients, even those statically configured, register their A resource record with the DNS server. The client's PTR record is registered in DNS by the DHCP server if the client is configured to obtain an IP address from the DCHP server. If the client is statically configured, it tries to register both its A and PTR records with the DNS server. To enable DHCP servers to update DNS when the zone is configured for secure dynamic updates, the DHCP servers must be added to the DnsUpdateProxy group. The configuration of secure dynamic updates requires the zone be an Active Directory integrated zone. Secure dynamic updates enable only computers that are members of the Active Directory domain to dynamically update their records and only computers that previously registered their records to reregister them.

✔ **Objective 2.06: Implement a Delegated Zone for DNS**   Delegating zones enables you to assign responsibility or authority for a portion of the DNS namespace to a separate entity or other zone. Zone delegation is useful when you currently use a BIND implementation. You can create a subdomain in your current namespace and delegate authority to a Windows 2000 DNS name server. This would enable the integration of WINS with DNS and the use of Active Directory integrated zones.

✔ **Objective 2.07: Configure a Root Name Server**   A root name server should only be configured in a network that does not have an Internet connection or connects to the Internet through a proxy server. All entries in the cache.dns file can be deleted and entries for internal root name servers added.

✔ **Objective 2.08: Configure a Caching-Only Server**   A caching-only server is useful in networks where the goal of the network is to eliminate zone transfer traffic across slow network connections while maintaining the ability to resolve host names.

✔ **Objective 2.09: Manage and Monitor DNS**   DNS can be managed and monitored using tools and utilities that include Dnscmd, Event Log, Network Monitor, System Monitor, and the DNS snap-in.

✔ **Objective 2.10: Test the DNS Server Service**   Nslookup and the Monitoring tab in the DNS server property dialog box can be used to troubleshoot DNS.

✔ **Objective 2.11: Configure a DNS Client**   The ipconfig /registerdns command can be used to forcibly register a client's resource records, and the ipconfig /flushdns command can be used to clear the client's DNS cache.

REVIEW QUESTIONS

1. You have installed and configured DNS on a Windows 2000 domain controller. You want to ensure that the primary zone is fault tolerant but do not want to install DNS on another server. Which of the following solutions enables you to accomplish this?

   A. Use the Task Scheduler to run the NTBackup utility every night at midnight to back up the DNS database.

   B. Configure the primary zone to enable zone transfers.

   C. Change the zone type to an Active Directory integrated zone.

   D. Change the zone to support only secure dynamic updates.

2. As the DNS administrator, you are responsible for changing the zone type on your DNS server from a standard primary zone to an Active Directory integrated zone. Which of the following must be true for you to accomplish this task?

   A. The primary zone must be installed on a member server in an Active Directory domain.

   B. The primary zone must be installed on a Windows NT 4.0 BDC in an Active Directory domain.

   C. The primary zone must be installed on a Windows 2000 domain controller.

   D. All DNS servers running secondary zones must have their DNS stopped.

3. Which of the following is required in order to configure a DNS zone running on a server configured as a Windows 2000 domain controller to accept only secure dynamic updates?

   A. All client computers must be running the Active Directory services client.

   B. All client computers must be configured as DHCP clients.

   C. The zone type must be a standard primary zone.

   D. The zone type must be an Active Directory integrated zone.

4. Your organization is considering a migration to Windows 2000 on both the server and desktop platform. Your network currently uses both WINS and a BIND 4.01 implementation for name resolution. Which of the following must be supported in your DNS implementation in order to properly install and configure the Active Directory?

   A. Dynamic update protocol

   B. Incremental zone transfers

    C. Secure dynamic updates

    D. Service resource records

5. You have just completed the migration to Windows 2000 on all of your servers. All of the clients in your network run Windows 95 and will be upgraded to Windows XP in one year's time. How can you configure DNS to resolve the Windows 95 clients computer names to IP addresses?

    A. Install Windows 2000 DNS and configure it for dynamic updates.

    B. Install Windows 2000 DNS and configure it with an Active Directory integrated zone that enables only secure updates.

    C. Install the Active Directory services client on all the computers running Windows 95.

    D. Install Windows 2000 DNS and add a WINS record to the zone.

6. You have just completed the migration to Windows 2000 on all of your servers, including two DNS servers. All of the clients in your network run Windows 95 and will be upgraded to Windows XP in one year's time. You would like to enable your DNS zones to use dynamic updates. Which of the following are valid options to accomplish this? (Choose all that apply.)

    A. Install the Active Directory services client on the computers running Windows 95.

    B. Configure the DHCP server to dynamically update client records on behalf of the clients.

    C. Configure the DNS zone to support dynamic updates from down-level clients in DNS.

    D. Install the Windows 2000 Terminal services client on the computers running Windows 95.

7. You have enabled dynamic updates for the Active Directory integrated zones on your Windows 2000 DNS server. The DNS server is configured with the default configuration. DHCP is also configured on the network, and all Windows 2000 Professional clients are configured to use DHCP. Which of the following events will trigger the reregistration of the client's A record with the DNS server?

    A. The client releases its DHCP address lease.

    B. The client system is rebooted.

    C. Running the command nbtstat -RR.

    D. Every 24 hours.

8. You have enabled dynamic updates for the Active Directory integrated zones on your Windows 2000 DNS server. The DNS server is configured with the default configuration. DHCP is also configured on the network and all Windows 2000 Professional clients are configured to use DHCP. The lease period set on the DHCP server is set to its default of eight days. What is the longest time that a client computer would ever wait to try to reregister its A resource record, assuming that it is not rebooted?

   A. 12 hours
   B. 4 days
   C. 24 hours
   D. 8 days

9. Which of the following client computer operating systems support dynamic updates?

   A. Windows 2000 Professional
   B. Windows 95
   C. Windows 98
   D. Windows NT 4.0 with SP4

10. You have enabled dynamic updates on your Windows 2000 DNS server. You have also configured scavenging and set the No-Refresh interval to 3 days and the Refresh interval to 5 days. After what number of days will DNS scavenging delete records?

   A. 3 days
   B. 5 days
   C. 8 days
   D. 1 day

REVIEW ANSWERS

1. **C** Changing the zone type from standard primary to Active Directory integrated enables the DNS database to be added to the Active Directory and replicated to other domain controllers during Active Directory replication. The need for zone transfers is no longer required.

2. **C** Changing the zone type of a standard primary zone to an Active Directory integrated zone requires that the primary zone be located on a server configured as a Windows 2000 domain controller.

3. **D** Only Active Directory integrated zones can be configured to accept secure dynamic updates.

4. **D** The proper installation and configuration of DNS only has one requirement for supporting DNS: SRV resource records. Dynamic updates would be very beneficial as well, but they are not required. Manual entry of all of the required service records will be necessary without DDNS but once created and maintained, Active Directory will function fine.

5. **D** Configuring your Windows 2000 DNS server with a WINS record enables DNS to query WINS for resolve computer names to IP addresses when the DNS server is unable to perform the resolution. This extended WINS integration is only available on Windows 2000 DNS servers as the WINS record is a nonstandard DNS resource record.

6. **B** By default, the client DHCP updates its own A resource record on the DNS server when dynamic updates are enabled. As Windows 95 clients do not support the dynamic update protocol, the DHCP server can be configured to dynamically update the client A resource record on the DHCP server.

7. **B** **D** The client reregisters its A resource record with the DNS server when the system is rebooted and every 24 hours. If your system is always running, it will re-register once a day.

8. **C** The longest time that a client would ever wait to reregister its A resource record is 24 hours, assuming that the DNS and DHCP servers were configured with the default settings.

9. **A** Windows 2000 is the only current Microsoft operating system that supports dynamic updates.

10. **C** When the No-Refresh interval is set to 3 days and the Refresh interval is set to 5 days, scavenging will delete records older than 8 days. A record is scavenged from the DNS database when the record is older than the sum of the no-refresh interval and the refresh interval.

WINS
Network
Infrastructure

ETA	NEWBIE	SOME EXPERIENCE	EXPERT
	5–7 hours	2–5 hours	1–2 hours

Your success on the Implementing and Administering a Microsoft Windows 2000 Network Infrastructure exam requires you to have a thorough understanding of the role the WINS service plays, of the proper configuration of WINS, of the different node types, and of the WINS replication options. You must also know how to configure the lmhosts file and how to manage and monitor WINS. Practical, hands-on experience is an asset that will increase your likelihood of passing this exam and is a good way to learn about WINS and become more comfortable with basic WINS concepts. Any experience that you have with WINS in a large network environment will also be an asset, as you are likely to run into questions about integrating WINS into a network environment that uses UNIX BIND servers and other non-WINS clients and servers.

Objective 3.01 Install, Configure, and Troubleshoot WINS

The installation of WINS is conducted through the Add/Remove Windows Components section of Add/Remove Programs in Control Panel. The configuration of WINS encompasses the configuration of both the WINS server and WINS clients. WINS client configuration can be accomplished manually through static TCP/IP configuration on each client or dynamically with the use of DHCP. In network environments with more than one WINS server, WINS replication must also be configured to enable the individual WINS databases stored on each of the WINS servers to send their information to each other. There are three types of replication that can be configured in WINS: push, pull, and push/pull. Before we explore each of the individual configuration options in detail, we will begin our journey with an overview of WINS and the NetBIOS name resolution process.

WINS Overview

The Windows Internet Naming Service (WINS) is a component of Windows 2000 that was carried forward from Windows NT. WINS has been replaced as the default and is a previously required service for name resolution in networks with down-level Windows operating systems. In Windows 2000, the DNS service is now the primary service for name resolution; however, in networks that consist of computers running both Windows 2000 and non-Windows 2000 operating systems, such as Windows NT, Windows 95, or Windows 98, it is recommended to use the WINS service in addition to DNS. The DNS service, as discussed in

Chapter 2, resolves host names or FQDNs to IP addresses. The WINS service, however, resolves NetBIOS names to IP addresses. The WINS service has been improved in Windows 2000 and offers a number of new features and enhancements that we will explore throughout the chapter, such as:

- Persistent connections for replication partners
- Manual tombstoning of WINS records
- Enhanced filtering and record searching in the WINS database
- The ability to delete both static and dynamic records from the WINS database
- The ability to export WINS data to a comma-delimited file

As with DNS, WINS makes it possible to configure clients in one of two ways with WINS server and node type information: statically or dynamically. Static configuration requires that each client be manually configured with the IP address of one or more WINS servers by editing the client's TCP/IP properties. Dynamic configuration can be accomplished by adding the IP address of one or more WINS servers and the appropriate node type information to the DHCP scope or server properties on the DHCP server. Once a client has been configured, they can participate in the NetBIOS name resolution process, which we will explore next.

Objective 3.02

Configure NetBIOS Name Resolution

The NetBIOS name resolution process varies in the sequence and number of steps according to the NetBIOS node type with which the client is configured. Four node types are supported and available in Windows 2000 and are listed and described in Table 3-1. The hybrid node type is the default for all Windows 2000 clients and down-level Microsoft clients.

TABLE 3.1	WINS Server Node Types
Node Type	**Description**
B-node	Broadcast node uses a broadcast for name registration and resolution.

(Continued)

TABLE 3.1	WINS Server Node Types (*Continued*)
Node Type	**Description**
P-node	Peer node queries a WINS name server for resolution. A requirement of P-node is that all computers be configured with the IP address of a WINS server; otherwise, communication will fail.
M-node	Mixed node combines the resolution strategies used by both B-node and P-node. In M-node, resolution of a NetBIOS name is first attempted by a broadcast, and, if unsuccessful, a query is sent to WINS server configured as the client's primary WINS server.
H-node	Hybrid node is the default node, and it too combines the resolution strategies used by B-node and P-node, but in the reverse order. H-node resolution begins with a query to a WINS server followed by a broadcast if the initial query to WINS does not resolve the NetBIOS name.

Local Lingo

node   The word "node" is commonly used to refer to a computer, a server, or a workstation on a network segment. "Node types" refers to the type of NetBIOS name resolution that an individual computer or node is configured to use. Don't confuse the term "node types" with the type of client computer (for example, a server or a workstation). To identify which node type a computer is configured as, open the Command Prompt, enter the command **ipconfig /all**, and press ENTER. The results of the ipconfig command will list the node type of the computer, as shown in Figure 3-1.

NetBIOS name resolution, by default, is a seven-step process in Windows 2000. The resolution process begins with a user entering a command such as the NET USE command to connect to another computer by NetBIOS name. An example of

```
C:\WINNT\System32\cmd.exe                                         _ □ ×
C:\>ipconfig /all

Windows 2000 IP Configuration

        Host Name . . . . . . . . . . . : noteadsrv
        Primary DNS Suffix . . . . . . . : imason.com
        Node Type . . . . . . . . . . . : Hybrid
        IP Routing Enabled. . . . . . . : No
        WINS Proxy Enabled. . . . . . . : No
        DNS Suffix Search List. . . . . : imason.com

Ethernet adapter External:

        Connection-specific DNS Suffix  . :
        Description . . . . . . . . . . : 3Com Megahertz 10/100 LAN CardBus PC
   Card #2
        Physical Address. . . . . . . . : 00-50-04-5B-E4-5F
        DHCP Enabled. . . . . . . . . . : No
        IP Address. . . . . . . . . . . : 192.168.1.200
        Subnet Mask . . . . . . . . . . : 255.255.255.0
        Default Gateway . . . . . . . . : 192.168.1.1
        DNS Servers . . . . . . . . . . : 192.168.1.10
                                          24.2.9.33
C:\>_
```

FIGURE 3-1   Identifying a client's node type

mapping a drive to a remote computer using a NetBIOS name is shown here:

```
net use x: \\server1\sharename
```

In the previous example, "server1" is the name of the computer on which the share titled "sharename" exists and "x:" is the drive letter that will be used to map a drive to that location from the computer on which the command is run.

NetBIOS Name Resolution in H-node

The execution of the above command requires that the NetBIOS name "Server1" be resolved to an IP address before the operation can complete successfully. The steps involved in the NetBIOS name resolution process are described next and assume that the WINS server node type is the default hybrid node type (H-node):

1. Once the "net use" command is executed by pressing ENTER, the computer on which the command was entered checks to ensure that the name entered is not its own. If the name is not its own, it then checks its NetBIOS name cache for the NetBIOS name to IP address mapping of Server1. Each NetBIOS computer maintains a name cache that consists of recently resolved NetBIOS names and preconfigured names.

2. If the name is not resolvable from the NetBIOS name cache, the computer queries its primary WINS server for resolution of the computer name.

3. If the primary WINS server does respond, the client resends the query to any additional WINS servers configured on the client.

4. If these additional WINS queries fail, the client broadcasts out on the network to try and resolve the computer name.

> **Exam Tip**
>
> A computer running Windows 2000 can be configured with the addresses of up to 12 WINS servers. Normally, you should not configure a client with more than two or three WINS servers.

5. If there is no response to the broadcast, the lmhosts file is checked to try and resolve the name.
6. If the lmhosts file does not contain the name to IP mapping, the computer's hosts file is checked.
7. If all of the preceding steps fail to resolve the name, one last resolution attempt is made by querying the DNS server if one is configured.

Computers running Windows 2000 are configured to use the H-node WINS server node type by default. The reason for this is simple: H-node reduces the amount of network traffic generated by WINS clients by always having them first try to resolve a NetBIOS name through a direct query to a WINS server. It is only when the answer is not found on the WINS server that the client broadcasts on the local network to try to resolve the name. The goal of H-node is to reduce the amount of broadcasts on the local network and thereby increase network performance.

> **Exam Tip**
>
> Become very familiar with the four different node types and the NetBIOS name resolution process as it pertains to each node type. The order in which the above steps are performed depends on the configuration of the node type on the computer where the command is executed.

NetBIOS Name Resolution in M-node

The steps in the NetBIOS name resolution process change when the WINS server node type is set to mixed node (M-node). The steps in the NetBIOS name resolution process when set to M-node are the following:

1. Once the "net use" command is executed by pressing ENTER, the computer on which the command was entered checks to ensure that the name entered is not its own. If the name is not its own, it then checks its NetBIOS name cache

for the NetBIOS name-to-IP address mapping of Server1. Each NetBIOS computer maintains a name cache that consists of recently resolved NetBIOS names and preconfigured names.

2. If the name is not resolvable from the NetBIOS name cache, the client broadcasts out on the network to try and resolve the computer name.

3. If the broadcast does not result in the name getting resolved, the computer queries its primary WINS server for resolution of the computer name.

4. If the primary WINS server does respond, the client resends the query to any additional WINS servers configured on the client.

5. If there is no response from any of the configured WINS servers, the lmhosts file is checked to try and resolve the name.

6. If the lmhosts file does not contain the name to IP mapping, the computer host's file is checked.

7. If all of the preceding steps fail to resolve the name, one last resolution attempt is made by querying the DNS server, if one is configured.

NetBIOS Name Resolution in B-node

The steps in the NetBIOS name resolution process are different when the client computer is configured with the broadcast WINS server node type (B-node). When configured for B-node, the NetBIOS name resolution process is as follows:

1. Once the "net use" command is executed by pressing ENTER, the computer on which the command was entered checks to ensure that the name entered is not its own. If the name is not its own, it then checks its NetBIOS name cache for the NetBIOS name-to-IP address mapping of Server1. Each NetBIOS computer maintains a name cache that consists of recently resolved NetBIOS names and preconfigured names.

2. If the name is not resolvable from the NetBIOS name cache, the client broadcasts out on the network to try and resolve the computer name.

NetBIOS Name Resolution in P-node

If the client computer's node type is changed to the peer WINS server node type (P-node), the NetBIOS name resolution process changes yet again and now follows the steps set out here:

1. Once the "net use" command is executed by pressing ENTER, the computer on which the command was entered checks to ensure that the name entered is not its own. If the name is not its own, it then checks its NetBIOS name cache for the NetBIOS name-to-IP address mapping of Server1. Each NetBIOS

computer maintains a name cache that consists of recently resolved NetBIOS names and preconfigured names.

2. If the name is not resolvable from the NetBIOS name cache, the computer queries its primary WINS server for resolution of the computer.

3. If the primary WINS server does respond, the client resends the query to any additional WINS servers configured on the client.

Lmhosts File

As mentioned earlier in the chapter, the lmhosts file is the predecessor of WINS, which required manual configuration by an administrator followed by distribution to all NetBIOS clients in a network to enable NetBIOS name resolution to occur. The lmhosts file is not extinct and can be a very valuable tool in the optimization of the name resolution process.

When a NetBIOS computer initializes, the contents of the lmhosts file are read and written into the computer's NetBIOS name cache. In the NetBIOS name resolution process, the NetBIOS name cache is the first area that is checked after the client confirms that the name it is trying to resolve is not its own. The NetBIOS name cache is checked to see if the NetBIOS name that the client is attempting to resolve is in the cache, as this would then avoid the need for a direct query to WINS or a broadcast on the network and the speed of the resolution request would be greatly improved. The lmhosts file can be a powerful tool when you want to ensure that specific computers such as domain controllers and global catalog servers are found quickly. To accomplish this, an lmhosts file must be created and new name to IP address mappings added to the file. The file must then be saved in its default location on all clients that you want to take advantage of these mappings.

By default, only a sample lmhosts file is included with Windows 2000. This sample file is named lmhosts.sam and is stored in the %systemroot%\system32\drivers\etc folder. This file can be used as a guideline in the creation of your lmhosts file, as it offers explanations about the configuration of the file. You can also simply modify and resave the sample file without a file extension. The lmhosts file can be edited with any text editor such as Notepad, but when saved, it must not

Travel Assistance

Save the lmhosts file in the %systemroot%\system32\drivers\etc folder and do not give it a file extension.

have a file extension. Let's have a look at how to create an lmhosts file and what the different configuration options are. To begin this process, we will open the lmhosts.sam sample file and make modifications to it by following these steps:

1. Open Notepad.
2. Select File, select Open, and browse to your %systemroot%\system32\drivers\etc folder and select the lmhosts.sam file.
3. Click Open.
4. Make the required changes to the file and select File, Save.
5. Open Windows Explorer and browse to the %systemroot%\system32\drivers\etc folder, right-click the lmhosts.sam file, select rename, delete the .sam file extension, and click ENTER.

When you make the required changes in step 4 to the lmhosts.sam file, adding only name to IP address mappings without using any of the available extensions within the file will not be as effective as you may want. By default, NetBIOS names are only kept in the NetBIOS name cache for 15 minutes, after which time they expire unless they have been used in that time period and were refreshed. To add a simple NetBIOS name mapping for a computer named "server1" with an IP address of 192.168.1.10, enter the following code:

```
192.168.1.10     server1
```

Be sure to use the TAB key to separate the IP address from the NetBIOS name in your entries. The unfortunate thing about the previous simple name mapping is that it will expire from the name cache after 15 minutes if it is not used. The #PRE extension can be used to preload the mapping into the NetBIOS name cache and not enable it to expire. The NetBIOS name cache file is read sequentially by the operating system, meaning that performance can be improved by placing the most frequently accessed computer mappings at the top of the list in the lmhosts file. The mappings that use the #PRE tag should be located near the bottom of the list, because they are loaded when TCP/IP initializes and are not accessed again. To change the previous simple name mapping to be preloaded, enter the following code:

```
192.168.1.10     server1     #PRE
```

A second extension known as the #DOM <domain> can be used to associate a mapping with the <domain> specified in the name mapping. The #DOM <domain> extension must be used in combination with the #PRE extension.

Changing the previous command to identify the domain mcsejobs.net can be accomplished by entering the following:

```
192.168.1.10      server1      #PRE #DOM mcsejobs
```

The third lmhosts file extension type that you should be familiar with is the #INCLUDE <filename>, which enables you to use a centralized lmhosts file that you configure for all clients to share through a Universal Naming Convention (UNC) path. This enables the local computer to parse the remote lmhosts file as if it were local to the computer, and it reduces the administration requirements as only one lmhosts file must be maintained and updated on a regular basis. A central lmhosts file stored on a computer named "server5" in a share named public with an IP address of 192.168.1.100 can be identified with the following entry:

```
192.168.1.100      server5      #PRE
```

```
#INCLUDE \\server5\public\lmhosts
```

One additional configuration step is required for the #INCLUDE extension to work. The public share on the remote server must also be listed in the client's LanManServer list of NullSessionShares to enable the clients to read the lmhosts file. To edit this list, open regedt32, browse to the key HKLM\System\Current ControlSet\Services\lanmanserver\parameters\nullsessionshares, and add public to the list found in that key.

Now that you are familiar with the steps involved in the name resolution process, we are going to continue our travels through the wonderful world of WINS by looking at the name registration and release process.

NetBIOS Name Registration and Release Process

In order for NetBIOS name resolution to work and support the resolution of NetBIOS names and network resources, NetBIOS clients must register name to IP mappings with a WINS server. When NetBIOS clients initialize, they attempt to register their name to IP information through a broadcast or through a directed message to a NetBIOS name server. Should a computer attempt to register a NetBIOS name that is already registered in the WINS database, the WINS server will send a name query request to the currently registered computer of the name to ensure that the record is still being used. If no response is received by the WINS server, the name is registered to the new computer. If a response is received, WINS sends a negative name registration response to the computer trying to register the duplicate name. This negative name registration response produces an initialization error message on the client stating that the NetBIOS name is already in use and it will be prevented from communicating via NetBIOS.

When trying to register its NetBIOS name, a WINS client tries three times to contact its primary WINS server. If all three attempts fail, the name registration request is sent to the secondary WINS server. Should the registration attempt fail, the client continues to try to register its NetBIOS name every 10 minutes.

Travel Advisory

NetBIOS computers generally request more than one name registration with the WINS server. A computer running Windows 2000 Professional, for example, would request name registrations for the workstation, server, and messenger services as well as the workgroup or domain that the computer is a member of and the name of the user currently logged on to the computer. This process enables WINS clients to query WINS for computers with specific capabilities. The registration of the Messenger service and the user's name enables network messages to be sent to that user.

WINS clients, although they have only one computer name, actually register their NetBIOS name three or four times. There are three types of WINS registrations:

- Computer names
- Domain names
- Special names used to maintain and retrieve browse lists

Listing the registered computer names for the computer you are logged on to is quite easy with the use of the nbtstat utility. To list the registered NetBIOS names for the local computer, follow these steps:

1. Click on Start, Programs, and Accessories, and select the Command Prompt.
2. At the Command Prompt, type **nbtstat –n** and press ENTER.

The result should be a listing of the different NetBIOS name registrations for each network adapter in your computer. Let's examine what each of these entries represents for a computer named lexus in the mcsejobs.net domain with an IP address of 192.168.1.1.

The \\lexus [00h] entry is the name registered for the WINS client workstation name.

The \\lexus [03h] registration is the name registered for the messenger service.

The \\lexus+++++++++++ [BFh] entry is a group name and only appears if the Network Monitor agent is installed and started on the computer. This name is padded with + signs when, as in this case, the computer name is not 15 characters in length.

The \\lexus [BEh] entry is a unique computer name entry for the Network Monitor agent service and again only appears when the Network Monitor Agent is installed and running.

The \\lexus [1Fh] entry is registered for Network Dynamic Data Exchange (NetDDE) services and only appears if the NetDDE services are started. The NetDDE services are not started by default in Windows 2000.

The \\lexus [20h] entry is the name registered for the server service. The server service allows folders to be shared on the local machine for remote access.

The \\lexus [21h] entry is the name registered for the computer as an RRAS client.

The \\lexus [06h] entry is the name registered for the computer if it is configured as an RRAS server.

The \\mcsejobs [00h] entry is registered by the workstation service to allow it to receive browser broadcasts for LAN Manager-based systems. Computers running Windows 2000 do not make these types of broadcasts.

The \\mcsejobs [1Bh] entry is registered by the server service that is configured as the Domain Master Browser. The WINS server returns the IP address of the computer registered with this type of record when queried for a Domain Master Browser.

The \\mcsejobs [1Ch] name is registered by domain controllers. This entry allows for the identification of the domain controller configured as the PDC in a Windows NT 4.0 domain.

The \\mcsejobs [1Dh] entry is registered only by computers configured as a Master Browser. This name registration is used by Backup Browsers to identify and obtain the browse list from the Master Browser.

The \\mcsejobs [1Eh] entry is registered by all Browser and Potential Browser servers. This entry is used in the creation of the browse list and during Master Browser elections.

The .__MSBROWSE__ . [01h] entry is registered by the Master Browser. This entry is used to broadcast and receive domain announcements. This entry alerts Master Browsers to the names of other domains and the Master Browsers on those other domains.

The \\Administrator[03h] entry is the name registration for the currently logged on user. In this example, I am logged on as the Administrator. This registration allows the net send command to be used to send messages to the logged on user.

NetBIOS Name Renewal

To help ensure that the NetBIOS name registrations on the name server are current, clients are required to periodically renew their registrations. When clients are properly shut down, the client automatically sends a message to the name server to release their name to IP mapping and make it available to other computers.

The first renewal attempt is made when 50 percent of the renewal interval has expired. At this time, the WINS client sends a renewal request to the primary WINS server. If the client is unsuccessful in its attempt to renew the name registration it continues to send renewal requests to the primary WINS server at ten minute intervals for a one hour period. Should the one hour period pass and the client remains unsuccessful in its attempts to renew its name registration, it then sends a renewal request to the secondary WINS server. If the first renewal attempt is not successful on the secondary WINS server, it continues to send renewal requests every ten minutes for a one-hour period to the secondary WINS server. If after an hour, the client has still not been able to renew its name registration, it then tries again to renew with the primary, then secondary WINS servers for one-hour periods at ten minute intervals. This process is repeated until the name is renewed or the name expires.

The nbtstat command can also be used on the client to manually renew the client's name registration. Computers running both Windows 2000 and the Windows NT 4.0 with service pack 4.0 or higher support the use of the nbtstat –RR command. Entering nbtstat –RR at the Command Prompt allows for all of the NetBIOS names registered to the client to be renewed. Prior to this command, a WINS client would have had to be restarted in order to re-register its name with a WINS server. The use of this command can help improve administrative efficiency by removing the need to reboot the client operating system to force a NetBIOS name renewal.

> **Travel Assistance**
>
> For more information on the WINS service, reference Microsoft's white paper on WINS, which can be found at http://www.microsoft.com/windows2000/techinfo/howitworks/communications/nameadrmgmt/wins.asp. For more information on the specific NetBIOS names registered with WINS, type **Q119495** into the Internet Explorer browser.

Install and Configure WINS

In networks that have computers running previous versions of Windows operating systems that require the resolution of NetBIOS names, the WINS service can greatly simplify administration efforts and help these computers locate and communicate with network resources.

I find WINS to be the ignored network service in Windows 2000. It is typical in all industries, including the software industry, to tend to focus on the new features of a product and not the ones that have been carried forward. This theory applies to WINS more than any other network service in Windows 2000. DNS, the primary network service for name resolution, tends to receive all the focus and attention in Windows 2000, but WINS still plays a vital role in the name resolution process. If your network contains computers running any other Microsoft operating system other than Windows 2000, effective NetBIOS name resolution requires WINS. To understand this better, let's have a look at how name resolution took place prior to DNS and WINS.

Prior to WINS, NetBIOS name resolution required the configuration of a file known as the lmhosts file. This was an extremely tedious means of configuring name resolution, particularly in a large network with many computers, simply because the lmhosts file has to be created manually. The lmhosts file is a text file that contains the NetBIOS computer name-to-IP address mappings for all client computers, known as nodes, on the network. NetBIOS was originally designed to provide programs with a uniform set of commands used to request low-level network services that managed names, created sessions, and transmitted information between computers.

> **Exam Tip**
>
> NetBIOS names are 16 bytes in length, but only 15 characters can be used to define the computer name. The 16th character uniquely identifies each service that uses the computer name.

Installing the WINS service requires that you are a member of the local Administrators group on a Windows 2000 member server or domain controller and that the computer that you are installing WINS on has a static IP address. When you think about it, it makes a great deal of sense to require a static IP address. If you configure your DHCP server to distribute WINS server IP addresses and node types but those IP addresses are dynamically assigned, clients would not be successful in registering their name to IP mappings.

As with all other network services, WINS is installed from the Add/Remove Windows Components section of Add/Remove Programs in Control Panel.

Exam Tip

Once the WINS service is installed, it is recommended that you configure the server's Advanced TCP/IP settings so that it is a client of itself, which ensures that the WINS server is registered in its own database.

To configure the WINS server as a WINS client, follow these steps:

1. Right-click My Network Places and select Properties.
2. Right-click the Local Area Connection and select Properties.
3. Select Internet Protocol (TCP/IP) and click Properties.
4. Select the Advanced button and choose the WINS tab, as shown in Figure 3-2.
5. Click Add, enter the IP address of a WINS server, and click OK four times to close all open dialog boxes.

Configuration Options for Non-WINS Clients

WINS was designed by Microsoft to work with Microsoft operating systems, enabling them a means of NetBIOS name resolution. Unfortunately, WINS was not a service that was ever standardized among multiple operating system vendors. There are two options available to configure WINS to support non-WINS clients: the first option is WINS proxy and static WINS mappings, and the second option is the integration of WINS with DNS.

The WINS Proxy

A proxy, by definition, is a trusted third party that acts on your behalf. If you have ever owned common shares in a publicly traded company such as Microsoft, each

- NetBIOS name registrations to be made on behalf of WINS clients located on subnets that do not contain a WINS server.
- NetBIOS names of non-WINS clients to be resolved on a WINS server if the non-WINS client has a static mapping in the WINS server database.
- UNIX clients to resolve NetBIOS names. A WINS server will not respond directly to WINS queries from UNIX clients, requiring a WINS proxy to exist on the same subnet as the WINS server. Better yet, move the UNIX clients to a different segment and place a WINS proxy on that segment.

A WINS proxy does not enable the following:

- Register non-WINS clients on a WINS server.

Computers configured as WINS proxies also play an important role in the NetBIOS name registration process. As discussed earlier in the chapter, WINS client computers broadcast their NetBIOS name registrations on the network upon initialization. Should a WINS server not exist on the subnet that the client is broadcasting on, the client's name registration broadcast would not get to the WINS server. A WINS proxy can assist in this process. Configuring a computer as a WINS proxy on a subnet on which there is no WINS server enables for name registration requests to be received by the WINS proxy and forwarded to the WINS server for all WINS clients on the subnet.

As you can see, computers configured as WINS proxies help non-WINS clients in the resolution of NetBIOS names, but one more configuration step is required to enable WINS clients to resolve the NetBIOS names of non-WINS clients: static name mappings. Because non-WINS clients cannot register their NetBIOS names, static name mappings must be created on the WINS server for non-WINS clients. To configure a static mapping on the WINS server, follow these steps:

1. Click Start, Programs, Administrative Tools, and WINS, and expand the entry for the WINS server on which you want to create a static mapping.
2. Right-click Active Registrations, then click New Static Mapping. The dialog box shown in Figure 3-3 will appear.
3. In the New Static Mapping dialog box, in the Computer Name box, type the name of the non-WINS client.
4. In the NetBIOS Scope box, you have the option of specifying a scope.
5. From the Type drop-down menu, specify the type of entry that you are creating. A computer is a Unique type.
6. In the IP address box, enter the IP address of the non-WINS client, then click OK.

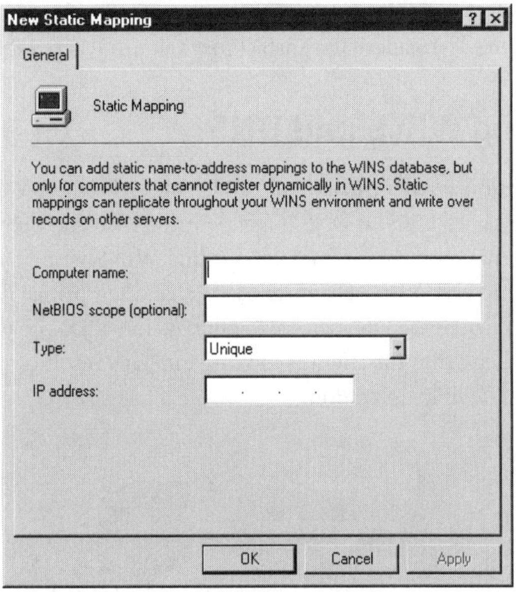

FIGURE 3-3   The New Static Mapping dialog box

One important point to remember about static name mappings created for non-WINS clients is that static mappings are not released from the WINS database when the non-WINS client shuts down or when NetBIOS name-to-IP address information about the client changes. If changes are made to the name or IP address of the WINS server, it is important to also change the static name mapping in the WINS database to reflect the changes. Deleting a record in WINS, whether it is a dynamic or a static record, marks the record for deletion by enabling the tombstone attribute on the record. In an environment with only a single server, the record disappears from view and that is the end of it. However, in an environment with multiple WINS servers, replication of the records from the WINS server on which it was deleted must occur with all of the other WINS servers. When the record is replicated, the WINS server receiving the replication observes the tombstone attribute, which indicates the record is to be deleted, and updates its WINS database by removing the record.

Configuring a WINS Proxy

Configuring a WINS proxy requires the registry of that computer to be edited. A registry editor like Regedt32 can be used to do this. Simply open the registry to

HKEY_LOCAL_MACHINE\SYSTEM\CurrentControlSet\Services\NetBT\ Parameters, set the data value of the EnableProxy value to 1, and restart the computer.

Integrating WINS and DNS

The second option available to extend WINS support to non-WINS clients is to integrate WINS with DNS, as DNS is a network service that the vast majority of operating systems natively support. Integrating WINS with DNS enables both WINS clients and non-WINS clients to use DNS as their primary means of name resolution but enables the DNS service to query WINS if DNS is unable to resolve the NetBIOS name that the client is looking for. This resolution process is displayed in the following illustration.

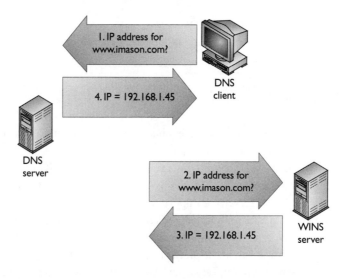

Exam Tip

Only Windows 2000 and Windows NT 4.0 DNS servers support the nonstandard WINS lookup record.

The integration of WINS with DNS becomes a little more complicated when your network uses non-Windows DNS servers. If you administer in an environment that uses non-Windows DNS servers, Microsoft recommends that you create a new DNS child domain and zone and delegate authority of the zone to a

Windows 2000 DNS server. The following illustration displays the DNS zone configuration on your network prior to the integration of WINS and DNS in the domain mcsejobs.net, which is hosted by non-Windows DNS servers, which are and need to remain authoritative.

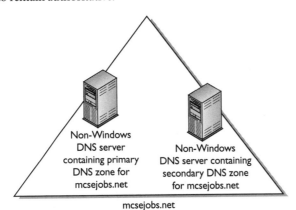

mcsejobs.net

The following illustration shows the approach that Microsoft recommends in the integration of WINS in this environment. This recommended approach involves the creation of a child DNS domain for which authority is then delegated for a new DNS zone to the newly configured Windows 2000 DNS server. This enables the non-Windows DNS server in the original DNS zone to remain authoritative for the mcsejobs.net domain while enabling the integration of DNS and WINS for extended name resolution in the child domain and new zone. In the following illustration, WINS client computers would register their name to IP address mapping with the WINS server (192.168.1.5). All clients, WINS and non-WINS, would then be configured to use DNS as their primary means of name resolution, and should DNS fail to resolve the name resolution request, it would contact the WINS server to try and resolve the name. DNS would locate the WINS server through the WINS record created on the Windows 2000 DNS server. The Windows 2000 DNS server in the wins.mcsejobs.com domain would also have to be configured to use WINS for forward lookup queries.

Exam Tip

When forced to integrate WINS with non-Windows 2000 DNS servers, create a new DNS zone with authority delegated to a Windows 2000 DNS server and integrate WINS with the new zone.

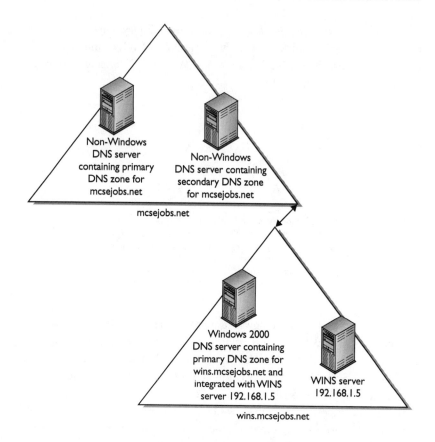

The configuration of WINS and DNS integration is accomplished through the DNS MMC snap-in. To configure your Windows NT 4.0 or Windows 2000 DNS server to integrate with WINS, follow these steps:

1. Click Start, Programs, Administrative Tools, and DNS.
2. Right-click the DNS zone that you wish to integrate with DNS, and select Properties.
3. In the DNS Zone Properties dialog box, select the WINS tab as shown in Figure 3-4.
4. Place a check mark in the box next to Use WINS Forward Lookup, or Use WINS-R Lookup in the case of a reverse lookup zone.
5. Enter the IP address of the WINS server into the IP address box, and click Add. When you are finished adding WINS servers, click OK.

One last WINS configuration scenario should be considered before moving on. This last configuration scenario involves a domain in which DNS resolution

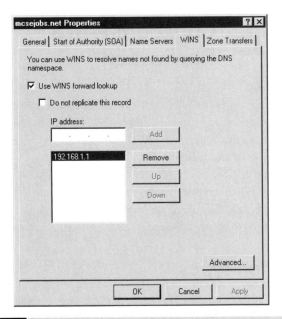

FIGURE 3-4   Integrating WINS with DNS for NetBIOS name resolution

is handled by a Windows 2000 DNS server configured with the primary zone for
the domain and integrated with WINS for resolution. The other DNS servers that
are configured with secondary zones are running BIND implementations of DNS,
which don't support the nonstandard WINS resource record. If you encounter a
configuration similar to this, revisit the WINS tab of the DNS Zone Properties dialog box that would exist on the Windows 2000 DNS server hosting the primary
zone, and place a check mark in the box next to Do Not Replicate This Record.
This will result in the record existing only on the Windows 2000 DNS server that
supports that type of resource record.

Exam Tip

WINS resource records are not standardized and, therefore, are supported only
by Windows 2000 DNS servers. When working in a DNS environment that
contains DNS servers running on other operating systems, select Do
Not Replicate This Record when configuring WINS integration on the
Windows 2000 DNS server.

Objective 3.03

Configure WINS Replication

A single server running the WINS service is able to handle a very high volume of name registrations and name resolution requests, but by itself, it is not fault tolerant. A network that requires the WINS service should always be configured with two WINS servers for redundancy and fault tolerance. This recommendation of more than one WINS server results in a new WINS configuration requirement: replication. Each WINS server maintains its own WINS database; therefore, for all WINS servers to share their database information, replication between servers must be configured to ensure database consistency in your network.

Replication Types

A WINS server can be configured to be one of three types of replication partners: pull, push, or push and pull.

Exam Tip
WINS servers only replicate changes to their database, not the entire database.

A *pull partner* requests or pulls new database entries from its replication partners at specific intervals. The default interval is every 30 minutes, but is configurable to meet your unique needs. Pull partners are ideal for networks that require the WINS database to be replicated across slow network links, as they can be configured to replicate at specific times. The downside to pull replication configured to occur at specific intervals is that in environments in which changes occur often, the different WINS databases can become less synchronized quickly.

A *push partner* notifies its replication partners of changes once the number of changes exceeds a specified threshold. The replication partners respond to the notification with a replication request to which the push partner sends its new database records. Replication traffic generally increases when WINS servers are configured as push partners. This type of configuration is great when your network links are fast and helps to ensure a higher level of database consistency.

A *push/pull partner* is the default replication configuration and gives you the best of both worlds. This replication type enables you to configure both a replication interval and replication threshold, which ensures that the databases will be synchronized.

> **Exam Tip**
>
> Configure the primary and secondary WINS servers as push/pull partners of one another to ensure that the databases are synchronized.

Configuring the replication settings is accomplished through the following steps:

1. Click Start, Programs, Administrative Tools, and WINS.
2. Expand the WINS server that you wish to configure as a replication partner and select Replication Partners.
3. From the list of servers, right-click the server that you want to replicate and select Properties.
4. Select the Advanced tab, as shown in Figure 3-5, and select a Replication Partner Type from the drop-down menu. Configure the appropriate settings based on the replication partner type that you choose.

Both push and pull replication types have an additional configuration setting, persistent connections, which is enabled by default. The persistent connections setting is used to maintain connections between WINS servers, which in turn increases the speed of WINS replication by avoiding the necessity to constantly reestablish new replication connections between partners. The persistent connections setting should be disabled when replication is to occur across slow connections.

Automatic Partner Discovery

WINS replication partners generally have to be added to the Replication Partners section of the WINS snap-in and configured for the type of replication that you are interested in using. The identification of WINS replication partners can, however, be configured to discover replication partners automatically if your network supports multicasting. Configuring your WINS servers for automatic replication partner discovery configures WINS to use the multicast address 224.0.1.24 for the discovery of other WINS servers. All WINS servers that are automatically discovered

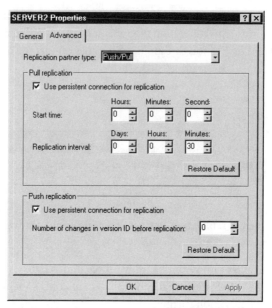

FIGURE 3-5   The Advanced Tab of the WINS Replication Partner Properties dialog box

are configured as push/pull partners with a pull replication interval set to two hours by default. To enable automatic replication partner discovery follow these steps:

1. In the WINS snap-in, right-click the Replication Partners folder and select Properties.
2. Select the Advanced tab in the Replication Partners Properties dialog box and place a check mark in the box next to Enable automatic partner configuration, as shown in Figure 3-6.

The use of automatic partner discovery requires the configuration of a multicast scope on your DHCP server to allow the WINS servers to obtain multicast addresses.

Optimizing WINS Replication

In a large network environment, you will be required to configure WINS to ensure consistent network-wide name resolution. The recommend strategy to accomplish database consistency throughout the WINS servers in your network is to use

Replication Partners Properties   ? X

General | Push Replication | Pull Replication | Advanced |

Block records for these owners:

IP Address		Add...
		Remove

☑ Enable automatic partner configuration

The WINS server can use multicast to automatically configure itself for
replication. Use this option only on small networks.

	Hours:	Minutes:	Seconds:
Multicast interval:	0	40	0
Multicast Time to Live (TTL):			2

OK   Cancel   Apply

FIGURE 3-6   Enabling Automatic WINS Replication Partner Discovery

a hub-and-spoke WINS topology. This will enable convergence times to be mini-
mized and name replication consistency to be optimized.

In a hub-and-spoke topology, one WINS server is configured as a push/pull
partner with all other WINS servers, as shown in the following illustration. This
enables one centralized server to receive WINS replication updates from all other
servers and then replicate those changes out to all its replication partners, resulting in the least amount of convergence time and least amount of latency.

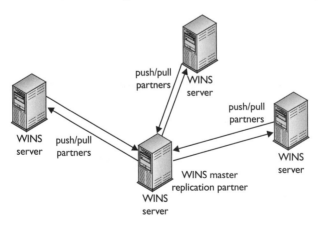

Manage and Monitor WINS

WINS is used to store NetBIOS-to-IP address mappings. The WINS database has the ability to change constantly in networks where client computers are powered on and off regularly. The integrity of the name-to-IP mappings in the WINS database is very important for effective name resolution.

Throughout your administration of a WINS server, you will need to delete WINS records to maintain the integrity of the WINS database. Deleting a WINS record is simple. Start by searching the Active Registrations in the WINS snap-in for the record you wish to delete, right-click the record, and select Delete. After choosing Delete, you are prompted with the dialog box, shown in Figure 3-7, which asks you to choose one of the two options.

Choosing to delete the record only from this server does not affect any of the server's replication partners records, only its own. Selecting to replicate the deletion of the record to other servers enables a tombstone attribute for the record that notifies the server's replication partners of the deletion the next time replication occurs.

The size of your WINS database will depend on the size of your organizations. In smaller organizations, finding the records that you wish to delete may not be an issue, but manually locating a single record in a WINS database containing thousands of entries would be a time-consuming process without the use of any filtering or searching tools. Luckily, searching and filtering tools are included with the WINS service and are available for you to use in your administrative efforts. To search for a record in the WINS database follow these steps:

1. Open the WINS snap-in and expand the WINS server to enable you to see both the Active Registrations and Replication Partners folders.

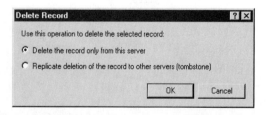

| FIGURE 3-7 | Deleting WINS records |

2. Select the Active Registrations folder.
3. From the menu, select View and Find by Name Results.
4. In the Find by Name dialog box, shown in Figure 3-8, enter the name that you wish to find and press Find Now. By default, all searches will look for entries that match the name you have entered in both uppercase and lower-case characters. If you want to configure the search to be case specific, place a check mark in the box next to Match case.

The size of the WINS database will vary according to the number of clients on your network and the frequency at which they register and unregister. The more often these registrations and unregistrations occur, the larger the database tends to get. Windows 2000 is configured to automatically compact the WINS database, but it can also be compacted manually with the jetpack command by following these steps:

1. Click Start and select Run.
2. In the Open box, type **cmd**, and click OK.
3. Type the command **net stop wins** and click ENTER.
4. Change to the %systemroot%\system32\wins directory, enter the command **jetpack wins.mdb temp.mdb**, and click ENTER.
5. Type the command **net start wins**.

When a WINS client shuts down properly, it sends a release message to the WINS server configured as its primary WINS server, notifying the server to release its mapping. Releasing a record does not delete it from the WINS database, as the record remains but is marked with a tombstone attribute to notify the WINS server's replication partners of the deletion. Periodically, it is necessary to clear each of the released entries that have not been removed. This can be accomplished both manually and automatically.

To manually clear entries in the WINS database, right-click the server name in the WINS snap-in and select Scavenge Database.

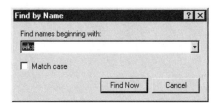

FIGURE 3-8   Finding names in WINS

Automatic removal of entries from the WINS database at specified intervals can be accomplished through the Intervals tab in the WINS server's properties dialog box, shown in Figure 3-9. The renewal interval defines how often a WINS client renews its name registration with the WINS server. The extinction interval is the time from when an entry is marked as released and the time when it is marked as extinct. The extinction timeout is defined as the time between when an entry is marked extinct and the time when the entry is removed or scavenged from the WINS database. The verification interval is the time period after which the WINS server will verify that the names that have been replicated from other WINS servers are still active.

Think of these definitions in the context of buying fresh fruit. Using this analogy, the renewal interval is how often you must shop for fruit. The extinction interval is the time from when your fruit goes bad (is released) in the fridge to when you throw it in the garbage in your kitchen (is extinct). The extinction timeout is defined as the time between when you throw the bad fruit in the garbage to when you take the garbage out to the curb for pickup.

Verifying the consistency of records in your WINS database is also very important in a network environment with more than one WINS server. The verification process forces the WINS server to compare all of the entries in its database with the

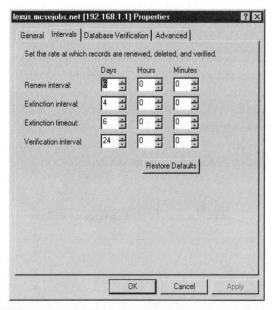

FIGURE 3-9   Configuring the automatic scavenging of records in the properties of a WINS server

entries in its replication partners databases. This process can be very resource inten-
sive in a large WINS database and can significantly increase network traffic; hence,
schedule verification to occur during off hours.

Figure 3-10 shows the Advanced properties tab on the WINS server's dialog
box. It is on this tab that you can configure advanced features such as detailed logging, burst handling, the database path, and down-level compatibility.

By default, the WINS service logs to the System event log. The detailed logging
option is helpful when trying to troubleshoot a problem with your WINS server
but should not be on continuously, as it degrades system performance.

Burst handling is a feature that is useful for WINS servers located in networks
that have large volumes of simultaneous requests. Burst handling enables the
WINS server to issue short leases to clients when it is under high load and would
normally not be able to service all of the requests due to the volume of requests.
These short leases are not recorded to the WINS database, but simply enable the
clients to return a short time later to register a mapping that is written to the database when the volume of requests has decreased.

The default storage location of the WINS database and log files is in the %sys-
temroot%\system32\wins folder. The Advanced tab of the WINS server's Properties
dialog box enables for this location to be changed. Should you need to change the
location of the database and log files, you are required to restart WINS.

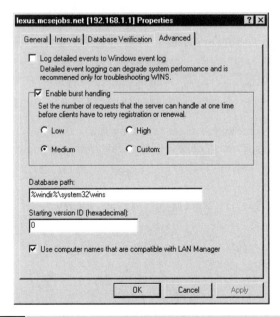

FIGURE 3-10   Configuring the advanced options on a WINS server

Troubleshooting WINS

If an entry or group of entries in the WINS server database does not replicate to its replication partners, there are two things to look into. First, confirm that the times on each of the WINS servers are synchronized. The requirement for time synchronization has to do with the expiration date value added to every entry in the WINS server database. The expiration date is derived by taking the WINS server's data and time and adding the extinction timeout value. This expiration date value is compared against the time on the WINS server that the entry is to be replicated to. If the dates are past those in the entries, the entries are removed. This process can cause the entries that are attempting to be replicated from being added to the WINS server's replication partner.

A second potential cause of this problem is the extinction timeout value. If the extinction timeout value is set to a time less than the value defined for a push/pull session to take place, the timeouts might occur before replication has an opportunity to occur. If the extinction timeout value is set to less than the values defined for push/pull replication, increase the value of the extinction timeout.

Nbtstat

As discussed earlier in the chapter, the nbtstat command can be used to manually force a renewal of a client's NetBIOS name registration on the WINS server. The command to accomplish this is nbtstat –RR. The nbtstat command can also be helpful when troubleshooting NetBIOS over TCP/IP problems. Some examples of what the nbtstat command can do for you are

- List the contents of the NetBIOS name cache
- List the active NetBIOS sessions and the ports that NetBIOS is listening on

The other nice feature of the nbtstat command is that it can be used to troubleshoot the local computer on which it is run or a remote computer, allowing you to perform remote administration.

Backing Up and Restoring WINS

Backing up the WINS database is very important and should be a part of your administrative preventative maintenance procedures. To back up your WINS database, follow these steps:

1. In the WINS snap-in, right-click the name of the server and select Properties.
2. On the General tab of the Properties dialog box, type the name of the directory in the Default Backup Path box, as shown in Figure 3-11.

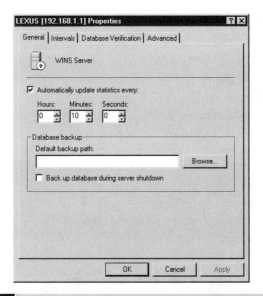

FIGURE 3-11   Configuring the WINS database backup path

Once the backup path has been defined, WINS will perform a complete backup to that directory location every three hours. Information on the WINS server's replication partners is stored in the registry; hence, a complete WINS backup strategy should also include backing up the system state on the WINS server.

To restore a WINS database, follow these steps:

1. Stop the WINS service.
2. In Windows Explorer, open the folder that contains the WINS database and log files and delete all the files. The default location is %systemroot%\system32\wins, but it is configurable in the Advanced tab of the WINS server's Properties dialog box.
3. In the WINS snap-in, right-click the name of the server that you are configuring and select Restore Database. (The Restore Database option is available only on WINS servers on which the WINS service is stopped.)
4. In the Browse For Folder dialog box, select the folder that you backed up your WINS database to and click OK.

Command line Administration

WINS is a network service that can be administered at the command line with a tool created just for that purpose. Winscl.exe is a command line tool that will allow you to perform some or all of your administration of WINS servers from the command line. Some examples of what you can do with the Winscl command are

- Initiate push or pull replication with a WINS replication partner.
- Delete all or simply a range of records.
- List records by name or version number.
- Back up and restore the WINS database.
- List information about WINS, the address of the WINS server, and domain names.

You can find out more information about the various administrative tasks Winscl will allow you to perform by following these steps:

1. Click on Start, Run, then type **cmd** and press OK.
2. At the Command Prompt, type **winscl /?**.

CHECKPOINT

✔ **Objective 3.01: Install, Configure, and Troubleshoot WINS** The WINS service is installed through the Add/Remove Windows Components section of Add/Remove Programs in Control Panel. Only Windows NT 4.0 and Windows 2000 DNS servers support the nonstandard WINS resource record and can be configured to forward resolution requests to WINS servers.

✔ **Objective 3.02: Configure NetBIOS Name Resolution** A WINS server should also be configured as a WINS client to ensure that its NetBIOS name is registered in the WINS database. NetBIOS names are registered dynamically when computers and services start and when users log on. There are four node types: B-node, P-node, M-node, and H-node. H-node is the default node type. WINS clients configured to use H-node will try to resolve a name in their local name cache, then query a WINS server, and lastly, try to resolve the name via a broadcast. The lmhosts file can be used to configure a client with preloaded NetBIOS name to IP address mappings in its name cache. #PRE specifies that the mapping be preloaded. #DOM specifies an associated domain and requires that #PRE also be used. #INCLUDE enables a client to be directed to a central lmhosts file and also requires the #PRE also be used. WINS clients that are not properly shut down do not release their name registrations leading to outdated registrations in the WINS database. Static mappings enable non-WINS clients to be resolved via WINS. WINS proxies are used to forward WINS name resolution requests to a WINS server on a different subnet, receive the name resolution response, and forward it back to the original requesting client. WINS servers will not respond to WINS queries made by UNIX clients. To enable UNIX clients to get a response from WINS, a WINS proxy must be located on the same segment as the UNIX client to query WINS on its behalf.

✔ **Objective 3.03: Configure WINS Replication**   A network should always have more than one WINS server for redundancy and fault tolerance, and the WINS servers should be configured to replicate their databases to each other. There are three types of WINS replication: push, pull and push/pull. WINS servers can be configured to automatically discover their replication partners if your network supports multicasting. When multicasting and automatic discovery is enabled, WINS servers use the multicast address 224.0.1.24. The default pull interval is two hours.

✔ **Objective 3.04: Manage and Monitor WINS**   Jetpack is a utility that can be used to compact a WINS database (wins.mdb). Restoring a WINS database can be accomplished only when the WINS service is stopped. The Winscl command line utility can be used to administer the WINS service from the Command Prompt and provides all of the functionality available in the WINS snap-in.

REVIEW QUESTIONS

1. You are trying to map drive letter x: to the apple share on Filsrv1. Filsrv1 is configured to use M-node for NetBIOS name resolution. The client you are trying to create the drive mapping on is configured to use P-node. Which of the following represent the correct sequence of resolution steps that will take place?

   A. Broadcast
   B. WINS server query
   C. Broadcast, WINS server query
   D. WINS server query, Broadcast

2. You would like to configure a static NetBIOS name mapping on your computer running Windows 2000 Professional that maps the IP address of a computer on a remote subnet to the computer's NetBIOS name. You connect to this computer occasionally through a virtual private network (VPN) connection and have been having trouble resolving resources using the computer name followed by the share name. Which file will you edit to accomplish this?

   A. lmhosts.sif
   B. lmhosts
   C. lmhosts.sam
   D. lmhosts.txt

3. You would like to configure two-hundred client computers running Windows 2000 Professional on your multiple subnet network with two WINS server IP addresses; 192.168.1.2, 192.168.1.3. You also want to configure these same client computers to use M-node resolution. Which of the following network services can be used to accomplish this?

   A. DNS
   B. WINS
   C. DHCP
   D. RRAS

4. Which of the following node types does Windows 2000 default to when no WINS servers are configured?

   A. B-node
   B. P-node
   C. M-node
   D. H-node

5. You have decided to use the lmhosts file for all NetBIOS name resolution in your small network that consists of only ten computers. Which of the following statements are correct?

   A. The lmhosts file must be stored on each individual computer on the network and distributed by DHCP.
   B. The lmhosts file must be stored on each individual computer on the network and manually maintained.

    C. The lmhosts file must be unique to each individual computer on the network and distributed by File System Replication (FRS).

    D. The lmhosts file must be unique to each individual computer running the server service on the network and must be updated regularly through Active Directory replication.

6. Which two of the following will result in the proper release of a WINS client's name registration in the WINS database?

    A. Logging off the computer

    B. Shutting down the computer

    C. Nbtstat -RR

    D. Netstat -r

7. You have a number of non-WINS client computers on multiple subnets. Your internal DNS servers are all BIND implementations. Which of the following is the recommended method for enabling the non-WINS clients to resolve names through WINS without requiring that an additional computer be added to the network?

    A. Install the WINS service on a server that already exists on each of the subnets.

    B. Install a WINS proxy on the subnet where the WINS server is located.

    C. Install a WINS proxy on the subnets where the WINS server is not located.

    D. Configure the BIND implementation of DNS to integrate with WINS.

8. You wish to configure the WINS database to automatically scavenge records every 36 hours. When you open up the WINS snap-in, you proceed to open up the properties of the WINS server and select the Interval tab. Which of the following settings will you set to 36 hours to accomplish this?

    A. Renewal interval

    B. Extinction interval

    C. Extinction timeout

    D. Verification interval

9. You have discovered that the database on one of the WINS servers on your network has become corrupted. Luckily, you have a backup from the day before that you can use to restore the database. After you delete all of the corrupted database and log files from the %systemroot%\system32\wins directory, you open the WINS snap-in to proceed with the restore. When you right-click the WINS server, you don't receive the option to restore the database. You refresh the WINS snap-in several times but continue to have the same problem. Which of the following is most likely to be causing this problem?

A. You are not a member of the local Administrators group.
B. The WINS server must be restarted after the database and log files are deleted.
C. The WINS service is not stopped.
D. The Default backup path specified in the Advanced tab of the server's Properties dialog box is different from the default location.

10. You want to ensure that the WINS servers on your network can handle large volumes of registrations and requests. Which of the following will enable you to accomplish this goal?

A. Enable burst handling on all WINS servers.
B. Disable detailed logging.
C. Move the WINS database and log files to separate partitions or disks.
D. Increase the renewal interval on all WINS servers.

REVIEW ANSWERS

1. **B** P-node name resolution sends a query to the WINS server.

2. **B** The lmhosts file is the file to use to add static entries outside of the WINS database. Static entries added to the lmhosts file are only available on the computer on which the lmhosts file resides. The lmhosts file should not have a file extension.

3. **C** The only network service that can be used to assign IP address configuration information like WINS server addresses and node types to multiple client computers is DHCP.

4. **A** B-node is the default resolution node type in Windows 2000 when no WINS servers are configured.

5. **B** The lmhosts file must be stored on each individual computer on the network and manually maintained. The lmhosts file is stored in the %systemroot%\system32\drivers\etc folder on each computer.

6. **B** **C** Properly shutting down the computer and using the nbtstat –RR command at the command prompt will both result in the name to IP mapping in the WINS database being released.

7. **C** Installing a WINS proxy on the subnets where the WINS server is not located would enable non-WINS broadcasts to be forwarded to a WINS server and the resolution for the name to IP forwarded back to the non-WINS client computer. BIND implementations of DNS do not support the nonstandard WINS record.

8. **C** The extinction timeout is the interval between the time when an entry is marked as extinct and the time when the entry is removed or scavenged from the WINS database.

9. **C** The WINS service must be stopped before the Restore Database option is available.

10. **A** Enabling burst handling on all WINS servers will enable the WINS servers to respond to all incoming requests during periods of high volume by issuing short leases to clients and not writing those leases to the WINS database.

Windows 2000 PKI and IPSec Network Infrastructure

Certificate Services and Public Key Infrastructure

	NEWBIE	SOME EXPERIENCE	EXPERT
ETA	5–7 hours	2–5 hours	1–2 hours

Your journey of studying for and passing the Implementing and Administering a Windows 2000 Network Infrastructure exam (70-216) continues with a look at the Public Key Infrastructure and Internet Protocol Security components that have been updated and added to Windows 2000.

Certificate Services are not new in Windows 2000 but have been updated and improved. You are required to have a solid understanding of the different Certificate Authority (CA) configurations and be knowledgeable in the different areas in which certificates can be used.

One of these areas is in the security and protection of IP traffic across both public and private networks using IP Security (IPSec). IPSec is new to Windows 2000 and, like all new features, tends to carry a heavier weight on the exam. Part II of this book explores the different default IPSec configurations and what each are intended to be used for. We will also discuss how to effectively plan and deploy your IPSec policy depending on the type of network environment in which you work.

Passing what has been referred to by many as the most difficult of the Windows 2000 core exams requires that you have a very solid understanding of the features and configuration options associated with both Certificate Services and IPSec. Your exam preparation should include setting up a computer with Windows 2000 Server and configuring Certificate Services in each of the available configurations as well as working with and assigning IPSec policies in a domain environment to give you the hands-on experience that is necessary to pass this Windows 2000 MCSE exam.

Network security is a very big concern to almost all network administrators. The thought of having proprietary data or confidential information stolen or simply read by unauthorized users is enough to give any manager nightmares. The use of certificates as a component of your network security is not a new concept in Windows 2000, but it's one you must be familiar with for the Implementing and Administering a Windows 2000 Network Infrastructure exam. If you have worked with Certificate Services in Windows NT 4.0, you will notice a number of changes, improvements, and additions that were not included in earlier releases of the service.

This chapter will cover the ins and outs of certificates, starting with a look at the components of a certificate, the different uses, and the certificate hierarchy. You'll also see how to install, configure, manage, and troubleshoot a certificate service. When you are familiar with the installation and configuration, we will explore the different options available to issue and obtain certificates. The last section of this chapter will end our journey with a look at the Encrypting File System (EFS), what it is used for, what is required for its use, and how to remove the keys of the data recovery agent for security purposes.

Install and Configure a Certificate Authority

Objective 4.01

The installation of Certificate Services is accomplished through the Add/Remove Windows Components section of Add/Remove Programs in Control Panel. The installation of Certificate Services also requires that you provide answers to a number of configuration questions in order to install the service. We will explore each of the installation and configuration options in detail, but before we delve into that, let's take a step back and begin with a look at the components that make up Certificate Services and what certificates can be used for.

Public Key Infrastructure (PKI) Basics

The Public Key Infrastructure (PKI) was designed to support and enhance two fundamental security operations: encryption and authentication. In their most basic form, certificates provide a means of digital authentication and allow you to either encrypt data or authenticate users. The encryption of data prevents the data from being seen and read by unauthorized individuals. The authentication of users allows one individual to prove to another individual that the data or message received actually came from the correct individual. Alternatively, authentication can be used to grant access into a secure part of a corporate network such as an intranet or extranet. Uses of certificates include the following:

- **Server authentication**   In e-commerce, certificates are used to authenticate servers to clients.
- **Client authentication**   In remote access solutions, certificates can be used to authenticate clients to servers.
- **Code signing**   In software distribution, certificates can be used to prove that the software about to be installed is from a specific software development company, such as Microsoft.
- **Secure e-mail**   E-mail can be encrypted or digitally signed, or both, for security and authentication.
- **EFS**   The Encrypting File System in Windows 2000 uses certificate/key pairs to allow files stored on the NTFS file system to be encrypted and unencrypted.
- **IPSec**   Certificates can be used to encrypt IP-based network traffic between IPSec-enabled clients and servers.

> **Exam Tip**
>
> Certificate Services do not need to be configured for EFS or IPSec, because both features are capable of providing their own certificates. A Certificate Authority, however, is required to issue certificates to IPSec clients not running Windows 2000 or a supported version of Kerberos.

Digital Encryption

Think of data encryption as a digital form of scrambling the contents of a message so that if the message is intercepted on the way to its intended recipient, the spy who intercepts it will not be able to read the message contents until it's unencrypted. In digital encryption, an encryption key known as a *session key* is used to encrypt and decrypt the data. The proper security of the session key is very important, because anyone who has access to the key has the ability to encrypt as well as decrypt all messages.

Symmetric Key Encryption

Symmetric key encryption involves the use of the session key to encrypt and decrypt data. The problem with symmetric key encryption is that both parties that wish to communicate must share the key. The question then becomes: how do the two parties that wish to communicate share the key in a secured manner? Simply sending the key across the network in an e-mail isn't secure and could lead to someone in addition to the intended recipient gaining access to the key. Anyone with the key could then capture the traffic on the network and use the key to decrypt the data. Therefore, symmetric key encryption, by itself, is not an adequate solution.

Public Key Cryptography

Public key cryptography is an encryption technology that uses two keys, known as a *key pair*, to encrypt data or authenticate users through the use of digital signatures. The two keys used in public key cryptography are the *private key* and the *public key*. The public key and the private key are mathematically related, allowing for a message encrypted with the private key to be unencrypted only by its associated public key, and vice versa. As the name suggests, the intent of the private key is to be kept private or confidential. The public key, on the other hand, is available to the general public and does not require the secrecy associated with the private key.

> ### Local Lingo
>
> **cipher text**   Text that has been encrypted using an encryption key. Without the proper decryption key, cipher text is unreadable.

The following illustration shows an example of public key cryptography used for data encryption, where encrypted data is sent from the user Rory to the user Dina. In this example, Rory encrypts the message with Dina's public key and sends the data across the network as cipher text. If anyone intercepts that data from the network, they would require Dina's private key to decrypt it. Dina receives the data and decrypts it using her own private key, which no one else aside from Dina has access to. The entire encryption/decryption process is typically transparent to the actual sender and receiver and is managed by PKI-enabled applications such as Microsoft Outlook, Internet Explorer, Internet Information Services, and Outlook Express.

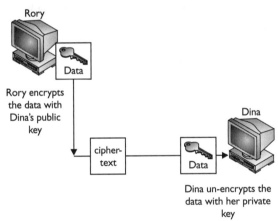

> ### Exam Tip
>
> Public key cryptography uses the recipient's public key to encrypt the message data and the recipient's private key to decrypt the message data.

Public key cryptography can also be used for authentication, allowing a user to send a message to another user with their certificate attached and encrypted using their private key. This attached, encrypted certificate is often referred to as a *digital signature*. The recipient is able to prove authenticity—that is, who the message came from—by decrypting the digital signature with the sender's public key. In this example, because only the sender should have access to their private key, using the sender's publicly available public key to decrypt the message proves the authenticity of the sender. Both data encryption and user authentication via digital certificates make use of public key cryptography. Digital signatures, however, are not transparent to the user. PKI-enabled applications such as Outlook Express and Outlook allow a user to specify that the message they wish to send be digitally signed.

Digital signatures were designed to authenticate and verify the originator of e-mail, e-commerce, or other digital transactions. The following illustration shows an example of a digital signature being used to prove that Rory is the original sender of the e-mail to Dina. In this example, Rory sends a message to Dina and uses his private key to digitally sign the message. When Dina receives the message, she uses Rory's public key, which is publicly available to decrypt the digital signature. If Dina is able to successfully decrypt the digital signature with Rory's private key and Rory is the only user with access to his private key, Dina can be certain that the message came from Rory. Digital signatures are useful when you want to send a message to another person and you want that person to be confident that the original message arrived in tact, without being tampered with or changed, and that the message was truly sent by you.

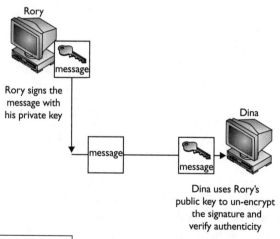

Rory

Rory signs the
message with
his private key

Dina

Dina uses Rory's
public key to un-encrypt
the signature and
verify authenticity

Exam Tip

Digital signatures authentication use the sender's private key to digitally sign the message, and the recipient uses the sender's public key to decrypt the signature. Digital signatures do not encrypt data.

A digital signature uses an algorithm known as a *hash algorithm*. Hash algorithms are designed to ensure that if the message data is tampered with at all during transmission, the modifications corrupt the digital signature and alert the recipient to the fact that the message may have been modified during transmission.

Travel Assistance

To learn more about the different types of encryption algorithms and key lengths, which help to determine the level of sophistication and security, check out http://www.verisign.org/repository/index.html.

Both symmetric key encryption and public key cryptography are used in a number of other encryption technologies. The encryption technology that you probably use most often that employs both of these technologies is Secure Sockets Layer (SSL). SSL is an encryption standard used to secure HTTP communications and can be seen on almost all e-commerce sites as well as banking and brokerage sites. In the case of an e-commerce transaction, SSL uses public key cryptography to secure the initial communication between the Web client and the Web server. Once a secure channel has been established, SSL uses symmetric key encryption to create a unique session key for this and only this session. This session key will be used to encrypt all data sent between the client and the server in this session. The sequential steps involved in an SSL session are described here:

1. The Web client sends an HTTPS GET request to the Web server. This communication generally takes place on TCP port 443, the default port for SSL.
2. The Web server responds by sending the client its digital certificate, which includes its public key.
3. The Web client then sends a message to the Web server requesting the highest level of encryption that the client supports be used. This message is encrypted with the public key of the Web server.
4. The Web server decrypts the message using its private key and responds with a message stating that it either supports the requested level of encryption or suggests an alternative encryption level. This message is encrypted using the Web server's private key. The available encryption levels are either 40 or 128 bit.
5. The Web client receives this message and decrypts it using the Web server's public key. Up to this point, public key cryptography has been used to create

a secure communication channel. Now symmetric key encryption is used to create a unique session key. The Web client then generates a unique session key and sends this session key to the Web server encrypted with the Web server's public key.

6. The Web server receives and decrypts the session key using its private key.

7. The actual data transmission is now set to begin, and all data sent to and from both the Web client and the Web server will be encrypted with the unique session key. This unique session key will only be used for this one session. If the session terminates for any reason, this entire process will have to be repeated to ensure that the Web client and the Web server each have a unique session key.

Certificate Authorities

Installing Certificate Services on a Windows 2000 server requires that you create a Certificate Authority (CA). A Certificate Authority is responsible for issuing and revoking certificates and keys for encryption, decryption, and authentication. The Certificate Authority's role is to act as a trusted third party, much like the Department of Motor Vehicles office, which is responsible for issuing drivers' licenses.

A driver's license is very similar to a certificate in that it contains a unique key (the driver's license number), attributes about the licensee (the driver's hair and eye color, height, and weight), and an expiration date. It is also generally laminated to deter or prevent people from tampering with it. Each Certificate Authority requires a certificate to confirm its own identity. Certificates are signed by the CA that issues them. The CA guarantees that the public key attached to the certificate belongs to the owner of the certificate. Certificates can be issued to a computer, a user account, or a service.

The Certificate Authority that issues a certificate can be either internal or external. Examples of external CAs include companies such as VeriSign, Entrust, Equifax, and Thawte. These companies allow organizations to buy certificates and are recognized and trusted by most PKI-aware applications. An example of this can be seen in Internet Explorer, a PKI-aware application that comes with the Windows 2000 operating system. To see all the Certificate Authorities trusted, by default, by your Internet Explorer Web browser, follow these steps:

1. Open Internet Explorer.
2. From the Tools menu, select Internet Options.
3. In the Internet Options dialog box, select the Content tab and then the Certificates button.

4. In the Certificates dialog box, select the Trusted Root Certificate Authorities tab, shown in Figure 4-1, and you will see all the Certificate Authorities trusted, by default, by your Internet Explorer Web browser.

An alternative way to view all the Certificate Authorities trusted by default is to use the Certificates snap-in and follow these steps:

1. Click Start | Run. Type **mmc** in the Open text box and click OK.
2. Select Console | Add/Remove Snap-in.
3. Click the Add button and select Certificates. Then click Add again. Select what you want the snap-in to manage certificates for. The three choices are My User Account, Service Account, or Computer Account. Click Finish, Close, and then OK.
4. Expand Certificates and Trusted Root Certification Authorities and select the Certificates folder.

An internal CA can be used inside a corporation where all computers can be configured to trust what is, by default, an "untrusted" CA. The certificate issuance

FIGURE 4-1   Viewing the default trusted root Certificate Authorities in Internet Explorer

process for an internal CA is very simple and consists of the following four steps:

1. A certificate request is made to a CA.
2. The CA verifies the requester's information based on the requirements defined in the CA's policy module.
3. The CA applies a digital signature to the certificate using its private key.
4. The CA issues the certificate.

The CA is also responsible for maintaining a list of revoked certificates, known as a *certificate revocation list* (CRL).

Local Lingo

policy module The criteria or attributes required by the CA for the successful issuance of a certificate. Required information could include company letterhead stamped with the corporate seal, a driver's license, a credit card number, proof of address via a utility bill or any other form of identification, or personal characteristic such as hair or eye color.

The configuration of all computers inside an organization to trust an internal CA is much simpler than configuring numerous external computers to trust the CA because, as the administrator, you have greater control over the internal computers. Features such as group policy in an Active Directory domain can be used to publish a list of trusted Certificate Authorities to all computers within a single-domain or multiple-domain environment. This level of administrative permission simply isn't available for computers that you do not directly manage.

Certificate Authority Hierarchies

All Certificate Authorities belong to a CA hierarchy, which is used to establish the model of trust through parent/child relationships. The use of certificates and their associated keys is all about trust. Take the example of three people named Mary, Rory, and Bill. If Mary trusts Rory, and Rory trusts Bill, but Mary and Bill don't know one another, Bill can trust Mary thanks to Rory's trust in Mary. The key to this trust example is that it must start somewhere, and that somewhere is referred to as the *root Certificate Authority*. The root Certificate Authority is the most trusted Certificate Authority in the hierarchy. Examples of trusted root Certificate Authorities are the external CAs mentioned earlier and displayed in Figure 4-1: VeriSign, Entrust, Equifax, and Thawte. The root CA must be guarded carefully and protected from unauthorized access, because if the root Certificate Authority ever becomes compromised, all certificate-based security becomes vulnerable. There are two classes of Certificate Authorities included in the Windows 2000 Certificate Services: enterprise and stand-alone. Within both classes, you are able to configure a single root Certificate Authority and multiple subordinate Certificate Authorities.

Exam Tip

The root CA must adhere to the strictest of security because if it were every compromised, the entire certificate hierarchy from the root down would be compromised.

The CA at the top of a CA hierarchy is generally referred to as the *root CA*. Root CAs are generally used only to issue certificates to other CAs, known as *subordinate CAs*. The subordinate CAs are also often referred to as *intermediate* or *issuing CAs*, where a CA that issues certificates to entities other than other CAs is referred to as an *issuing CA*. *Intermediate CA* refers to a CA that is not a root CA but only certifies other CAs. An example of these different CA types is shown here:

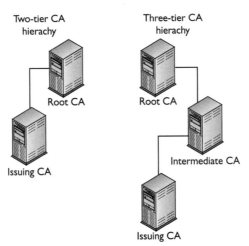

The integrity of the root CA and of the certificates that it issues is very important to the overall structure. Therefore, the policy module on root CAs tends to be more detailed and requires increased levels of authentication. A root CA can be created in both Certificate Authority classes as either an enterprise root CA or a stand-alone root CA.

> **Exam Tip**
>
> There is no requirement that all CAs share a common top-level CA parent (or root).

There are a number of benefits to deploying multi-level or Three-Tier CA hierarchies as opposed to simply creating a single root CA and using that CA to issue all certificates. These benefits include

- The security of the root CA is much higher, as limited direct access to the root CA is required by the intermediate and issuing CAs and no access to the root CA is required by the objects requesting the certificates.
- All CAs can be centrally administered from a single MMC console ensuring administrative simplicity.
- Intermediate CAs can be created and managed by independent business units if required.
- The cost and impact of a compromised or failed CA diminishes.
- Flexibility in the configuration of the CA security environment is achieved as key strength, physical protection, and protection against network attacks can be controlled either centrally or independently.
- Frequent renewals of keys and certificates are possible for those intermediate or issuing CAs that have a higher security risk.
- It allows for a branch of your CA hierarchy to be shut down without affecting the rest of the CA hierarchy.

The Enterprise Root CA   An enterprise root CA is the top-level CA in a certificate hierarchy and, as the top-level CA, it signs its own CA certificate. Enterprise root CAs can run on any Windows 2000 Server platform, including a domain controller, but they do require the Active Directory to be available on the network in order to be installed and configured. The Active Directory is used to store Certificate Services information and to determine the identity of the certificate requester and verify that the requester has the required permissions to request a particular type of certificate.

Enterprise root CAs should be used when you are planning on issuing certificates only to users and computers within your own organization. The recommended use and configuration would have the enterprise root CA only issue certificates to enterprise subordinate CAs and remain offline and stored in a very secure location, physically disconnected from the network, the remainder of the time to prevent against tampering. The name you give the enterprise root CA is also very important because CA names are bound into their certificates. This restricts you from changing the name of the CA; therefore, you should take into consideration the naming conventions you use within your organization.

> ## Exam Tip
>
> Enterprise root CAs require Active Directory and require that the individual installing them be a member of the Enterprise Admins group.

The installation of an enterprise root or enterprise subordinate Certificate Authority requires the following:

- The user performing the installation must be a member of the Enterprise Admins group.
- The network must have a DNS server and a Windows 2000 domain controller hosting the Active Directory.
- Administrative privileges are needed on the DNS, Active Directory, and CA servers.

> ## Exam Tip
>
> To publish certificates in the Active Directory, the Windows 2000 server running Certificate Services must be a member of the Cert Publishers group, which is done automatically upon the installation of Certificate Services.

During the installation process of an enterprise root CA, a self-signed CA certificate is automatically generated using the CA's key pair. Information about the CA is also written to the Active Directory in the CA object, which provides members of the domain with information about available CAs and the types of certificates they are configured to issue. Once a root CA has been installed, it is possible to install either an intermediate or issuing CA.

The Stand-Alone Root CA   The stand-alone root CA is also a top-level CA in the certificate hierarchy and may or may not be a member of a domain. Because membership in a domain is not necessary for the installation of a stand-alone root CA, Active Directory is not a requirement either.

Stand-alone root CAs should be used when you are planning on issuing certificates to users and computers outside of your own organization. The recommended use and configuration has the stand-alone root CA issuing certificates only to stand-alone subordinate CAs and remaining offline the remainder of the time to prevent against tampering.

Exam Tip

Stand-alone root CAs do not require Active Directory but do require the individual installing them to have local administrative privileges.

The lifetime of certificates issued by stand-alone CAs is determined by two registry keys:

- HKLM\System\CurrentControlSet\Services\Certsvc\Configuration\Stand-alonCA\ValidityPeriod
- HKLM\System\CurrentControlSet\Services\Certsvc\Configuration\Stand-alonCA\ValidityPeriodUnits

In each of the above registry key paths, the Stand-alone CA entry is the name of the installed CA, and the value of ValidityPeriod is stated in days, weeks, months or years. The ValidityPeriodUnits value is the number of days, weeks, months or years that represents the lifetime of the certificates issued. By default, certificates issued by stand-alone CAs have a lifetime of one year.

The Enterprise Subordinate CA   Enterprise subordinate CAs are used to issue certificates within an organization and are the children of enterprise root CAs in the hierarchical CA structure. An enterprise subordinate CA cannot be created without an existing enterprise root CA. This is a simple principle to remember if you liken it to the idea that every child must have a parent. This principle, however, differs slightly when talking about stand-alone CAs.

By default, certificates issued by enterprise CAs have a maximum lifetime of two years. The lifetime of each type of certificate issued on a single CA can be different. The lifetime of each type of certificate is determined by the certificate template. Each type of certificate has its own certificate template. For example, the default lifetime of two years is configured for the following certificate templates:

- CEP encryption
- Enrollment agents
- IPSec
- Web server

The default lifetime for the following certificates is set to five years:

- Domain controllers
- Subordinate CA

The Stand-alone Subordinate CA The stand-alone subordinate CA can operate as an isolated certificate server or within a CA trust hierarchy. The requirement of a parent differs slightly when applied to the stand-alone subordinate CA. The stand-alone subordinate CA can have an internal parent of a stand-alone root CA within the organization or can be the child of an external commercial CA that provides the subordinate with its server certificate. Stand-alone subordinate CAs are generally used to issue certificates to users outside of your organization, so it is generally recommended that you obtain the subordinate CA's certificate from a trusted commercial CA that all Internet browsers are configured to trust.

An example of this is an e-commerce site that uses Secure Sockets Layer (SSL) for secure transactions. If the site were to issue its own certificate, no client browser would trust the Certificate Authority that issued it. If, on the other hand, the site were to apply for and receive a certificate from a commercial CA such as VeriSign, all clients with browsers configured to trust VeriSign would be able to securely connect to the e-commerce site without interruption.

Installing Certificate Services

The Certificate Services feature is included with all three versions of the Windows 2000 Server operating system but is not installed by default. Like all other services in Windows 2000, Certificate Services can be installed through the Add/Remove Windows Components section of Add/Remove Programs in Control Panel.

Exam Tip
Once Certificate Services is installed, the server cannot be renamed, added, or removed from a domain.

The installation of Certificate Services is more involved than the installation of the other network services we have looked at thus far, such as DNS, DHCP, and WINS. During the installation of Certificate Services, you will be asked to choose the type of certificate server you wish to install from the dialog box shown in Figure 4-2.

Exam Tip

You will not be tested on the Advanced Options settings and should only change them if you require a specific cryptography configuration.

To configure advanced options, place a check mark in the box next to Advanced Options. The Advanced Options section allows you to configure the cryptography service provider (CSP), which in turn affects which hash algorithm you are able to choose. Based on the hash algorithm you choose, you can specify the key length to be used by the certificate service. The default is a 512-bit key length, but the larger the key length, the more secure the level of encryption. The last of the advanced options includes the ability to use existing keys. Use this option when you are relocating or restoring a previously installed CA. If you are restoring or relocating a CA and select to use an existing key, you should also place

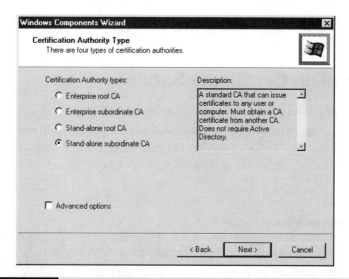

FIGURE 4-2   Selecting a CA type

a check mark in the box next to Use the Associated Certificate. This ensures that a certificate identical to the previous CA's certificate is used and avoids potential certificate problems. These various configuration settings are displayed in the dialog box shown in Figure 4-3.

The second step in the installation process requires that you enter the information needed to identify your CA. The information required from the default policy module for a stand-alone subordinate CA is shown in the dialog box in Figure 4-4. The CA Name field is used to identify the CA object and therefore must be unique for each CA you install in your organization. The Country/Region section requires that you specify the two-character country/region code required by the X.500 Naming Scheme standard. The default code is the United States code US. The Valid For section is grayed out when you're installing a subordinate CA because it can only be set when you're configuring a root CA. The validity duration is the length of time for which certificates will be valid from their original data and time of issue. The recommended time period is two years.

The third step in the installation process requires that you specify a location where the certificate database and certificate database log files will be stored. This information is specified in the dialog box shown in Figure 4-5. The default location of the Certificate Services database and log file, as shown in Figure 4-5, is in the %systemroot%\system32\certlog directory. Performance can be improved by storing the files on different physical drives.

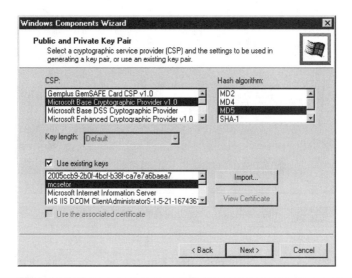

FIGURE 4-3   Configuring advanced options

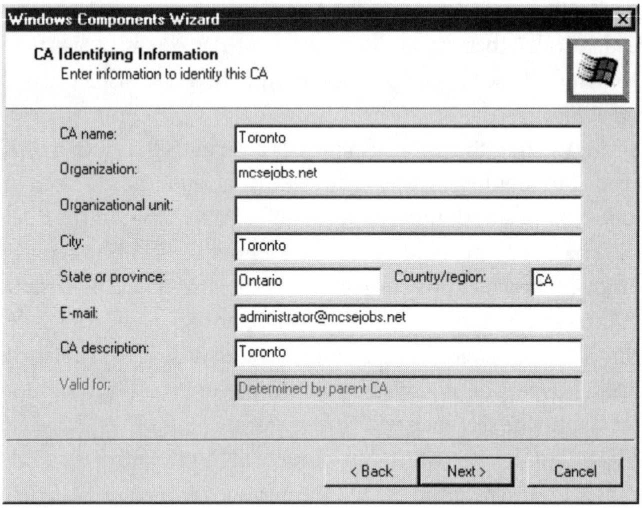

FIGURE 4-4   Entering CA identification information

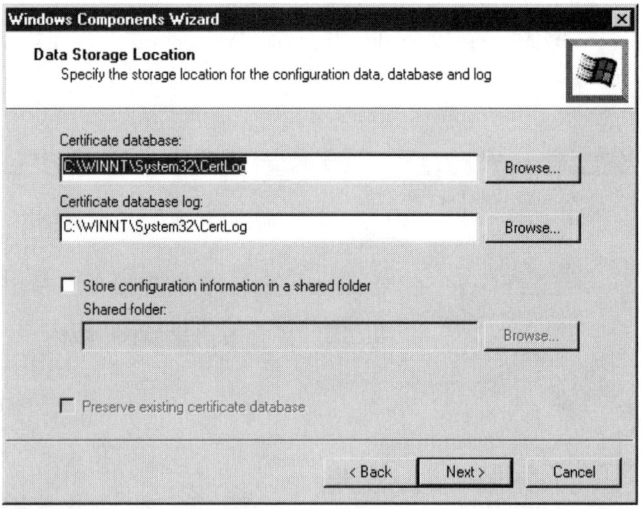

FIGURE 4-5   Configuring the Certificate Services database location

As discussed earlier, a subordinate CA must have a certificate that is issued from a root CA. The issuer of this certificate can be a CA within your organization or an external, commercial CA. Which CA issues this certificate will depend on the type of subordinate CA you have chosen to install. In the example we have been using, a stand-alone subordinate CA is being installed. To obtain a certificate if a parent CA is available online, select the option Send the Request Directly to a CA Already on the Network, as shown in Figure 4-6. If the parent CA is not online, the certificate request can be saved to a file by selecting the second option, Save the Request to a File, and specifying a location where the file can be saved. This saved certificate request file must then be submitted to the parent CA when it is available online again in order for a certificate to be issued.

Once the certificate has been issued to the subordinate CA, it must be installed. To install the certificate from a file, follow these steps:

1. Open the Certification Authority snap-in found under Start | Programs | Administrative Tools.
2. Right-click the name of the CA and select All Tasks from the context menu, followed by Install CA certificate.
3. Browse for the file received from the parent Certificate Authority, select the file, and click Open.

Backing Up and Restoring Certificate Services

Proper backup of the server running Certificate Services requires backing up the system state using the NTBackup utility or a third-party vendor's utility. It is

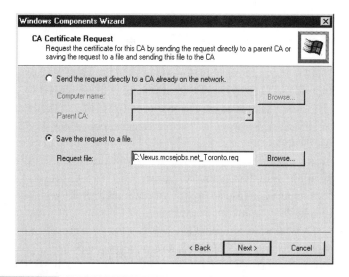

FIGURE 4-6   Obtaining a certificate for a subordinate CA

possible to back up the Certificate Services database without performing a full backup; however, this method is discouraged if used as a recurring backup methodology.

To back up only the Certificate Services database, use the Certification Authority snap-in. In order to perform the backup operation, you have to be a member of the Backup Operators or Administrators group. In the Certificate Authority snap-in, right-click the CA you want to back up and select All Tasks, followed by Backup CA. This will open the Certification Authority Backup Wizard, which will require you to answer a couple questions before the backup takes place.

Restoring the CA from a backup is done through the same snap-in. The steps are almost identical, with the only change being that you select Restore CA as opposed to Backup CA. The restore process also launches a wizard, which asks you for the location of the backup file and where you wish to restore it to. After restoring the CA, check to make sure that your IIS service starts properly. If not, you will need to restore the metabase from a previous backup and then try to start the IIS service. Oftentimes, a corrupt or damaged metabase will prevent IIS from starting, which in turn prevents Certificate Services from starting. If the IIS service starts properly, Certificate Services should start properly as well—or at the very least you have ruled out the problem being attributed to IIS.

Now that you have learned how to install, configure, back up, and restore Certificate Services, we will look at the ins and outs of issuing and revoking certificates.

Troubleshooting Certificate Services

The best place to start when troubleshooting problems with Certificate Services is the System log in Event Viewer. Oftentimes, a problem with the Certificate Services database is a dependency problem. Because proper functionality of Certificate Services depends on IIS, event messages about other services should also be investigated.

Certificate Services can also be run in diagnostics mode by running the Certsrv.exe utility from the Command Prompt. This starts Certificate Services as a stand-alone application instead of as a Windows 2000 service and displays a log of its actions in the Command Prompt window. Certificate Services cannot be running as a service when you run Certsrv.exe; the service must first be stopped and then Certsrv.exe run. Once Certificate Services is stopped, open a command prompt and enter **certsrv –z** to start Certificate Services in diagnostic mode.

Issue and Revoke Certificates

Objective 4.02

A number of alternatives are available for the distribution and issuing of certificates in the Windows 2000 network. The automatic distribution of certificates is configurable in the Public Key Policies section of a group policy. It is also possible to explicitly request a certificate using either the Certificate Request Wizard or the Certificate Services Web pages.

The policy module of Certificate Services is responsible for determining whether a request is approved, denied, or left pending for an administrator to approve or deny. The default policy module varies according to the type of CA. For example the enterprise CA policy is configured to always issue or deny a certificate request immediately. The enterprise CA policy uses the Active Directory to determine the identity of the user, computer, or service requesting the certificate and to determine whether the requesting object has the required permissions to obtain the type of certificate being requested. The stand-alone CA policy sends a certificate request to a pending queue for an administrator to approve or deny it. This default setting can be changed on a stand-alone CA to allow for the immediate issuance or denial. The reason that the certificate request is queued up by default is that a stand-alone CA does not verify the identity of the requester because it does not require or use the Active Directory. Therefore, issuing a certificate without any way of verifying the identity of the user could pose a security risk. To avoid this security risk, the request is queued and an administrator can make the final approval or denial decision.

> **Exam Tip**
>
> Automatic certificate request settings can be defined in the Public Key Policies section of a group policy. This approach greatly simplifies administration.

Regardless of the method used to obtain certificates, once they're obtained, the certificates are stored in one of five standard certificate stores:

- My Store contains a user's or computer's certificates, which have associated private keys.

- The CA store contains issuing or intermediate CA certificates used in the building of certificate hierarchies.
- The trust store contains certificate trust lists (CTLs), which allow you to control the purpose and validity period of certificates issued by external CAs.
- The root store contains only self-signed CA certificates for trusted root CAs.
- The UserDS store provides a logical view of the certificate repository stored in Active Directory.

Certificate requests can be divided into two types: simple and advanced. The intended purpose of the certificate determines which type of request is necessary. Certificates to be used for IPSec, client authentication, and server authentication require advanced certificate requests. As we look at the steps involved in requesting a certificate using both methods, we will explore the choices available in both the simple and advanced certificate requests.

Using the Certificate Request Wizard

The Certificate Request Wizard can be used only to request a certificate from an enterprise CA. The selection of different certificate types is dependant on the user's access rights. The use of the Certificate Request Wizard allows the request to be processed immediately, and a certificate is either refused or granted.

Exam Tip

The Certificate Request Wizard can be used only to request a certificate from an enterprise CA.

To request a certificate using the Certificate Request Wizard, follow these steps:

1. Click Start | Run and type **mmc** in the Open text box. Click OK.
2. In the empty MMC, select Action | Add/Remove Snap-in.
3. In the Add/Remove Snap-in dialog box, select Add.
4. Select the Certificates snap-in from the list of available snap-ins and click Add. From the dialog box that appears, select the account for which you want to request a certificate. This account can be My User Account (the account you are currently logged on as), Computer Account (the account of the local

computer), or Service account (which will prompt you to select a service running on the local computer). For this example, select My User Account. Click OK, Close, and then OK again.

5. Expand Certificates – Current User, right-click a logical store name (Personal, Enterprise Trust, and so on), and select All Tasks, followed by Request New Certificate.

6. Click Next to start the wizard. Select a certificate template on the Certificate Template page and, if required, select Advanced Options. The advanced options will allow you to configure the CSP and give you the choice of enabling strong private key encryption, which requires a password to be entered every time the private key is used. In Advanced Options, you are also able to specify the name of the CA that issues the certificate. This is important in an environment with multiple CAs.

7. Enter a display name for the certificate, and when the wizard is finished select Install Certificate.

Exam Tip

When you're requesting a certificate for a computer account, be sure to select Store in Local Machine Store.

Using the Certificate Services Web Pages

Using the Certificate Services Web pages is the second method available to explicitly request a certificate. The installation of Certificate Services creates the Web pages that allow for both simple and advanced certificate requests.

Exam Tip

For a stand-alone CA, using the Web pages is the only method available to request a certificate.

To submit a certificate request via the Web, follow these steps:

1. Open Internet Explorer and browse to http://*servername*/certsrv, where *servername* is the name of the CA.

2. On the Welcome page, choose the radio button next to Request a Certificate and then click Next.

3. On the Choose Request Type page, select User Certificate Request followed by the type of certificate you wish to request. Then click Next. This is also where an advanced request could be selected instead of a user certificate request.
4. Fill in the identifying information and click Submit.

On a stand-alone CA, the certificate is not available immediately to install. An administrator must first issue the certificate.

Issuing Pending Certificates

Once a certificate request has been made through the Web interface on a stand-alone CA, the certificate must be issued by an administrator. This process allows the administrator to approve or reject individual requests and adds a human level of consistency checking. This approval and rejection procedure applies only to certificates requested from a stand-alone CA that is configured to mark every incoming certificate request as pending, which is the default setting. To reject or approve pending certificates, follow these steps:

1. Open the Certification Authority snap-in and select Pending Requests.
2. Right-click the certificate you wish to process and select All Tasks, followed by either Issue or Deny.

Using Auto-Enrollment to Issue Certificates

The process of requesting, receiving, and installing certificates can be automated using the automatic certificate settings in public key policies. Public key policies comprise a component of group policy and can be applied at one of three levels in the Active Directory structure. In the physical structure of Active Directory, group policy objects (GPOs) can be applied at the site level. In the logical structure of Active Directory, GPOs can be applied at the domain and Organizational Unit level.

If you want to create a GPO that will apply the automatic certificate settings to all computers in the domain, it should be created at the domain level. This way, all users and computers in the domain will pick up and apply the policy and automatically request, receive, and install a certificate. The key concept to keep in mind when planning the design of your organization's Active Directory is the simplicity of future administration. The use of group policy to automatically enroll each computer-related certificate works towards this goal of administrative simplicity and efficiency.

Revoking Issued Certificates

Once a certificate has been issued, the integrity of an organization's public key infrastructure is maintained through proper revocation of compromised or unneeded certificates. For example, if an employee leaves the organization, their certificate should be revoked at the same time their account is disabled. Another example of where a certificate should be deleted is if the private key of a certificate becomes compromised, which could occur if a notebook is stolen and the private key was stored locally on the notebook. Both of these examples are times when the user's certificate should be revoked to maintain the integrity of the Certificate Services database. To revoke an issued certificate, follow these steps:

1. Open the Certification Authority snap-in and select Issued Certificates.
2. Right-click the certificate you want to revoke and select Revoke Certificate.
3. In the Reason Code drop-down box, select the reason for the revocation and click Yes. Selecting the reason code Certificate Hold allows the certificate to be unrevoked or for the reason code to be changed at a later date. Think of this as being similar to disabling a user account as opposed to deleting it. Disabling the account allows it to be re-enabled in the future where deleting requires it be re-recreated.

The integrity achieved by the revoking of certificates is only as good as the associated certificate revocation list (CRL) and the client settings for checking this list, which we will explore next.

The Certificate Revocation List (CRL)

Every CA automatically publishes an updated CRL at intervals specified by the administrator. CRLs can be created manually using the CRL Publishing Wizard without affecting the automatic publishing schedule. The only reason to publish a CRL manually is if a number of certificates in the Certificate Services database have recently been revoked—you alert clients to manually connect to the CA with the updated CRL and download a more recent copy. The key reason for this is to maintain the integrity of the Certificate Services. To generate a CRL manually, follow these steps:

1. Open the Certification Authority snap-in and right-click Revoke Certificates. Select All Tasks, followed by Publish.
2. Choose Yes from the dialog box that appears. This dialog box states that the last published CRL is still valid and can be used by clients, and it asks whether you are sure you want to publish a new CRL.

Exam Tip

Clients continue to use their cached copy of the CRL until it expires and do not automatically retrieve updates. Updated CRLs must be manually downloaded by the client, which can be done in their browser by going to http://*servername*/certsrv.

By default, both enterprise CAs and stand-alone CAs publish a CRL weekly. The enterprise CA publishes the CRL to the active directory, and the stand-alone CA publishes the CRL to the %systemroot\system32\certsrv\certenroll directory on the computer on which the stand-alone CA is installed.

Exporting and Importing Certificates

Depending on the certificate settings defined on the CA that issued the certificate, it may be possible to import or export user, computer, and service account certificates. The exporting and importing of certificates may be required if a user is assigned a specific computer for their own personal use and that computer is upgraded over the course of time. Because the user's certificate is stored in the local certificate store, exporting it would allow it to be imported to the new computer and allow the user to continue to work uninterrupted. The option to export a certificate only appears if the private key is marked as exportable, and, as the user, you have access to the private key. This setting is configured on the certificate server. Exporting a certificate does not remove the certificate from the local certificate store. To remove it from the certificate store, use the Certificates snap-in to delete the certificate.

To export a certificate, follow these steps:

1. Open the Certificates snap-in and expand the Personal logical store, followed by the Certificates store.
2. Right-click the certificate you want to export and select All Tasks, followed by Export.
3. In the Certificate Export Wizard, click Next and choose to either "Yes, Export the Private Key" or "No, Do Not Export the Private Key." The option to export the private key only appears if the private key is marked as exportable. Click Next.
4. Select the file format you want to export the certificate in and click Next. Enter a file name and path and then click Next, followed by Finish.

To import a certificate, follow these steps:

1. Open the Certificates snap-in and expand the Personal logical store, followed by the Certificates store.
2. Right-click the Certificates logical store and select All Tasks, followed by Import.
3. In the Certificate Import Wizard, click Next and browse for the certificate file. Click Next.
4. Specify the certificate store in which to import the certificate and click Next and then Finish.

Supporting Authentication of External Users

To support the authentication of users external to your organization, a few additional steps must be taken. The authentication of external users requires that the external user have the following items:

- A valid certificate issued by a trusted CA or by a CA that is listed in the Certificate Trust List
- A user account in the organization's domain
- A name mapping that maps the external user certificate to the user account in the domain

Prior to creating a name mapping, it is important that you decide upon a name-mapping strategy. You have three name mapping strategies to choose from. The first allows you to map one certificate to one user account and is referred to as a *one-to-one name mapping*. The second allows you to map any certificate with identical subject values to a single certificate. This is known as a *many-to-one mapping*. The third and final option is to map any certificate that uses the same issuer to a single user account and is also referred to as a *many-to-one mapping*. To map an account to a certificate, follow these steps:

1. Open Active Directory Users and Computers and from the View menu select Advanced Features.
2. Double-click the domain name to display the containers within the domain and then select the container where the user account you want to map to exists.
3. Right-click the user account and select Name Mappings.
4. On the X.509 Certificate tab, click Add and enter the name and path to the CER file for the certificate you want to map the user account to.

5. For a one-to-one mapping, select the check boxes next to Use Issuer for Alternate Security Identity and Use Subject of Alternate Security Identity. For a many-to-one mapping of certificates with identical subject values, clear the check box next to Use Issuer for Alternate Security Identity and place a check mark in the box next to Use Subject of Alternate Security Identity. For a many-to-one mapping of certificates with identical issuers, place a check mark in the box next to Use Issuer for Alternate Security Identity and clear the box next to Use Subject of Alternate Security Identity.
6. Click OK.

The Windows 2000 PKI also allows you to issue Authenticode certificates, which allow employees to verify the origin and integrity of applications downloaded from their own corporate intranet.

Removing the Encrypting File System (EFS) Recovery Keys

Objective 4.03

The removal of the Encrypting File System (EFS) recovery keys is something that all administrators should know how to do and is a skill that is measured on the exam. However, it is not the only thing that you should know. Before we explore the removal process, we will discuss EFS and explore what EFS is intended to be used for.

The Encrypting File System is a new feature in Windows 2000 that allows you to configure specific files, folders, or entire drives formatted with the NTFS file system to be encrypted and decrypted using certificates. EFS does not require Certificate Services be installed, because it is capable of issuing its own certificates for the sole purpose of EFS.

There are a number of important points to remember about EFS, including:

- EFS is only available on partitions, volumes, or drives formatted with NTFS.
- The use of EFS requires a recovery agent certificate.
- EFS is used to encrypt and decrypt data on a disk but does not encrypt data that is sent across the network.
- EFS does not allow system files or folders to be encrypted.
- Compression and encryption are mutually exclusive.
- Copying a file into an encrypted folder encrypts the file, but moving the file into an encrypted folder does not—the file remains unencrypted.

- Backing up encrypted files preserves the encryption attribute, but moving or copying them to another file system results in the encryption attribute being lost.
- NTFS permissions are not affected by EFS and may allow a user who cannot open an encrypted file to be able to delete it.

Each EFS user generates a public-key pair and obtains an EFS certificate upon the first attempt by a user to encrypt a file. The certificate can be issued by an enterprise CA in a Windows 2000 domain, although EFS can also generate a self-signed certificate for stand-alone operation. The EFS feature in Windows 2000 also includes an EFS recovery policy that uses trusted recovery agents. The administrator of the domain or local computer is the default recovery agent; however, additional recovery agents can be added. Each recovery agent generates an EFS recovery public-key pair and is issued an EFS recovery certificate by EFS or by an enterprise CA if one is installed. EFS recovery agent certificates are published to domain clients with the group policy object and allow a recovery agent to decrypt files, folders, or drives encrypted by another user. This procedure provides a means of recovery in case the user loses their EFS certificate and is unable to decrypt their encrypted data.

EFS generates a random key (like a session key) for each file, folder, or drive that is to be encrypted. Each file that is encrypted has its own unique, random key used for encryption. The user's EFS public-key pair is not used to encrypt the file but instead used to encrypt the unique, random session key. This way, only the user who encrypted the file is able to use their private key to decrypt the unique, random session key and decrypt the file. When encrypting the unique session key, the user uses their EFS public key so that only their EFS private key can be used to decrypt the session key. One last step is also incorporated into the EFS encryption process. A copy of the unique session key is encrypted with each recovery agent's EFS public key and is associated with the file. This approach allows for the recovery agent to decrypt the file in the event the user loses their EFS key. No plain-text copy of the secret key is ever stored in the system, making it difficult or impossible for others to decrypt files encrypted by other users.

You could think of the EFS process as being similar to the use of a security deposit box. If you rent a security deposit box, the box itself along with many others are generally stored in a safe or vault. When the vault is opened, you are escorted into where your safety deposit box is. You have a key for that box. That key can be likened to the unique session key used to encrypt a file in EFS. Only you have a copy of that key, and without that key, you would not have access to your items in the safety deposit box. When you are done adding or removing items from the safety deposit box, you store your key at home in a locked cabinet. The storage of the key in a locked cabinet can be likened to the encrypting of the session key with a user's EFS public key, because it is a way of protecting that session (safety deposit box) key.

Encrypting Files, Folders, and Drives

Encrypting files and folders is a very simple process and can be accomplished in one of two ways. The easiest way for most users is to use Windows Explorer and follow these steps:

1. Open Windows Explorer.
2. Right-click the file on an NTFS partition that you wish to encrypt.
3. Select Properties from the context menu.
4. On the General tab of the Properties dialog box, click the Advanced button.
5. In the Advanced Attributes dialog box, shown in Figure 4-7, place a check mark in the box next to Encrypt Contents to Secure Data.
6. Click OK twice to close all open dialog boxes.

Exam Tip	
Deleting an encrypted file is not limited to the person who encrypted the file.	

The second means available to encrypt and decrypt files, folders, and entire drives is a command-line tool known as Cipher.exe. Cipher can be used to encrypt

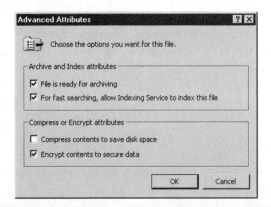

FIGURE 4-7   Encrypting a file in Windows Explorer

and decrypt files at the Command Prompt and can also be scripted to encrypt or decrypt files. The **cipher** command has a number of switches that can be displayed with explanations by typing the following at the Command Prompt:

```
Cipher /?
```

The most important switches to be aware of are listed here:

- **/e** Used to encrypt a specified directory and configure the directory to encrypt all files created in the directory in the future.
- **/d** Used to decrypt a specified directory and configure the folder to no longer encrypt files added to it.
- **/s** Used to indicate that the immediate directory and all subdirectories should be encrypted or decrypted. This switch should be used in conjunction with the /e or /d switch.

Exam Tip

If a folder is encrypted and you had access to the folder prior to it being encrypted, you are still able to access the folder. Encrypting a folder only marks the folder as encrypted so that all files in the folder are encrypted as they are created, but it does not prevent access to the folder.

Decrypting Files, Folders, and Drives

Both Windows Explorer and the command-line tool Cipher can be used to decrypt files, folders, and drives stored on a partition or volume formatted with the NTFS file system. To decrypt a file using Windows Explorer, follow these steps:

1. Open Windows Explorer.
2. Right-click the file on an NTFS partition that you wish to decrypt.
3. Select Properties from the context menu.
4. On the General tab of the Properties dialog box, click the Advanced button.
5. In the Advanced Attributes dialog box, shown previously in Figure 4-7, remove the check mark in the box next to Encrypt Contents to Secure Data.
6. Click OK twice to close all open dialog boxes.

EFS can be used to encrypt and decrypt files and folders on both a local drive and a remote drive of another computer. When using EFS across the network on a remote drive, however, remember that your data is not protected when accessing it across the network. When a user opens an encrypted file stored on a remote server, the file is decrypted on the remote server and sent across the network in clear text. Other security protocols and features, such as IPSec, PPTP and SSL, can be used to secure the transfer of data across the network, but that is not the function of EFS.

Backing Up EFS Certificates and Keys

EFS is designed to allow only the user who encrypted the file and the data recovery agent to decrypt the file; therefore, it is important to back up the EFS certificate and associated private key for important users, particularly users who are configured as data recovery agents. That way, in the event of a disk failure and loss of the data recovery agent's encryption certificate, the data recovery agent is able to restore the certificate and continue to access the encrypted files.

As the recovery agent, it is critical that you use the Export command from the Certificates MMC to back up the recovery certificate and associated private key to a secure location. After performing the backup, you should use the Certificates MMC to delete the recovery certificate from your personal store, *not* from the recovery policy. By doing this, you reduce the number of places that your recovery agent information is stored and improve the overall security of your EFS implementation.

When the time comes that you need to perform a recovery operation for a user, follow these steps:

1. As the data recovery agent, restore the recovery certificate and associated private key to the recovery agent's personal store using the **Import** command in the Certificates MMC.
2. Then, again as the recovery agent, decrypt the data and change the encryption attribute.
3. Once the data has been recovered, the data recovery agent should again *delete the recovery certificate* from the recovery agent's personal store on the user's computer. This time, however, you don't have to perform the export process. The deletion of the recovery agent's recovery certificate from the user's computer and the storage of that certificate in a secure location apart from the computer is an additional security measure that is highly recommended for the protection of sensitive data.

Exam Tip

Removing the data recovery agent prevents users from using EFS, because at least one data recovery agent is required for EFS functionality.

The default recovery policy is configured locally for stand-alone computers. For computers that are part of a network, the recovery policy is configured at either the domain, organizational unit, or individual computer level, and it applies to all Windows 2000-based computers within the defined scope of influence. Recovery certificates are issued by a Certificate Authority (CA) and managed using the Certificates MMC.

Travel Assistance

For more information on how to restore the recovery agent's certificate, read Knowledge Base article Q242296. Did you also know that you can type any Knowledge Base article number into the location bar of your Internet Explorer browser and it will open up the article. Neat, eh?

Moving and Copying Encrypted Files

The moving and copying of encrypted files has the potential to affect the encryption attributes of these files. Remember that EFS is only available on volumes formatted with the NTFS file system. Therefore, if you have read permission for a file that has been encrypted by another user and are prevented from opening the file, you are still able to access the file by copying it to a FAT-formatted volume or partition, where the encryption property will be lost.

The outcome of copying and/or moving files between NTFS partitions or volumes is simple to understand. Regardless of whether an encrypted file is moved or copied between NTFS partitions, it will always maintain its encryption attribute.

Exam Tip

Remember that EFS is a feature of the NTFS file system and is therefore not available for drives or partitions formatted with the FAT or FAT32 file system. Copying an encrypted file to a FAT-formatted volume results in the file being decrypted.

Disabling EFS

EFS can also be disabled to prevent users from encrypting files. In an Active Directory domain, the easiest way to disable EFS is through the use of a GPO that is applied to all users and computers in the domain. A group policy can also be used to disable EFS at the OU level, allowing you to disable EFS for specific users but not all users. The most effective way to disable EFS is to configure a group policy with an empty recovery policy.

Exam Tip

The absence of a recovery policy or a recovery policy with no recovery agent produces the same end result—EFS is disabled.

Troubleshooting EFS

Allowing users to encrypt files and folders can lead to a number of problems. For example, a user could save a file that they created into a shared folder that was encrypted by another user. The user that created and saved the file wouldn't realize that the file then becomes encrypted, preventing other users from accessing the file. One of the first steps in solving encryption-related issues is to understand what files are encrypted and who encrypted the files or folders.

A second example of where an encryption problem could result is when a user loses their EFS certificate and is unable to decrypt a file they had originally encrypted. The user may or may not even realize that the data recovery agent is able to decrypt the file, but even if they do realize it, they may not know who the data recovery agent is. Identifying the data recovery agent of the encrypted file of folder is the first step to recovery.

In both of these examples, a utility known as Efsinfo can be used to identify the files and folders that are encrypted, the users who encrypted them, and the certificate thumbprints of the certificate required to decrypt them.

To use Efsinfo, open a command prompt and change the drive letter and directory path to represent the drive and directory on which you wish to identify encrypted files and folders. Then simply type **efsinfo**, and the results should be similar to those shown in Figure 4-8. The example in Figure 4-8 shows Efsinfo being used to query the folder named "encrypted" on the C drive. The results show one file named new.txt as being encrypted and indicate that the file was encrypted by a user named Osborne in the Mcsejobs domain. The results also indicate that a second file, not encrypted.txt, is not encrypted but located in the same folder.

The Efsinfo utility comes with a number of switches, each of which can be helpful in the troubleshooting process:

```
C:\WINNT\System32\cmd.exe                                    _ □ ×

C:\encrypted>efsinfo

C:\encrypted\

new.txt: Encrypted
    Users who can decrypt:
        MCSEJOBS\osborne (CN=osborne,L=EFS,OU=EFS File Encryption Certificate)

not encrypted.txt: Not Encrypted

C:\encrypted>_
```

FIGURE 4-8   Identifying encrypted files and folders with Efsinfo

- **/U**   Displays user information (the default option)
- **/R**   Used to display recovery agent information
- **/C**   Used to display certificate thumbnail information
- **/I**   Instructs Efsinfo to continue performing what it has been programmed to do even after errors occur
- **/Y**   Used to display your current EFS certificate thumbnail on the local PC
- **/S**   Instructs Efsinfo to perform its operation on the current directory and all subdirectories

Let's go back to the second example, where a user wants to identify the recovery agent for a particular file. This can be accomplished using the following command:

```
Efsinfo /R new.txt
```

In this command, the file new.txt, which we identify as being encrypted, could be specified so that only recovery agent information for that file is displayed. However, the command will still execute correctly without a file being specified. To identify the certificate thumbprint for the certificate that is able to decrypt the file, the following command can be used:

```
Efsinfo /c
```

Travel Advisory

For more information on EFS, check out the "Step-by-Step Guide To Encrypting File System (EFS)" at http://www.microsoft.com/windows2000/techinfo/planning/security/efssteps.asp

CHECKPOINT

✔ **Objective 4.01: Install and Configure a Certificate Authority**   To send data encrypted across the network, use the recipient's public key to encrypt the data. The recipient will then use their private key to decrypt the data. To digitally sign a message, use the sender's private key to sign the message. The recipient will use the sender's public key to decrypt the message and prove authenticity. There are two classes of Certificate Authorities: enterprise and stand-alone. Within each of these classes are two types of Certificate Authorities: root and subordinate. Enterprise root certificate servers should be used when issuing certificates only to users within your own organization. Stand-alone certificate servers should be used when issuing certificates to users outside of your organization. Enterprise root CAs and enterprise subordinate CAs require Active Directory to exist prior to installation because the Certificate Services feature uses the Active Directory to store information. An enterprise root CA must exist and be available in order for an enterprise subordinate CA to be installed. A parent or stand-alone root CA is not required for the installation of a stand-alone subordinate CA. To install an enterprise-class Certificate Authority, you must be a member of the Enterprise Admins group. Certificate Services can be run in diagnostic mode by first stopping the service and then executing the command certsrv.exe –z at the Command Prompt.

✔ **Objective 4.02: Issue and Revoke Certificates**   For an enterprise root or enterprise subordinate CA to publish certificates in the Active Directory, the server must be a member of the Cert Publishers group. Certificates can be explicitly requested using either the Certificate Request Wizard or the Certificate Services Web pages. The Certificate Request Wizard can only be used to request a certificate from an enterprise CA. On a stand-alone CA, the Web pages provide the only method available to request a certificate.

✔ **Objective 4.03: Remove the Encrypting File System (EFS) Recovery Keys**   Cipher is a command-line tool that can be used to encrypt and decrypt files, folders, and entire drives. Encrypting a folder only marks the folder as encrypted so that all files in the folder are encrypted as they are created. However, it does not prevent access to the folder but rather only to the files within the folder. Copying and/or moving an encrypted file between NTFS partitions or volumes results in the file always maintaining its encryption attribute. The absence of a recovery policy or a recovery policy with no recovery agent produces the same end result—EFS is disabled. The Efsinfo utility can be used to list all encrypted files on a specific drive or within a specified directory. It can also be used to list the users who have the ability to decrypt the encrypted object and display their certificate thumbprint.

REVIEW QUESTIONS

1. Your organization has an extranet that allows suppliers to view your inventories in real time. You have been asked to change the security model for the extranet to limit access to only individuals with valid certificates issued from a certificate server that you have been asked to install. What type of certificate server will you install first to accomplish this goal, assuming that the certificate for this server will be purchased from an external commercial CA?

   A. Enterprise root CA
   B. Stand-alone root CA
   C. Enterprise subordinate CA
   D. Stand-alone subordinate CA

2. A colleague has asked you to describe the use of data encryption to the management team in your organization to assess whether it is something that management would like to implement for all corporate e-mail in an effort to increase security. Which of the following statements correctly describes the keys used in the encryption of data?

   A. The sender's private key is used to encrypt the data.
   B. The recipient's private key is used to encrypt the data.
   C. The sender's public key is used to encrypt the data.
   D. The recipient's public key is used to encrypt the data.

3. You have been asked to configure a Certificate Services hierarchy to issue certificates to users in your organization for the purpose of client authentication against specific servers that contain R&D information. Which of the following hierarchical configurations would you implement?

   A. Enterprise root CA, enterprise subordinate CA
   B. Stand-alone root CA, stand-alone subordinate CA
   C. Enterprise root CA, stand-alone subordinate CA
   D. Stand-alone root CA, enterprise subordinate CA

4. You are the administrator of your organization's network. One of your responsibilities is the installation of the enterprise certificate hierarchy, which consists of one enterprise root CA and four enterprise subordinate CAs. One of the servers configured as an enterprise subordinate CA needs to be replaced. You have purchased a new server, installed Windows 2000 Server, and configured the server as a member server in the mcsejobs.net Active Directory domain. After you install Certificate Services on the new server and configure it as an enterprise subordinate CA, what must you do?

   A. Change the name of the server to include CA in its name.
   B. Add the local Administrator account to the Cert Admins group.
   C. Add the computer account to the Cert Publishers group.
   D. Add the local Administrator account to the Cert Publishers group.

5. Which of the following groups must you be a member of in order to install an enterprise root CA?

   A. Domain Admins
   B. The local Administrators group on the server
   C. Enterprise Admins
   D. Cert Publishers

6. When preparing for a disaster-recovery situation, which one of the following components, if backed up, will allow you to successfully restore the Certificate Services database for a stand-alone root certificate server?

   A. System State
   B. Metabase
   C. Certificate Services database
   D. Active Directory database

7. You have just completed the installation of an enterprise subordinate CA and wish to test the server to ensure that it is working and capable of issuing certificates. Which of the following items will you use to explicitly request a certificate? (Choose all that apply.)

   A. The Certificate Request Wizard in the Certificates snap-in
   B. The Certificate Services Web pages
   C. Group Policy
   D. The Certificate Request Wizard in the Certification Authority snap-in

8. You have just completed the installation of a stand-alone CA and wish to test the server to ensure that it is working and capable of issuing certificates. Which of the following will you use to explicitly request a certificate?

   A. The Certificate Request Wizard in the Certificates snap-in

   B. The Certificate Services Web pages

   C. Group Policy

   D. The Certificate Request Wizard in the Certification Authority snap-in

9. What two requirements must be present prior to the installation of an enterprise subordinate CA?

   A. DNS

   B. Active Directory

   C. Enterprise root CA

   D. Stand-alone root CA

10. Which two of the following types of Certificate Authorities require Active Directory prior to their installation?

   A. Enterprise root CA

   B. Enterprise subordinate CA

   C. Stand-alone root CA

   D. Stand-alone subordinate CA

REVIEW ANSWERS

1. **D** A stand-alone subordinate CA should be installed if a certificate for this server is going to be published from an external commercial CA.

2. **D** When sending a message whose contents you wish to encrypt, the recipient's public key is used to encrypt the data so that only the recipient's private key can be used to decrypt the data.

3. **A** The recommended CA hierarchy would consist of an enterprise root CA and one or more enterprise subordinate CAs. The root CA would issue certificates to the subordinate CAs, which in turn would issue certificates to the users in the organization.

4. **C** The server's computer account must be added to the Cert Publishers group in order to allow the CA to publish certificates in the Active Directory.

5. **C** In order to install an enterprise root CA, you must be a member of the Enterprise Admins group.

6. **A** Backing up the System State component will allow you to successfully restore the Certificate Services database for a stand-alone root certificate server if it crashes.

7. **A** **B** On an enterprise subordinate CA, both the Certificate Services Web pages and the Certificate Request Wizard can be used to request a certificate.

8. **B** Stand-alone CAs only support the Certificate Services Web pages as a means of explicitly obtaining a certificate.

9. **B** **C** Both the Active Directory and an enterprise root CA must be available on the network prior to the installation of an enterprise subordinate CA. This is a trick question not unlike the ones you will see on the real exam. DNS is a requirement of Active Directory, and Active Directory is required to install an enterprise root CA. Therefore, it can be assumed that DNS already exists on the network and is not a direct requirement for the installation of an enterprise subordinate CA.

10. **A** **B** Both the enterprise root and enterprise subordinate CAs require Active Directory to be installed and online prior to their installation.

Network Protocol Configuration

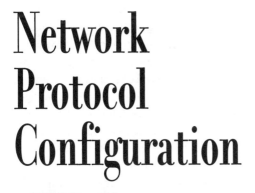

	NEWBIE	SOME EXPERIENCE	EXPERT
ETA	7–10 hours	4–7 hours	2–4 hours

The configuration of network communications is fundamental to the successful deployment and support of Windows 2000 in all networks. Understanding the installation and configuration process of each of the protocols that Windows 2000 supports is the first step in this process. Troubleshooting any communication problems that arise is the next concept that we will examine in this chapter. Once you understand the fundamentals of network protocols and their configuration, we will look at a new feature in Windows 2000 known as IP Security (IPSec). Familiarity with and a thorough understanding of IPSec is required for success on the Implementing and Administering a Microsoft Windows 2000 Network Infrastructure exam. This chapter will cover the ins and outs of IPSec and then close with a look at using Network Monitor to capture, monitor, and display network data as a part of the troubleshooting process.

Objective 5.01

Install, Configure, and Troubleshoot Network Protocols

Windows 2000 supports network protocols, allowing it to interoperate with a variety of different operating systems. The network protocols supported by Windows 2000 include the following:

- TCP/IP
- NWLink (IPX/SPX)
- NetBEUI
- AppleTalk
- Data Link Control (DLC)

TCP/IP is the default network protocol and is installed with the Windows 2000 operating system. To install additional network protocols, follow these steps:

1. Open Network and Dial-up Connections and right-click the name of the connection you wish to bind another network protocol to (for example, Local Area Connection).
2. Select Properties from the context menu and on the General tab click the Install button.
3. From the Select Network Component Type dialog box, choose Protocol and select the Add button.
4. From the Select Network Protocol dialog box, shown in Figure 5-1, select the protocol you wish to install and click OK.

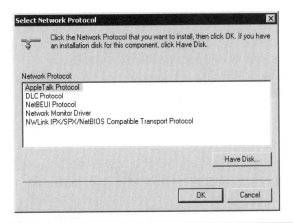

FIGURE 5-1   Adding additional network protocols

Once you have added the protocols, some configuration may be required. Because the configuration requirements for the various protocols differ, we will look at each protocol individually.

Objective 5.02

Install and Configure TCP/IP

Like all other network protocols, TCP/IP is installed as described in the preceding section. The configuration of TCP/IP can be accomplished one of two ways. As discussed in Chapter 1, the DHCP service can be used to automatically lease out IP addresses to numerous clients from a configured scope of IP addresses and administer them centrally on the DHCP server. An alternative to automatic distribution and configuration is static or manual configuration of IP addresses. Normally, client computers on a network are configured to dynamically obtain an IP address from a DHCP server, and servers are configured statically to ensure that their IP addresses do not change.

Exam Tip

Static IP address configuration only requires that an IP address and subnet mask be entered. A default gateway address is not a requirement for static configuration and is only required when operating in a routed network environment.

To configure TCP/IP with either a static or dynamic IP address, follow these steps:

1. Open Network and Dial-up Connections and right-click the name of the connection that you have bound TCP/IP to (for example, Local Area Connection).

2. Select Properties from the context menu. On the General tab, select Internet Protocol TCP/IP from the list of protocols and then click the Properties button.

3. On the General tab of the Internet Protocol TCP/IP dialog box, shown in Figure 5-2, choose the radio button next to Obtain an IP address Automatically for dynamic IP address assignment or choose the radio button next to Use the Following IP Address for static configuration.

4. If you selected the dynamic configuration option, click OK. If you selected the static configuration choice, an IP address and subnet mask is required. The address of a default gateway is optional but should be entered in a routed network environment. A preferred DNS server IP address should also be entered because DNS is required for name resolution. Once this information

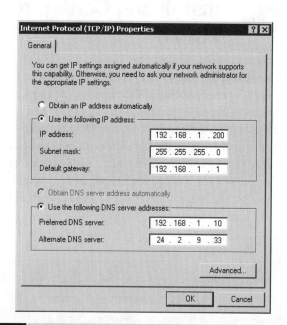

FIGURE 5-2   Configuring TCP/IP properties

has been entered, you can click OK to finish or continue to provide more configuration information through the Advanced button on the dialog box.

The Advanced button on Internet Protocol TCP/IP Properties dialog box opens the Advanced TCP/IP Settings dialog box, which contains four tabs: IP Settings, DNS, WINS, and Options.

The IP Settings tab allows you to bind multiple static IP addresses to one network interface and specify multiple gateway addresses.

The DNS tab, shown in Figure 5-3, allows you to specify multiple DNS servers and list them in order of use. It also provides the ability to specify different DNS suffixes, which instruct Windows 2000 to query those domain suffixes in the name-resolution process. The DNS tab is also used to configure dynamic DNS, which is accomplished by selecting the option Register This Connection's Addresses in DNS.

The WINS tab is used to identify and list multiple WINS servers and specify the order of use. It is also used to enable LMHOSTS lookups, which are enabled by default, and gives you the opportunity to disable NetBIOS over TCP/IP.

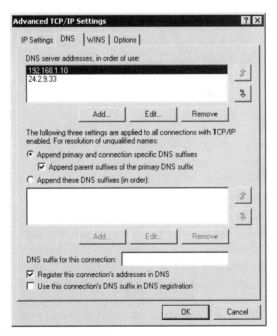

FIGURE 5-3   Configuring DNS settings in the Advanced TCP/IP Settings dialog box

Disabling NetBIOS over TCP/IP should only be done in a native Windows 2000 environment in which all computers are running a version of the Windows 2000 operating system.

Objective 5.03   Configure TCP/IP Packet Filters

The Options tab in the Advanced TCP/IP Settings dialog box allows for the configuration of IP Security (IPSec) and/or Internet Protocol (IP) filtering. We will explore the configuration of IPSec in Objective 5.08 and will focus on TCP/IP filtering in this section. TCP/IP filtering allows you to control the type of IP traffic that reaches the computer.

Exam Tip
Assigning TCP/IP packet filters through the TCP/IP properties will result in those filters applying to all network adapters on the local computer. This can result in communication problems on a multihomed computer.

IP traffic is broken into two types: User Datagram Protocol (UDP) and Transmission Control Protocol (TCP). Different services use different IP types and service ports to allow IP communication across a network. Figure 5-4 shows the TCP/IP Filtering dialog box, which is used to filter out specific types of IP traffic (UDP and/or TCP) by specifying the port number associated with the service you wish to filter out. For example, the HTTP service uses TCP port 80 for incoming and outgoing requests. Leaving the default Permit All setting enabled allows all TCP traffic to be sent and received by the computer. Changing the setting to Permit Only and clicking Add prompts you to enter a port number. Entering port 80 and clicking OK allows only traffic on TCP port 80 to be sent and received.

The name of the dialog box, TCP/IP Filtering, is a little bit misleading because more protocols than simply TCP and UDP can be filtered. Each protocol type is represented by a number that you are able to enter into the IP Protocols box to enable filtering of that specific protocol. The associated protocol numbers can be

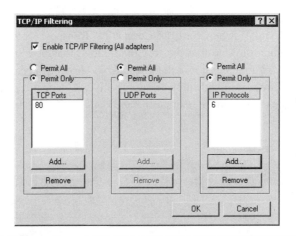

FIGURE 5-4   Configuring TCP/IP filtering

found in a file named protocol in the path %systemroot%\system32\drivers\etc. The two most common protocols, TCP and UDP, are represented by the numbers 6 and 17, respectively.

If you are not familiar with the port number(s) that a specific service operates on, a second file, named services, in the same directory can be used to obtain service port number associations. TCP/IP filtering is disabled by default and must be configured on a computer-by-computer basis.

Exam Tip

You cannot filter Internet Control Message Protocol traffic with TCP/IP filtering; however Routing and Remote Access Service can also be configured for IP filtering and does support the filtering of ICMP traffic.

Objective 5.04

Install the NWLink Protocol

Like all other network protocols, NWLink is installed through Network and Dial-up Connections, but the configuration of NWLink is much simpler than

TCP/IP because there is only one potential configuration requirement. Figure 5-5 shows the NWLink IPX/SPX/NetBIOS Compatible Transport Protocol Properties dialog box, which allows you to choose either auto or manual frame type detection. In a network that uses only a single frame type, leaving the default setting of auto is fine. However, if your network uses both 802.2 and 802.3 frame types, change the detection mode to manual and add both frame types to the list.

Exam Tip

When Windows 2000 is configured for auto detection and both 802.2 and 802.3 frame types are detected, only 802.2 will be supported.

NWLink is required for computers running Windows 2000 and configured with the Client Service for NetWare (CSNW) or clients that are accessing Windows 2000 file and print services through Gateway Services for NetWare (GSNW).

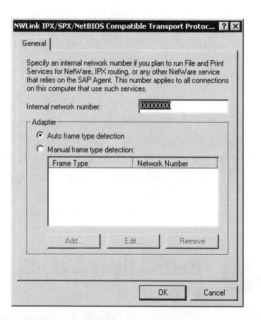

FIGURE 5-5   Configuring NWLink properties

> **Exam Tip**
>
> Installing the Novell Client is the only way to use IP-based printing, the Novell Distributed Printing Service (NDPS), or the Novell Enterprise Printing Service (NEPS) because these are not supported through CSNW or GSNW.

To install the Client Service for NetWare on a computer running Windows 2000, follow these steps:

1. Click Start | Settings | Network and Dial-up Connections, then right-click the connection that you wish to install CSNW on and select Properties.
2. In the Properties dialog box for the connection, click the Install button and select Client. Click the Add button.
3. In the list of available services to install, select Gateway (and Client) Services for NetWare and click OK.
4. In the Select NetWare dialog box, select either a Preferred Server or a Default Tree and Context and click OK.
5. Click the Yes button in the Network Logon dialog box that prompts you to restart your computer for the changes to take effect.
6. Click Close on the Properties dialog box for your network connection.

Well done! You have now installed the Client and Gateway Services for Netware!

Configuring Data Link Control, AppleTalk, and NetBEUI

The remaining three supported protocols—DLC, AppleTalk and NetBEUI—require no configuration once installed. I hesitate to say no configuration because AppleTalk can be further configured by adding support for file and print sharing, but for the most part they require little additional configuration.

DLC

DLC is not like other protocols in the sense that it is not designed for communication between computers. Instead DLC provides applications with direct access to the data link layer in the OSI model. DLC is not used for normal session communication but is included in Windows 2000 for two primary reasons:

- To support access to IBM mainframes (SNA servers)
- To support printing to Hewlett-Packard printers that are connected directly to the network, usually through a JetDirect box

In the case of printing to network-connected HP printers, DLC should be installed on the computer running Windows 2000 that is configured as the print server.

NetBEUI

NetBEUI was originally introduced by IBM back in 1985 and is still in use today. Now that's pretty impressive when you think about how often standards and technology change today! NetBEUI has a number of advantages, particularly in a small network environment, including:

- Provides fast and efficient communication on small networks
- Requires no configuration after installation
- Offers good error protection
- Uses a very small amount of memory

That being said, two of the biggest drawbacks to NetBEUI in a larger organization are that it is not routable and that it can be very chatty.

AppleTalk

The AppleTalk protocol allows for the integration of computers running Windows 2000 and Macintosh operating systems and allows users on both platforms to share files and printers. There are three components to an AppleTalk network:

- File server for Macintosh
- Print server for Macintosh
- AppleTalk

To install print services for Macintosh, follow the steps:

1. Click Start | Settings | Control Panel, and double-click Add/Remove Programs.
2. Click Add/Remove Windows Components and select Other Network File and Print Services (select the text, not the check box). Click the Details button.

3. Place a check mark next to Print Services for Macintosh and click OK and then Next. To install File Services for Macintosh, you can also place a check mark next to File Services for Macintosh. The installation of File Services for Macintosh requires that one of the volumes on the computer running Windows 2000 be formatted with the NTFS file system.

4. When the configuration is complete, click Finish.

Following these steps installs the AppleTalk protocol automatically with the installation of Print Services for Macintosh. If you simply want to install the AppleTalk protocol, follow these steps:

1. Click Start | Settings | Network and Dial-up Connections, then right-click the connection you want to bind the AppleTalk protocol to and select Properties. (For example Local Area Connection.)

2. Click the Install button and select Protocol in the list of network components and click Add.

3. In the Select Network Protocol dialog box, select AppleTalk and click OK.

One important point to be aware of is that the installation of the AppleTalk protocol occurs on all LAN adapters regardless of whether you chose a single network adapter. To unbind the AppleTalk protocol from any LAN adapter that you do not want AppleTalk to be bound to, follow these steps:

1. Click Start | Settings | Network and Dial-up Connections, then right-click the connection you want to unbind the AppleTalk protocol from. (For example Local Area Connection.) Select Properties from the context menu.

2. In the list of installed protocols, remove the check mark next to AppleTalk.

When AppleTalk is installed it does have one configuration setting that can be set. By exploring the properties of the protocol you are able to configure AppleTalk to accept inbound connections on the adapter and select a zone for the computer to appear in. To configure the acceptance of inbound connections, follow these steps:

1. Click Start | Settings | Network and Dial-up Connections, then right-click the connection you want to configure AppleTalk on and select Properties.

2. Select AppleTalk from the list of installed protocols and click the Properties button.

3. On the General tab of the AppleTalk Protocol Properties dialog box, place a check mark in the dialog box next to Accept inbound connections on this adapter and from the drop-down menu select a zone for the computer to appear in.

Objective 5.05 Configure Network Bindings

Configuring network bindings allows you to change the order in which protocols are bound to network providers, such as the workstation and server services, allowing you to improve network communication performance. For example, if your organization's network uses both TCP/IP and NetBEUI, but TCP/IP is the primary protocol for network communication, TCP/IP should be listed at the top of the network bindings, making it the first protocol used to try to establish a connection. To configure the binding order, follow these steps:

1. Open the Network and Dial-up Connections dialog box and on the Advanced menu select Advanced Settings.
2. In the Advanced Settings dialog box, shown in Figure 5-6, select the protocol that you wish to make the primary protocol and use the up-arrow button on the right side of the dialog box to move it to the top of the list for each provider. Then click OK.

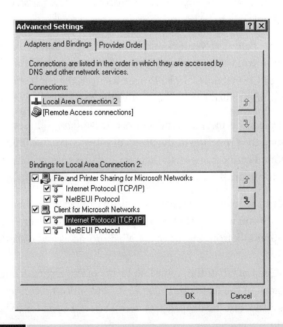

FIGURE 5-6 Configuring network bindings

> ### Exam Tip
>
> You must be a member of the Administrators group to change the network binding configuration.

Objective 5.06 Manage and Monitor Network Traffic

A number of tools and utilities are available to manage, monitor, and troubleshoot problems with network protocols. This section focuses on how to use these tools most effectively to resolve problems quickly using a solid methodology.

The first step in troubleshooting any type of problem should be to try to pinpoint the actual problem. Many times, variables that relate to a problem or are part of the cause of a problem overshadow the real problem you are trying to solve. A number of tools are available to help you hone in on the actual problem, and we will explore these tools in this section of the chapter.

Ipconfig

One excellent tool for providing great information and a starting point in your troubleshooting process is the ipconfig command, which is used to display your current IP configuration. Typing **ipconfig /all** at the command prompt will display the IP information for all the adapters on the local computer. The use of this command is sometimes enough to identify the problem and allow you to take steps to resolve it. For example, if the ipconfig /all command displays the IP address bound to your network card as 169.254.23.45, you know that the IP address has been assigned by the Windows 2000 default IP address assignment. Chapter 1 discusses how APIPA can be disabled by editing the registry. An IP address obtained through APIPA tells you one of two things: Either the static IP address configured for the local machine conflicts with another IP address on the network, thus making it unusable by the local computer, or, if the client is configured to obtain an IP address dynamically, the client has been unable to obtain an IP address, thus pointing to potential client connectivity problems or problems with the DHCP server or DHCP relay agent.

Ipconfig has a number of switches you should be familiar with for your day-to-day administration as well as for the exam. Table 5-1 lists the switches and what they can accomplish.

TABLE 5.1	Ipconfig Switches

Switch	Description
/all	Lists all the IP configuration information for all adapters on the local machine
/release	Releases all leased IP addresses
/renew	Attempts to renew IP addresses for all adapters configured to obtain an IP address from a DHCP server
/flushdns	Deletes all entries in the local DNS cache
/registerdns	Attempts to refresh all DHCP leases and reregister the client's DNS information with a DNS server configured to support dynamic DNS
/displaydns	Displays the contents of the DNS resolver cache on the local computer
/showclassid	Lists all the DHCP class IDs
/setclassid	Allows you to modify the DHCP class ID

Ping

Ping is a popular command used to verify IP-level connectivity. The ping command sends an Internet Control Message Protocol (ICMP) echo request to the hostname, the fully qualified domain name, or the IP address entered after the command. For example, to "ping" a computer named server1, you would use the following command:

```
ping server1
```

If this command generates the message "Unknown host server1," it could indicate a DNS problem. To eliminate DNS from the equation, try to ping server1 using its IP address, as shown here:

```
ping 192.168.1.1
```

The ping command is useful when you want to try to narrow down where the problem is actually occurring. If a computer on your network is having trouble communicating with another computer, ping can be used to verify whether each computer can be reached and a response returned. For example, if workstation1 is having problems connecting to server1, but other computers can connect to server1, then workstation1 could be pinged from another computer. If a response is returned, communication at the IP level would be confirmed successful and troubleshooting in other areas could continue. If a response isn't received, other variables affecting connectivity could be investigated, such as the network cable, the network card, the IP configuration of workstation1, or its IPSec settings.

Tracert

Tracert is a routing utility that uses the IP time-to-live (TTL) field and ICMP error messages to determine the route from one host to another through a network. Tracert allows you to see the route your IP packets take to their destination and identify the time it takes to move from router to router until the packets reach their final destination. If any one of the routers fails to route the IP packets, tracert identifies this, making you aware of where the problem exists. If the problem is a router on your network, you can then take the corrective action to identify and fix the problem. An example of the tracert command is shown here, where it is used to trace the route to the host web site at the Microsoft.com site:

```
tracert www.microsoft.com
```

Pathping

The pathping command is a route-tracing tool that combines the functionality of ping and tracert and provides the degree of packet loss at any given router. This additional information allows you to pinpoint which router(s) is causing the network problems. Using the pathping command is as simple as typing **pathping** *hostname* or **pathping** *IP address*, where *hostname* is the name of the destination computer and *IP address* is the IP of the destination computer. To see the difference between Ping and Pathping, open the Command Prompt and trace the route to the host Web site at Microsoft.com site by entering the following and pressing ENTER:

```
Pathping www.microsoft.com
```

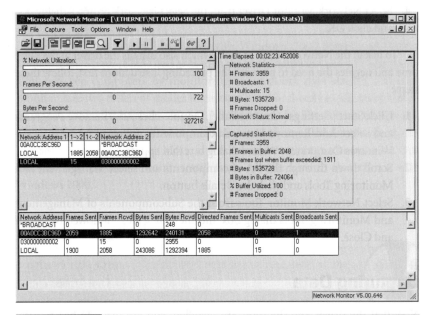

FIGURE 5-7   Network session capture statistics displayed in the Network Monitor capture window

The default settings in Network Monitor are configured to capture all the network traffic coming in and out of the local network interface card, thus capturing a lot of traffic that you may not need. There are two solutions to this—one is proactive, and the other reactive. The proactive solution is to configure a capture filter prior to starting the capture. The purpose of a capture filter is to process each packet based on a set of filter criteria and discard any packets that do not meet the criteria. This helps to reduce the amount of unnecessary traffic captured but increases the performance burden on the CPU of the computer. The second solution is to capture all the data and run a display filter on the results once the capture is complete. If you decide to capture all the data, make sure you set your capture buffer size large enough to accommodate the traffic you intend to capture. The default capture buffer size is 1MB. You might want to increase it to at least 4MB and possibly 10MB or higher to prevent frames from being overwritten. The required size of the capture buffer is relative to the amount of data you want to capture and the use of capture filters, which can make your capture more specific and result in an overall smaller capture.

Configure and Troubleshoot Network Protocol Security

Objective 5.07

Network protocol security can be achieved in a number of different ways, with the end goal being to protect the data transported across the network. One of the ways that data can be protected while traveling across the network is through the use of a virtual private network (VPN). In Windows 2000, a VPN can be configured to use one of two different encryption protocols: Point-to-Point Tunneling Protocol (PPTP) or Layer 2 Tunneling Protocol (L2TP). PPTP uses Microsoft Point-to-Point Encryption (MPPE) to encrypt data, whereas L2TP uses IPSec for encryption. Chapter 6 discusses the use, implementation, and configuration of VPNs. The use of IPSec is not, however, limited to VPNs, as you will see in the next section of this chapter. IPSec really has two uses:

- Defend against network attacks
- Protect IP packets

IPSec requires system medications on the computers participating in the secured communications. IPSec is sometimes referred to as an end-to-to security model, meaning that the computer sending the information secures the data prior to transmission and that the receiving computer knows that the data will be secured and decrypts the data only after receipt. IPSec works at Layer3 of the OSI model, the network layer, meaning that it is transparent to the user and that it does not require configuration on a per application basis.

To better understand how IPSec works, let's look at an example of two computers named wks1 and wks2 configured with an active IPSec policy. Rory is the user at wks1 and wishes to send data to the user Dina at wks2 encrypted using IPSec. The steps to the communication process follow:

1. Rory decides to send a file to Dina at wks2 using FTP. Dina's computer, wks2, is set up as an FTP server and configured to allow Rory to both read and write data to the FTP site.
2. Before the FTP session can be established, but behind the scenes to both Rory and Dina, the IPSec driver on wks1 checks its stored IP Filter Lists to identify whether the FTP packets should be encrypted. The IPSec driver determines from the rules in the IPSec policy that the all IP traffic should be encrypted.
3. The IPSec driver on wks1 notifies Internet Key Exchange (IKE) to begin negotiations.

4. The IKE service on wks2 receives a message from wks1 requesting a security negotiation. This assumes that a security negotiation has not already been negotiated between the two computers.

5. Wks1 and wks2 establish a security association (SA) and shared master key. This step is skipped if wks1 and wks2 have already established a security association.

6. Wks1 and wks2 then establish two more SAs, one for outbound communication and the other for inbound communication. Each SA has unique encryption keys used to encrypt and decrypt either outbound or inbound data.

7. The IPSec driver on wks1 uses the outbound SA to sign and/or encrypt the packets and passes the packets to the IP layer to be sent to wks2.

8. The encrypted packets are received by the network adapter on wks2 and passed to the IPSec driver.

9. The IPSec driver on wks2 uses the inbound SA to check the integrity signature and/or decrypt the packets.

10. The IPSec driver then passes the decrypted packets to the TCP driver, which passes the data to the FTP server application on Dina's computer wks2.

Network protocol security can also be achieved through the use of packet filters that prevent protocols on all or only specific service ports to enter or leave network devices like routers and firewalls. The use of packet filtering at the adapter level is discussed in Objective 5.03. The implementation of IP filters through RRAS is discussed in Chapter 7.

Objective 5.08
Configure and Troubleshoot IPSec

With security being such a big concern when discussing and planning external network architectures, it is often forgotten that the majority of proprietary information that is stolen or compromised occurs within the internal network. In fact, a 1999 survey by the CSI/FBI titled "Computer Crime & Security" revealed that an astonishing 97 percent of unauthorized usage came from within the corporation. IP security (IPSec) is one of the new features in Windows 2000 that can help address the issue of security both internally and externally. In a Microsoft Windows 2000 network, IPSec can provide authentication, packet filtering, and encapsulation (also known as *tunneling*).

Travel Assistance

IPSec is not a protocol that is proprietary to Microsoft. It is a security protocol developed by the Internet Engineering Task Force (IETF) whose implementation details can be found in RFC 2401 at http://rfc.net. Microsoft also has a whitepaper on IPSec titled "IP Security for Windows 2000 Server," which can be found at http://www.microsoft.com/windows2000/techinfo/howitworks/security/ip_security.asp.

From an authentication perspective, IPSec can be implemented to allow computers wanting to communicate the ability to confirm the authenticity of the other prior to exchanging any data. IPSec can also be used to establish a security association between two computers, allowing for the transfer of encrypted data without the requirement of any intermediary device, such as a router or switch, to support IPSec. IPSec uses standard IP packet formats to to accomplish this. Only the source and destination computers are required to support IPSec.

To configure your computer running Windows 2000 Server with a local IPSec Server (Request Security) policy, follow these steps:

1. Click Start | Programs | Administrative Tools and select Local Security Policy.
2. Select IP Security Policies on Local Machine and right-click Server (Request Security) policy and select Assign.

Congratulations! You have now configured your Windows 2000 server with a local IPSec policy.

Objective 5.09 Enable IPSec

In Windows 2000, IPSec is implemented through IPSec policies. IPSec policies can be applied to the local computer, at the site, domain, or organizational unit (OU) level, or simply for a group of computers within one of the aforementioned Active Directory components using a group policy.

As an open-standard security protocol, IPSec is supported by numerous vendors of both hardware- and software-related products, allowing the implementation of IPSec in Windows 2000 to interoperate with other implementations that may exist within your network or within one of the networks you wish to connect with.

IPSec exists below the Transport level in the Open Systems Interconnection model, as shown in the following illustration, and it allows information to be sent from the sender to the receiver with only those two parties knowing the security key used to encrypt the data. The layer of the OSI model that IPSec is located at is sometimes referred to Layer 3. IPSec ensures authentication and encryption by mixing public-key cryptography and secret-key encryption and managing all the required keys, thus increasing the level of security and the speed of information transfer. Additionally, because IPSec works below the Transport level, it is transparent to both users and applications, meaning that all applications can use IPSec without any additional application configuration requirements.

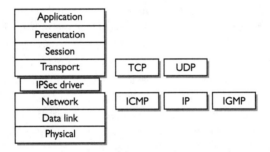

IPSec can be deployed by using one of two protocols: Authentication Header or Encapsulating Security Payload (as shown in the following illustration). Select the AH protocol when you require data authentication and data integrity but not data encryption. In other words, the AH protocol will guarantee that the recipient receives the data that the sender sent without any modifications or tampering while in transit. Select the ESP protocol when you require the sent data to be encrypted. Use both ESP and AH together to provide data authentication, integrity, and encryption.

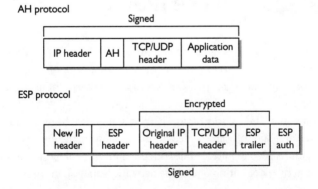

Exam Tip

IPSec only provides computer authentication, not user authentication. Use the ESP protocol to encrypt data and the AH protocol to authenticate computers.

The configuration of IPSec is accomplished through a policy and requires administrative rights on either the local computer or at the site, domain, or OU level. The IP Security Policy Management snap-in, shown in Figure 5-8, can be used to configure and manage IPSec policies. Other Microsoft Management Console snap-ins can also be used for the management of IPSec policies, such as the Active Directory Users and Computers snap-in for policies set at the domain or OU level and the Active Directory Sites and Services snap-in for policies set at the site level. The Local Security Policy snap-in can also be used for the creation of local computer IPSec policy.

Three IPSec policies are predefined, as shown in Figure 5-8:

- Client (Respond Only)
- Server (Request Security)
- Secure Server (Require Security)

All three of the predefined IPSec policies are designed for computers that are members of a Windows 2000 domain. Any of the three predefined policies can be assigned without any modification, or they can be modified to suit your unique requirements. Assigning a policy is as simple as right-clicking the policy in the IP Security Policy Management snap-in and selecting Assign from the context menu.

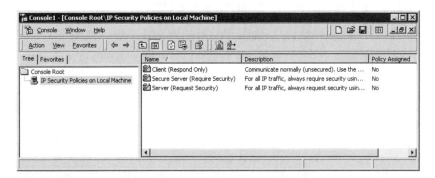

FIGURE 5-8 The IP Security Policy Management snap-in

Before we look at how to modify the three predefined policies, we will examine what each of the policies is designed to accomplish.

<table>
<tr><td>

Exam Tip

</td></tr>
<tr><td>

Only a single IPSec policy can be assigned to any one computer. Create a custom IPSec policy if you require a combination of the rules used in each of the default policies.

</td></tr>
</table>

Client (Respond Only) Policy

The Client (Respond Only) policy contains a default response rule that enables the client to negotiate a secure communication session using IPSec encryption with any requesting computer. The client itself, however, will never request a secure session because the policy is set to "respond only" and not request IPSec.

This policy should be applied to computers that do not require secure communications all the time but need the ability to communicate securely if requested. Think of the Client policy as proper etiquette in the context of sending out wedding invitations. Most wedding invitations will ask you to "RSVP" to let the wedding planner (generally the bride—at least in my case) plan for the number of guests that will be attending. Etiquette (the client policy) dictates that you respond. Proper etiquette (client policy) doesn't allow you to request that you attend; it only allows you to respond.

Server (Request Security) Policy

The Server (Request Security) policy is configured to always try to communicate securely but to allow the computer to accept unsecured communication between itself and another computer if the other computer does not support IPSec.

In the Microsoft family of operating systems, no other Microsoft operating system older than Windows 2000 supports the use of IPSec. The Server policy should be applied to Windows 2000 computers that you want to communicate securely with all other computers that support IPSec. The benefit of the Server policy is that it will always request secure communication but, like the Client policy, in the event that the computer it is trying to communicate with doesn't support IPSec, it can still communicate unsecured. For example, if your network consists of computers running both Windows 2000 and Windows NT 4.0 operating systems and you want all Windows 2000 computers to communicate using IPSec but also want all Windows NT 4.0 computers to be able to communicate unsecured with any other computer running either Windows NT 4.0 or Windows 2000, the Server policy would allow you to accomplish your goal. All communication between computers running Windows 2000 would use IPSec, and all communication between computers running Windows 2000 and Windows NT 4.0 would be unsecured.

Exam Tip

The Server policy is the most restrictive IPSec policy that can be used in a network that includes computers running both Windows 2000 and down-level Windows operating systems while still allowing the computers running the down-level operating systems to communicate with the computers running Windows 2000.

Secure Server (Require Security) Policy

The Secure Server (Require Security) policy is the most secure of the three default, preconfigured IPSec policies and requires IPSec be used for all communications. The Secure Server policy will not permit unsecured communications between the computer configured with the Secure Server policy and any other computer.

The Secure Server policy should be configured for servers that always require secure communications. These computers will only be able to communicate with other computers that support and are configured to use IPSec.

Exam Tip

If you apply the Secure Server policy to a computer running Windows 2000 on your network, no computers running any down-level version of a Microsoft operating system will be able to communicate with the computer running Windows 2000.

Before we talk about the components that make up individual policies, we are going to look at the two modes that IPSec can operate in: transport mode and tunnel mode.

Objective 5.10 — Configure IPSec for Transport Mode

Transport mode is the default mode for IPSec in Windows 2000 and provides end-to-end security through data authentication and data encryption. Transport mode is ideal for communication between two hosts on the same private network, where the traffic does not pass through a firewall. All traffic sent and received from the computers configured with an IPSec policy that meets the IP filter defined in the policy is encrypted between the two computers on the network. Now that you are familiar with the three default IPSec policies, let's discuss a scenario involving a fictional organization in which you will be required to apply your knowledge of these policies. The key components of the organization's network are shown in the illustration below. Use the illustration to assist you in the proper implementation of your IPSec policy.

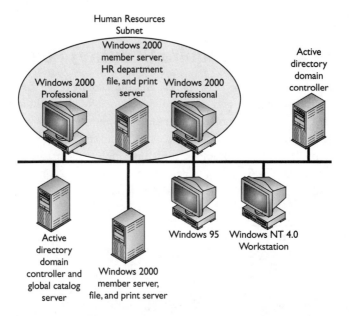

The fictional organization known as Mcsejobs uses the Active Directory domain mcsejobs.net as their Active Directory root domain. The computer in the domain runs a number of different operating systems, including Windows 2000 Server, Windows 2000 Professional, Windows NT 4.0 Workstation, and Windows 95. The organization's Active Directory structure takes advantage of OUs for the logical grouping of users and computers based on how they are administered. The IT model at Mcsejobs is centralized at the company's head office in Dallas. All domain controller objects reside in their default location while the computers and users for each department are located in a departmental OU named after the department. The organization's initial goal for the implementation of IPSec is to help protect all communications between computers in the Human Resources (HR) department. All of the client computers in the HR department are running Windows 2000 Professional. All of the company's HR data is stored on a File and Print Server that is configured with the highest security and permits access only to members of the HR department. This server is physically secured in the server room in a locked, caged area. Using the default IPSec security policies, how and where would you define the IPSec policy to meet the needs of the organization?

To answer this question, let's break it down into bite size pieces. First, let's answer the question of what do we need to accomplish. The end goal is to ensure that all communication between the computers in the HR department send information across the network encrypted by an IPSec policy. With that goal in mind, we need to assign two of the default IPSec policies. For the client computers running Windows 2000 Professional, we want to assign the Client (Respond Only) policy, and for the File and Print Server running Windows 2000 Server, we want to assign the Secure Server (Require Security) policy.

The next question is where do we want to apply this policy. Here we have a couple of options to choose from. We could configure individual local computer security policies for all computers in the HR department; doing that, however, would require more administrative time and effort than if we were to use a group policy. One of the intended benefits of the Active Directory is to reduce the amount of required administration. In an effort to achieve that benefit, we could create two group policies at the HR departmental OU—one for the computers running Windows 2000 Professional and the one for the computers running Windows 2000 Server—and change the security on the individual group policy objects to filter their application to the required computers. For example, we would remove the Read and Apply group policy permissions from the Authenticated Users group and add in the Domain Computers group granting it Read and Apply group policy permission. We would then add in the computer account for the HR department's File and Print server and configure it with Deny Read permission. Then, on the second GPO, which applies only to the HR departments File and Print server, we would again remove the Read and Apply group policy permissions from the Authenticated Users group and add in the specific computer account for the HR department's File and Print server and configure it with Read and Apply group policy permission.

By applying the policies at the OU level and filtering the application to the appropriate computer accounts, we can be confident that only the computers within that OU receive the policy, which is what we want to accomplish as our end goal. We can also be confident that no domain controllers will receive either policy, as all of our domain controller computer accounts are located in the Domain Controllers OU. This is a very important point because our domain contains computers running down-level operating systems. Should we purposely or accidentally configure a domain controller with the Secure Server (Require Security) IPSec policy, we would prevent all down-level client computers that do not support IPSec from logging on to the domain. With a Secure Server (Require Security) IPSec policy in place, all domain controllers would be required to accept only secured communications, even for authentication, to prevent down-level client computers from being able to authenticate with the domain controller. The key here: Plan carefully!

Now, just when you think we're done, we've still missed one key step. Have you figured it out yet? Well, the missing step is the creation of one more GPO. This last group policy object should be created and applied at the Domain Controllers OU. Yes, you heard me correctly: the GPO at the Domain Controllers OU should be configured with the Server (Request Security) IPSec policy. The reason for this is to allow the File and Print server to talk to the Kerberos service running on all domain controllers, so that authentication to shares on the File and Print server can take place. By placing an IPSec policy on the Domain Controllers OU that requests security, you are allowing the domain controllers to talk securely to all requesting computers while allowing the domain controller to communicate unsecured with all computers that either don't request IPSec or don't support IPSec.

Now let's review what we have accomplished. Creating a GPO for client computers in the HR department means that those clients are now required to request the use of secure communications when trying to communicate with any other computer in the domain; however, only computers that are configured with an assigned IPSec policy will reciprocate and allow the communications to be secure. Any communication with down-level operating systems or domain controllers will be unsecured as those computers are not configured with an assigned IPSec policy. Additionally, any incoming or outgoing communication with the HR departments File and Print server requires that the communication be secured. This will prevent all down-level operating systems from establishing a connection with the computer and prevent all computers running Windows 2000 that do not have an assigned IPSec policy from communicating with the File and Print server. By creating a GPO at the Domain Controllers OU, you have allowed for communication between the HR department's File and Print server and all domain controllers to occur, but have not prevented any client computers from being able to obtain authentication with the domain controllers. Congratulations, you've successfully applied the default IPSec policies at Mcsejobs!

Objective 5.11

Configure IPSec for Tunnel Mode

Tunnel mode allows for an IPSec tunnel to be created. Like a tunnel you might drive through in a car, an IPSec tunnel must have a starting point and an ending point, much like the tunnel entrance and tunnel exit. In the case of IPSec, the tunnel starting point is the IP address of one Windows 2000 Server, and the ending point is the IP address of another Windows 2000 computer. Generally, tunnel mode in IPSec is used when you wish to create a secure channel across a public network such as the Internet. One example of where an IPSec tunnel might be used is to connect a Windows 2000 Server at one branch office in your organization to another Windows 2000 Server at another office across the Internet.

Tunnel mode only secures communication between the computers configured as the start point and endpoint of the tunnel, but not the remaining computers on the local network, as shown here.

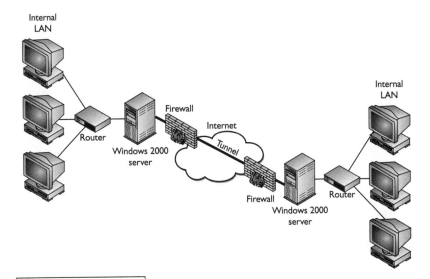

Exam Tip

To allow IPSec traffic to successfully pass through a firewall, the following rules must be configured: allow UDP port 500, allow protocol ID 51 for AH, and allow protocol ID 50 for ESP.

To create a local IPSec policy in tunnel mode IPSec between two computers named server1 which has an IP address of 192.168.1.10 and server2 which has an IP address of 192.168.1.100 follow the steps below:

1. On server1, click Start, Programs, Administrative Tools and select Local Security Policy.
2. Right-click Secure Server (Require Security) and select Properties.
3. In the Secure Server (Require Security) Properties dialog box, select the IP Security Rule All IP Traffic and click the Edit button.
4. In the Edit Rule Properties dialog box, select the Tunnel Setting tab and choose the radio button next to "The tunnel endpoint is specified by this IP address."
5. Enter the IP address **192.168.1.100**. Click Ok and Close.
6. Select IP Security Policies on Local Machine, right-click Secure Server (Require Security), and select Assign.
7. On server2, click Start, Programs, Administrative Tools and select Local Security Policy.
8. Right-click Secure Server (Require Security) and select Properties.
9. In the Secure Server (Require Security) Properties dialog box, select the IP Security Rule All IP Traffic and click the Edit button.
10. In the Edit Rule Properties dialog box, select the Tunnel Setting tab and choose the radio button next to "The tunnel endpoint is specified by this IP address."
11. Enter the IP address **192.168.1.10**. Click Ok and Close.
12. Select IP Security Policies on Local Machine, right-click Secure Server (Require Security), and select Assign.

Congratulations! You have now created an IPSec tunnel between server1 and server2 that requires all communication between the two computers to be encrypted using the secure server IPSec policy.

Objective 5.12 Customize IPSec Policies and Rules

IPSec policies use rules to govern when and how they are applied. Rules contain a number of components, as shown in the following list. A default response rule exists and is associated with all newly created policies by default, because each IPSec policy must have at least one rule. Here are the rule components:

- Tunnel endpoint

- Network type
- Authentication method
- IP filter list
- Filter action

The tunnel endpoint component only applies to rules used for IPSec connections configured in tunnel mode and defines the tunneling computer closest to the IP traffic destination. A connection in tunnel mode requires a minimum of two rules, one for each of the computers that make up the endpoints of the tunnel.

There are three choices for the type of network connection that you wish the IPSec rule to apply to. The rule can apply only to LAN traffic or only to remote access traffic, or it can be configured to apply to all network traffic.

There are also three authentication methods to choose from. The authentication method verifies the identity of a user. The default authentication method is the Kerberos version 5.0 protocol. This default can be used by any client computers that support the Kerberos protocol and are members of a trusted domain. A certificate is the second available authentication method. The use of certificates for authentication requires that a trusted Certificate Authority has been configured. The third available authentication method is a preshared key. A preshared key is a unique string of characters that two users agree upon and manually configure prior to use. The downside to using a preshared key is that it is the least-secure authentication method because it is viewable in the IPSec policies property pages. The upside is that it is quick to configure and doesn't require that the clients support the use of the Kerberos protocol.

The IP filter list defines the type of traffic that will be secured by the rule. The default filter can be used or custom filters can be created for specific types of IP traffic.

The filter action is the security action that will occur when traffic matches an IP filter. There are three filter actions to choose from: permit, block, and negotiate. Permit obviously allows traffic through, and block does not allow traffic through. The negotiate filter action negotiates the security for the given connection. You are able to specify one or more negotiated filter actions, with the actions at the top of the list taking priority. The filter actions are processed from the top of the list to the bottom until the negotiation of one of the filter actions is successful.

The Default Response Rule

The default response rule is the fallback rule used when a rule is not defined for secure communication requests. The default response rule is designated for all defined policies but may not be active. A check mark in the box next to the Default Response Rule indicates that it is activated. Removing the check mark deactivates the Default Response Rule.

The properties of the Default Response Rule state that all network connections, LAN and remote access, will use Triple Digital Encryption Standard (3DES) encryption when negotiating Security Associations. 3DES is the strongest encryption standard included with Windows 2000. The rule also states that Kerberos will be used for authentication.

Creating an IPSec Policy

IPSec policies can be created in a number of different locations. The location you choose to create the policy in will depend on the rights and permissions you have and what you are trying to accomplish. An IPSec policy applied at the local computer will apply to the local computer but can potentially be overridden by another conflicting policy configured at the site, domain, or OU level in an Active Directory domain environment. To create a new IPSec policy on the local computer, follow these steps:

1. Open the Local Security Policy snap-in found in Start | Programs | Administrative Tools.
2. Right-click IP Security Policies on Local Machine and select Create IP Security Policy.
3. The IP Security Policy Wizard will appear. Click Next to proceed.
4. Enter a name for the new policy and an optional description. Click Next.
5. The default response rule is enabled by default in the next dialog box that appears. Remove the check mark from this box and click Next to continue and create your own rules.
6. Click Finish. The New IP Security Policy Properties dialog box will appear, as shown in Figure 5-9. Click Add to create a new rule.

Clicking Add followed by Next launches the Security Rule Wizard. The first dialog box asks you to choose the mode for the IPSec connection. The default is to not specify a tunnel and use the default transport mode. If you decide to configure the IPSec policy in tunnel mode, the IP address of the tunnel endpoint must be specified. The next dialog box asks you to select one of the three network types: all network connections, local area connections, or remote access. Next, you are required to select an authentication type, with the default set to use Kerberos. The other two options are to use either certificates or a preshared key. The IP filter list

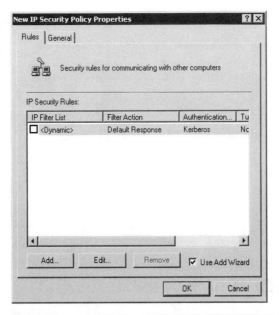

FIGURE 5-9   Creating a new IP Security policy rule

must be selected next. In this dialog box, shown in Figure 5-10, one of the two default IP filters can be selected or new IP filters can be created by clicking the Add button.

To create a new IP filter that applies to all HTTP traffic, click Add and give the new filter the name "http traffic" in the IP Filter List dialog box. Click the Add button to launch the IP Filter Wizard and then click Next. The source address should be the IP address of the computer on which you want to apply the IPSec policy. The destination address should be set to the IP address of a specific Web server or any IP address to apply to all Web servers that the computer might connect to. The protocol that HTTP uses is TCP and should be selected from the Protocol drop-down list. The IP protocol port that a Web request is sent from should be set to From Any Port, and port 80 should be specified in the To This Port box. Click Next and then Finish, and the rule is created. The next step in the policy-configuration process is to select a filter action for the type of traffic that the rule applies to and then select Next. Selecting Permit would allow unsecured HTTP traffic to pass through. Selecting Request Security would allow unsecured traffic, but only if secure communication cannot be established. The last option is to configure Require Security, which will force IPSec to be used for all HTTP communications.

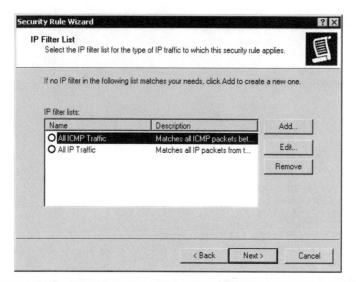

FIGURE 5-10 Configuring the IP filter list

Let's look at a more realistic scenario to make sure you understand how to apply IP filters to achieve your goals. You are required to create a security policy in your organization that ensures that all traffic between the HR department and all other departments is secure and confidential. The traffic within the HR department must be secure but does not have to be confidential. The HR department is the only department on the 192.168.1.0 network with a subnet mask of 255.255.255.0. All the other departments in your company are located on the 192.168.2.0 network, with a subnet of 255.255.255.0. To achieve these goals, you should create a security policy named HR and apply it at the domain level so that the policy agent on each computer in the domain would obtain the policy. You would also create two negotiation policies and associate them with the HR policy. Create the first negotiation policy and name it HR1 and configure it to use the ESP security protocol. Create the second negotiation policy and name it HR2 and configure it to use the AH security protocol. Next, create two IP filters, each to be associated with a negotiation policy. The source address for the first IP filter will be 192.168.1.0, and the destination address will be 192.168.2.0. The protocol for this filter will be set to Any. This first IP filter will then be associated with the HR1 negotiation policy. The second IP filter will have a source address of 192.168.1.0 and a destination address of 192.168.1.0, with the protocol also set to Any. It will be associated with the HR2 negotiation policy.

The result of this configuration is that when users in the HR department communicate with one another, the HR2 filter applies to that communication traffic because of the subnet of both the sender and the receiver; the traffic is secured but not encrypted with the AH protocol. When a user in the HR department communicates with a user in any other department on the network, the HR1 filter applies and the traffic is secured and encrypted using the ESP protocol. This configuration meets all the requirements specified.

Objective 5.13   Manage and Monitor IPSec

Once you have configured an IPSec policy, verifying that it is actually working can be accomplished with a number of troubleshooting tools. The first utility that can be used to identify whether IPSec is functioning correctly is the ping utility. When you ping a computer configured with an IPSec policy, the initial response returned should be "negotiating security." On the second ping attempt, the security should be negotiated—depending on the speed of the connection—and the ping request should complete successfully. Only one of the two computers that have been assigned the IPSec policy needs to run the ping command. The security negotiation will take place between them during the first ping attempt but will been seen only on the first computer to run the command. Once the security negotiation is complete, all subsequent ping attempts should receive a standard reply.

One of the drawbacks of IPSec is the increased burden that is places on the CPU of the computers configured with IPSec properties. As part of the ongoing management of your IPSec policy, you may want to consider network adapters with onboard IPSec support to enable the CPU to pass the encryption overhead to the network adapter, thereby freeing the CPU up for other tasks and applications.

The second tool that can be used is the IPSec Monitor. If an IPSec policy is negotiated, it should appear in the IPSec Monitor. To launch the IPSec Monitor, type **ipsecmon** in the Run dialog box.

A third tool that can be used to verify IPSec configuration is the Network Monitor tool. Configure a filter in Network Monitor to capture only Internet Security Association and Key Management Protocol (ISAKMP). If this protocol does not appear in the capture, communications are not using IPSec.

CHECKPOINT

✔ **Objective 5.01:** Install, Configure, and Troubleshoot Network Protocols
Windows 2000 supports five network protocols: TCP/IP (the default),
NWLink, NetBEUI, AppleTalk, and DLC.

✔ **Objective 5.02:** Install and Configure TCP/IP   Client computers can be
configured in one of two ways: statically or dynamically through DHCP.
Static TCP/IP configuration requires that a valid IP address and subnet
mask be entered. Statically configuring TCP/IP with the IP addresses of
primary and secondary DNS servers will override the DNS server settings
obtained through DHCP.

✔ **Objective 5.03:** Configure TCP/IP Packet Filters   TCP/IP packet
filtering can be configured through the advanced properties of a client's
TCP/IP properties. TCP/IP packet filtering configured through the
advanced TCP/IP properties does not permit the filtering of ICMP
traffic.

✔ **Objective 5.04:** Install the NWLink protocol   If your network uses multiple IPX/SPX frame types, set the detection mode to manual and add both
frame types; otherwise, only the 802.2 frame type will be detected.

✔ **Objective 5.05:** Configure Network Bindings   To optimize network
communication performance, the network protocol used most often on
the network should be bound at the top of the binding order. Changing
the binding order requires you to be a member of the Administrators
group.

✔ **Objective 5.06:** Manage and Monitor Network Traffic   Network traffic
can be monitored using a number of different tools and utilities, including
ipconfig, ping, tracert, pathping and Network Monitor. Data being transferred on the network can be captured using Network Monitor and should
be considered unsecured unless sent using encryption. There are two
version of Network Monitor: the version that comes with Windows 2000,
which only allows data coming in and out of the local computer to be
captured, and the Systems Management Server (SMS) version, which
allows traffic on the entire network segment to be captured.

✔ **Objective 5.07: Configure and Troubleshoot Network Protocol Security**
Network protocol security is related to any form of security used to secure
data transferred across a network.

✔ **Objective 5.08: Configure and Troubleshoot IPSec**   IPSec can use two
protocols: AH and ESP. The Authentication Header (AH) protocol is used
to ensure that transferred data is authentic and unmodified. The
Encapsulating Security Protocol (ESP) is used to ensure that transferred
data is confidential, authentic, and unmodified.

✔ **Objective 5.09: Enable IPSec**   IPSec policy can be applied to the local
computer, site, domain, or organizational unit (OU). There are three
default IPSec policies: Client (Respond Only), Server (Request Security),
And Secure Server (Require Security). Only a single IPSec policy can be
assigned to one computer. IPSec can operate in two modes: transport
and tunnel.

✔ **Objective 5.10: Configure IPSec for Transport Mode**   Transport mode is
the default mode for IPSec in Windows 2000 and provides end-to-end
security through data authentication and data encryption. Transport mode
is ideal for communication between two hosts on the same private network
where the traffic does not pass through a firewall.

✔ **Objective 5.11: Configure IPSec for Tunnel Mode**   Tunnel mode can
only be configured between two Windows 2000 computers. IPSec tunnel
mode is used when you wish to create a secure channel across a public network such as the Internet. To allow IPSec traffic to successfully pass through
a firewall, the following rules must be configured: allow UDP port 500,
allow protocol ID 51 for AH, and allow protocol ID 50 for ESP.

✔ **Objective 5.12: Customize IPSec Policies and Rules**   IPSec policies use
rules to govern when and how they are applied. Rules contain a number of
components, such as tunnel endpoint, network type, authentication
method, IP filter list, and filter action.

✔ **Objective 5.13: Manage and Monitor IPSec**   IPSec Monitor is a utility
that can be used to verify that IPSec is working properly. Network Monitor
can also be used to monitor IPSec by creating a filter to capture only
Internet Security Association and Key Management Protocol (ISAKMP).
If this protocol does not appear in the capture, communications are not
using IPSec.

REVIEW QUESTIONS

1. You wish to optimize the communication configuration of a file and print server on your network. The server, which is located in your organization's server room, hosts a domain DFS root and has two NIC cards, both configured with NetBEUI, TCP/IP, and NWLink and bound in that order to the Workstation and Server services. Your network is divided into six different subnets in two sites and a single Active Directory domain. The clients on your network only have TCP/IP and NetBEUI bound to their NIC cards, in that order. What can you do to optimize communication on your network?

   A. Change the network binding order on the file and print server to list TCP/IP at the top of the binding order.

   B. Change the network binding order on the file and print server to list TCP/IP at the bottom of the binding order.

   C. Change the network binding order on each client computer to list TCP/IP at the top of the binding order.

   D. Change the network binding order on each client computer to list TCP/IP at the bottom of the binding order.

2. You have been asked to configure a file and print server in your network with a static IP address. What information is required for the proper configuration of a static IP address? (Choose two.)

   A. IP address

   B. Default gateway address

   C. Preferred DNS server address

   D. Subnet mask

3. As the administrator in your domain, you have configured the primary and secondary DNS server IP addresses (10.10.1.4 and 10.10.1.250) statically on a computer running Windows 2000 Professional. Two months later you decide to change all the client computers on your network from static IP address configurations to DHCP-enabled clients. You have configured the DHCP scope to include the IP address of two different DNS servers: 192.168.1.4 and 192.168.4.250. Which DNS IP addresses will the Windows 2000 Professional client end up with once it begins obtaining an IP address from DHCP? (Choose two.)

   A. 192.168.1.4

   B. 192.168.4.250

    C. 10.10.1.4

    D. 10.10.1.250

4. As the administrator of your Windows 2000 network, you would like to configure a TCP/IP filter. The computer on which you want to create the filter is
in a kiosk-type environment. It is a standalone computer in the front lobby
of your corporation that allows guests to surf the Internet while waiting for
someone within the company. You would like to configure a filter that only
allows DNS and HTTP traffic to and from the computer. Which of the following filters would accomplish this?

    A. Select Enable TCP/IP Filtering and permit only TCP ports 80 and 53,
UDP port 53, and IP protocols 6 and 17.

    B. Select Enable TCP/IP Filtering and permit only TCP ports 80 and 53 and
IP protocol 6.

    C. Select Enable TCP/IP Filtering and permit only TCP ports 80 and 53,
UDP port 53, and IP protocols TCP and HTTP.

    D. Select Enable TCP/IP Filtering and permit only TCP ports 80 and 53 and
IP protocol 17.

5. You have enabled TCP/IP filtering through the advanced TCP/IP properties
on a computer running Windows 2000 Professional. This computer is also
configured for Internet Connection Sharing to allow five other clients on the
local area network to connect out to the Internet. The internal IP address of
the computer is 192.168.1.50, and the external IP address is 24.56.98.140. The
IP filter you have enabled through the advanced TCP/IP properties of the
external IP address permits only DNS, HTTP, and FTP traffic through on
their default service ports. Shortly after you configure the filter, users on the
network inform you that they are no longer able to connect to the Windows
2000 Professional computer to gain access to files and folders that they were
able to gain access to before. What is causing the problem?

    A. The Server service must be restarted on the computer after an IP filter is
configured.

    B. The IP filter was mistakenly configured on the internal IP address, not
the external IP address.

    C. The IP filter applies to both the internal and the external IP addresses,
thus preventing you from connecting.

    D. The users must log off and log back on to update their user access con-
trol list, which will now contain the permission to connect to the
Windows 2000 computer configured with an IP filter.

6. Which of the following types of traffic are you not able to filter through IP filtering?

   A. TCP
   B. ICMP
   C. UDP
   D. RDP

7. You are the network administrator for your organization. Your network uses both Novell 5.0 file servers and Windows 2000 file servers, with the default protocol of TCP/IP. You have installed Client Services for NetWare on all your client computers running Windows 2000 Professional but are still not able to connect to the Novell resources. What must you do to allow your clients to connect to the Novell servers?

   A. Install IPX/SPX on the Novell file servers.
   B. Bind TCP/IP to the top of the binding order for the Workstation service on the Windows 2000 Professional clients.
   C. Bind TCP/IP to the top of the binding order for the Server service on the Windows 2000 Professional clients.
   D. Install NWLink on all the client computers.

8. You wish to configure an IPSec policy to secure and encrypt all communications across the local area network. Which authentication protocol will you use to accomplish this?

   A. Kerberos
   B. EAP
   C. ESP
   D. AH
   E. TLS

9. Which utility will allow you to see all the hops that a packet takes on its way to its final destination IP address?

   A. Nslookup
   B. Ping
   C. Tracert
   D. Network Monitor

10. Which of the following utilities can you use to list IPSec policies that are enabled on the local computer?

A. IPSec Monitor
B. Netstat
C. Network Monitor
D. Pathping

REVIEW ANSWERS

1. **A** Changing the network binding order on the file and print server to list TCP/IP at the top of the binding order would be the best approach for optimizing network communication. The network protocol bound to the top of the network bindings list is the first protocol that the network service it is bound to attempts to use when making a connection to another computer.

2. **A D** Configuration of a static IP address requires both a valid IP address and a subnet mask. The default gateway and preferred DNS server are not mandatory requirements for proper configuration.

3. **C D** The two statically configured DNS entries will take precedence over the dynamically assigned DNS IP addresses.

4. **A** To configure an IP filter to only allow DNS and HTTP traffic in and out of the computer, TCP/IP filtering must be enabled and only TCP ports 80 and 53, UDP port 53, and IP protocols 6 and 17 should be permitted.

5. **C** IP filters apply to all network cards in a computer and cannot be configured on a per–network card basis. The IP filter must be removed to allow the internal clients to connect to shared files on the computer.

6. **B** ICMP traffic cannot be filtered through IP filtering in the advanced properties of TCP/IP. It can be filtered through an IP filter configured in RRAS.

7. **D** NWLink must be installed on all the computers running Windows 2000 Professional because it is still required for communication through the Client Services for NetWare.

8. **C** To encrypt and secure data through an IPSec policy, the ESP protocol should be used.

9. **C** Tracert is the utility to use to see all the hops that a packet takes on its way to its final destination IP address.

10. **A** IPSec Monitor is the utility to use to list the IPSec policies enabled on the local computer.

Windows 2000 Routing and Remote Access Infrastructure

Remote
Access
Infrastructure

	NEWBIE	SOME EXPERIENCE	EXPERT
ETA	7–10 hours	4–7 hours	2–4 hours

Your journey of studying for and passing the Implementing and Administering a Windows 2000 Network Infrastructure exam (70-216) concludes with a look at the routing and remote access network infrastructure in Windows 2000. This includes a detailed look at the Routing and Remote Access Service (RRAS), IP routing, and the two shared Internet connection options: Internet Connection Sharing (ICS) and Network Address Translation (NAT). Passing what has been referred to by many as the most difficult of the Windows 2000 core exams requires that you have a good understanding of the features and configuration options associated with RRAS. A number of new features have been added to RRAS in Windows 2000, including remote access policies, L2TP VPN support, RADIUS authentication and accounting, the Internet Authentication Service, Internet Connection Sharing, and Network Address Translation, to mention a few. Your exam preparation should include setting up a computer with Windows 2000 Server and configuring RRAS in a number of the configurations discussed in this part of the book to give you the hands-on experience necessary to pass this Windows 2000 MCSE exam.

The configuration of the Routing and Remote Access Service is necessary both for the exam and for your daily administrative responsibilities. Network communication no longer stops at the local area network (LAN) in an organization. With the popularity of the Internet and the economic focus on globalization, networks are in a state of constant change—whether that change involves expansion, contraction, or integration. The Routing and Remote Access Service can play a significant role in your network's routing and remote access strategy, because it offers a stable, scalable platform to meet the demanding requirements of the corporate world. Understanding the installation and configuration process of RRAS and the security configuration options available to you is a requirement for the exam and the day-to-day administration of your network.

We will begin our journey with a look at the fundamentals of this service, which include the installation options available to you when installing RRAS on a computer running Windows 2000 Server. Once you have learned how to configure the service, we will explore how to monitor the service and then how to secure the service. Once you have a solid understanding of the configuration of a single RRAS server, we will explore the configuration of multiple RRAS servers and how to centrally administer this group of servers using the Remote Authentication Dial-In User Service (RADIUS) and the Internet Authentication Service (IAS). To conclude the chapter, we will shift our focus to the configuration options available on a Windows 2000 client. The Routing and Remote Access Service has been thoroughly revamped from its implementation in Windows NT 4.0, so avoid making the assumption that because you knew RAS inside and out in NT 4.0 you can skip this section. You require a strong understanding of RRAS and its many new features for success on the Implementing and Administering a Windows 2000 Network Infrastructure exam. The RRAS component of the exam is one of the larger components, and this chapter will provide you with the information necessary to prepare for the exam.

Objective 6.01

Configure and Troubleshoot Remote Access

The Routing and Remote Access Service (RRAS) included in Windows 2000 provides the following features:

- Multiprotocol LAN-to-LAN or LAN-to-WAN connectivity
- Virtual private network (VPN) connectivity using Point-to-Point Tunneling Protocol (PPTP) or Layer Two Tunneling Protocol (L2TP)
- Network Address Translation (NAT) functionality for shared Internet access
- Dial-up and VPN access for remote clients
- Dial-on-demand functionality

Unlike in Windows NT 4.0 Server, RRAS in Windows 2000 Server is installed by default, but it's not configured or enabled. Let's explore how to configure RRAS.

Exam Tip

Unlike other services in Windows 2000, RRAS is installed by default. It must be configured and enabled using the RRAS snap-in but does not need to be installed through Add/Remove Windows Components in Add/Remove Programs in Control Panel.

Configuring and enabling RRAS is accomplished through the RRAS snap-in by following these steps:

1. Select Routing and Remote Access from the Administrative Tools menu.
2. Right-click the name of the server and select Configure and Enable Routing and Remote Access. This will launch the Routing and Remote Access Server Setup Wizard.

3. Click Next, and you'll be asked to choose from five different RRAS configurations, as shown in Figure 6-1. Each option will guide you through different configuration options that we will explore. Choose the option that best suits you and click Next.

Exam Tip

You must be a member of the Administrators group to configure and enable RRAS.

Once enabled and configured, RRAS can also be disabled. However, be aware that disabling RRAS causes all configuration information to be lost. Reenabling RRAS requires that it also be reconfigured, which can be a tedious task, depending on the complexity of your configuration.

Travel Advisory

The Netsh tool is a command-line utility that can be used to save and then reapply the configuration of an RRAS server. More information on Netsh can be found in the online help.

Routing and Remote Access Server Setup Wizard

Common Configurations
You can select from several common configurations.

- ● **Internet connection server**
  Enable all of the computers on this network to connect to the Internet.

- ○ **Remote access server**
  Enable remote computers to dial in to this network.

- ○ **Virtual private network (VPN) server**
  Enable remote computers to connect to this network through the Internet.

- ○ **Network router**
  Enable this network to communicate with other networks.

- ○ **Manually configured server**
  Start the server with default settings.

< Back   Next >   Cancel

FIGURE 6-1   Configuring RRAS

Configure Inbound Connections

Five configuration options are available to you when configuring and enabling RRAS on a computer running Windows 2000 Server:

1. Internet connection server
2. Remote access server
3. Virtual private network (VPN) server
4. Network router
5. Manually configured server

Let's take a look at what each of these five configuration choices allows us to do and what options become available with each of the configuration choices.

Internet Connection Server

The Internet Connection Server option allows you to configure the server to use either Internet Connection Sharing (ICS) or Network Address Translation (NAT). Both of these options allow multiple users on the local area network to access the Internet through a shared, single Internet connection. The advantages, disadvantages, and configuration options available are discussed and explained in detail in Chapter 8.

Internet Connection Sharing should only be used in small office networks and not for shared access in large corporate networks. NAT is the obvious choice for configuration in a large corporate network because it is much more scalable than ICS and offers the ability to use more than one external network adapter and multiple external IP addresses. ICS, on the other hand, is limited to one external IP address.

The use of Internet Connection Sharing requires that the server configured with ICS be multihomed and the internal network adapter have an address of 192.168.0.1. All other internal clients will receive an IP address on the 192.168.0.1/24 network from the ICS server. Another benefit of NAT over ICS is that it can be configured to use any internal range of IP addresses.

Remote Access Server

The Remote Access Server option allows you to configure the server to accept dial-in connections from remote clients. This option allows you to specify the network protocols you would like to support for dial-in access. The five network protocols supported in Windows 2000 are TCP/IP, IPX/SPX (NWLink), NetBEUI, AppleTalk, and DLC. As you can see in Figure 6-2, the default settings allow you to specify that all of the protocols installed on the server be supported. This can be changed, though, to allow you to select only the protocols you require, which will depend on your goals and configuration requirements.

Exam Tip

NetBEUI is not a routable protocol, except with an RRAS server. Remote access clients can be configured to dial in using NetBEUI and the RRAS server can allow them to connect to computers on the remote network.

As in Windows NT 4.0, both Serial Line Internet Protocol (SLIP) and Point-to-Point Protocol (PPP) are supported standards, but only for dial-in access. In other words, Windows 2000 Server cannot be configured as a SLIP server, capable

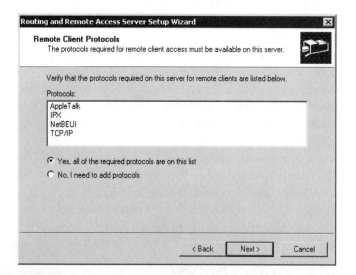

FIGURE 6-2 Selecting the supported dial-in protocols

of accepting dial-in connections from SLIP clients. A computer running Windows 2000 can, however, dial in to a SLIP server. SLIP is an older remote access standard that is typically used by UNIX remote access servers.

The configuration of the remote access server option will also require that you select how you want dial-in clients to obtain an IP address. The two options are dynamically through a DHCP server and from an IP address pool that you configure the RRAS server to use. Choosing to automatically assign IP addresses from a DHCP server does not require that the DHCP service be installed and configured on the network. If the DHCP service is not available on the network, RRAS will use its own built-in DHCP Allocator service to lease out IP addresses. For information about the installation and configuration of DHCP, see Chapter 1. For more information about the integration of the DHCP service with RRAS, see the section "Objective 6.04: Configure Routing and Remote Access for DHCP Integration."

Exam Tip

Choosing to automatically assign IP addresses from a DHCP server does not require that the DHCP service be installed and configured on the network. If the DHCP service is not available on the network, RRAS will use its own built-in DHCP Allocator service to lease out IP addresses on the 169.254.0.0/16 network.

The next step in the configuration of a remote access server is to select whether you want to configure the server to use an existing RADIUS server. The default is No, as shown in Figure 6-3. The use of the Remote Authentication Dial-In User Service (RADIUS) and the Internet Authentication Service (IAS) will be discussed in detail in Objective 6.11. Once you click Next in this dialog box, you can click Finish to complete the configuration of your remote access server. Congratulations! You're all set up for dial-in access. Well, almost done. Keep reading.

It is the second, third, and fifth options (remote access server, virtual private network server, and manually configured server) in the preceding list that we will focus on in this chapter, because other chapters in this book discuss and explain the other configuration options.

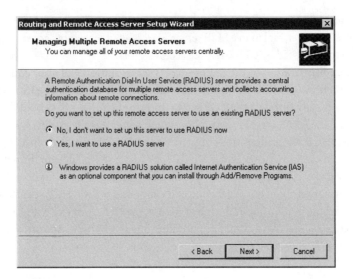

FIGURE 6-3 The RADIUS configuration options

Objective 6.03

Configure a Virtual Private Network (VPN)

The Virtual Private Network Server option allows you to configure an RRAS server to allow incoming VPN connections from remote access clients. The key difference between a VPN connection and a dial-up connection is that the information sent between the client and the server over a VPN is encrypted and therefore more secure.

Virtual private networks allow users to communicate securely with one another over private or public networks such as internal LANs or the Internet. A VPN client is able to establish an encrypted, point-to-point connection with another client or server across a public or private network. The ability to connect securely using a VPN across the Internet can result in a huge financial savings for large organizations whose previous alternative was to buy or lease expensive private, leased lines.

Windows 2000 supports two VPN protocols: Point-to-Point Tunneling Protocol (PPTP) and Layer Two Tunneling Protocol (L2TP). Both VPN protocols are used to encapsulate data packets inside PPP data packets, thereby allowing ordinary PPP packets to be sent and received across the Internet over TCP/IP. It is only when the PPP packet is opened that the encrypted data packet is seen and must be unencrypted in order for the data to be read. There are some key differences between PPTP and L2TP that you must be aware of.

PPTP will only work over IP intertransit networks. It offers no compression of the TCP/IP header and no tunnel authentication to prove that the remote computer is who it says it is, and it uses built-in PPP encryption known as *Microsoft Point-to-Point Encryption* (MPPE).

Exam Tip

L2TP uses IPSec for encryption and is therefore limited in use to only computers running Windows 2000. Prior to using L2TP for a VPN connection, IPSec must be configured on the two computers needing to establish the connection.

L2TP, on the other hand, can work over numerous types of intertransit networks, such as IP, Frame Relay, G3 Fax, ATM, and X.25. It also offers TCP/IP header compression and tunnel authentication, and it uses IPSec for encryption, which is much stronger and secure than PPP encryption. The downside to L2TP is that, because it uses IPSec for encryption, only computers that support IPSec can take advantage of L2TP, meaning that the use of L2TP is limited to computers running Windows 2000. Another drawback to L2TP is that it will not work through a NAT server. This is because L2TP encrypts the header portion of the IP datagram, which contains the UDP port number. NAT must be able to change the information in the IP datagram header, but if it does, it invalidates the checksum that IPSec has calculated on the packet, which indicates to the recipient that the packet has been tampered with and causes the receiving computer to request retransmission.

Exam Tip

L2TP cannot be used when access to the Internet is configured through a NAT server.

Configuring a VPN server requires that the RRAS server have two network adapters—one connected to the internal network and the other connected to the Internet. The connection to the Internet does not have to be a persistent connection, but it is recommended. Select the server's network adapter that is connected to the Internet from the list of available adapters, as shown in Figure 6-4.

Next, you will be required to choose how you want to provide IP addresses. The two options—automatically through a DHCP server or from a static IP address pool—are the same as when we examined the configuration of a remote access server. Next, you choose whether you want the VPN server to be a RADIUS server. Finally, click Next and then Finish, and you are done. The configuration of a VPN server is a straightforward process.

When you choose to install a VPN server, five PPTP and five L2TP ports, known as *WAN miniports*, are installed by default, allowing for only five PPTP and L2TP connections to be established. Depending on your requirements, the number of available ports can be increased or decreased. To change the port configuration, follow these steps below:

1. Open RRAS and Ports, located under the name of the RRAS server.
2. Right-click Ports and select Properties.
3. Select WAN Miniport (PPTP) or (L2TP) and click the Configure button.
4. In the Configure Device dialog box shown in Figure 6-5, the number of ports can be increased to a maximum of 16,384 or decreased to a minimum of 1 for PPTP. The maximum for L2TP is 30,000, and the minimum is 0.

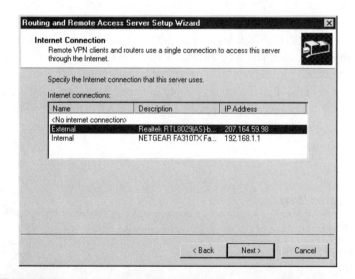

FIGURE 6-4   Specifying the internet adapter for a VPN server

---

Exam Tip

When the RRAS server is configured for VPN access, a default five PPTP and five L2TP ports are created. For security reasons, keep the number of VPN ports close to the maximum number of expected VPN connections.

Network Router

Configuring a computer running Windows 2000 Server as a network router allows the computer to route TCP/IP and/or IPX/SPX (NWLink) between different network segments. The only option you must configure if you choose the Network Router option is whether you wish to use demand-dial connections. After you make your decision, click Next and then Finish. Before you can use the router, however, you must use the RRAS snap-in to configure the routing protocols for each network interface. Windows 2000 supports two routing protocols: Routing Information Protocol (RIP) and Open Shortest Path First (OSPF). The

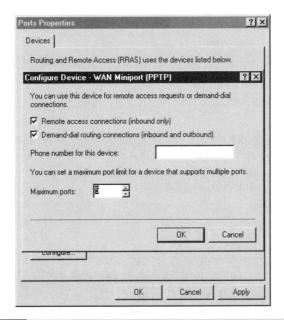

FIGURE 6-5 Configuring the number of available WAN miniports

configuration of the router may also require that static routes be added to the routing table. Chapter 7 will explore in detail the configuration options available when configuring a computer running Windows 2000 as a network router.

The Network Router option is useful for scenarios where you need to connect to separate IP segments but don't have a hardware routing device. The use of Windows 2000 as a router in a large network environment is not recommended, because the performance of a hardware device will be much higher. Other considerations to factor in when configuring a computer running Windows 2000 Server as a router are the other applications and services running on the computer and the performance degradation resulting from RRAS.

Manually Configured Server

The fifth and last configuration option available is Manually Configured Server. Choosing this option does not require you to enter any configure options in the RRAS Setup Wizard, because it simply configures the RRAS server with the default settings for a remote access server and router. These default options can then be modified using the RRAS snap-in, not through the RRAS Setup Wizard. To modify the default options, follow these steps:

1. Open RRAS and right-click the name of the server you wish to configure.
2. Select Properties from the context menu.
3. Proceed through the tabs of the Properties dialog box, configuring the options that you require.

The number of tabs that appear in the Properties dialog box will increase with the number of network protocols installed on the local server. In Figure 6-6, you can see from the tabs that TCP/IP, IPX/SPX (NWLink), NetBEUI, and AppleTalk are installed. You will also notice that there is a tab for the Point-to-Point Protocol (PPP) to allow configuration of PPP properties as well as individual network protocols. The difference here is that PPP is a dial-up protocol as opposed the TCP/IP, IPX/SPX (NWLink), NetBEUI, and AppleTalk which are network protocols that operate over the PPP dial-up protocol.

Travel Advisory

Each installed network protocol will have its own tab in the Properties dialog box of the RRAS server.

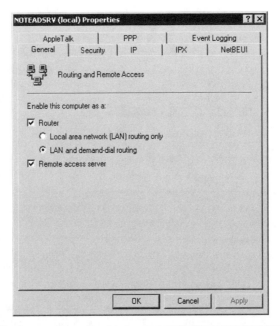

FIGURE 6-6   Configuring the general properties of the RRAS server

On the General tab of the Properties dialog box shown in Figure 6-6, you can enable the server as a router or a remote access server, or you may choose to configure it as both. Configuring the server as a router forces you to select one of the two suboptions underneath the router selection. The router can be configured for local area network routing only or for LAN and demand-dial routing.

Selecting the LAN Routing Only option instructs the RRAS server that demand-dial and VPN access is not required. Selecting the LAN and Demand-Dial Routing option provides support for demand-dial and VPN connections.

Figure 6-7 shows the two variables that can be configured on the Security tab: the authentication provider and the accounting provider. There are two choices for the type of authentication provider: RADIUS and Windows authentication. The default Windows authentication instructs the RRAS server to use the local account database if the server is configured as a member server that is not in a domain or to use the domain account database of the domain to which it is a member. As a member of a down-level Windows NT 4.0 domain, the computer would authenticate all remote access requests against the domain's Security Account Manager (SAM) database. If the RRAS server were a member of an Active Directory domain, the server would authenticate all remote access requests against

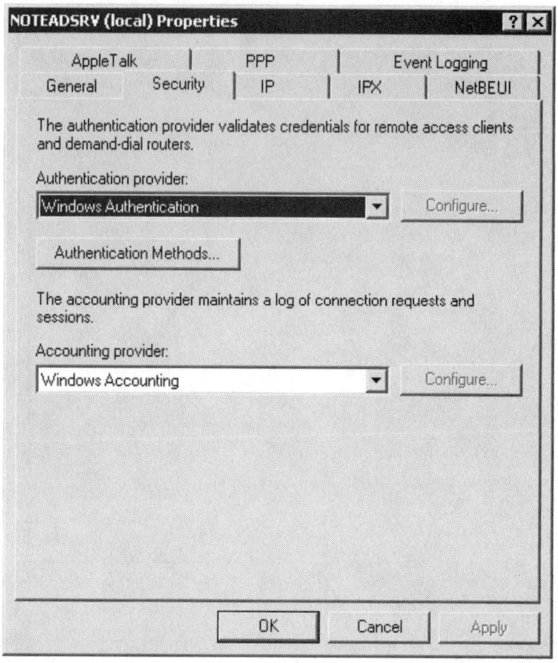

FIGURE 6-7 Setting the authentication and accounting providers

an Active Directory domain controller. The RRAS server is also configured to log all connection authentication information in the log files configured in the Event Logging tab. Choosing RADIUS authentication allows the authentication to be handled by a RADIUS server.

The Authentication Methods button underneath the Authentication Provider drop-down box allows you to configure the different types of available and supported authentication methods, as shown in Figure 6-8. We will discuss each of the different authentication methods in Objective 6.09.

The Accounting Provider setting can also be configured through the Security tab of the Properties dialog box. The default accounting provider is Windows Accounting, which instructs the server to log connection information in the log files that are configured in the properties of the Remote Access Logging folder in RRAS. The two other choices are RADIUS and None, allowing either for a RADIUS server to log the connection information or for no connection information to be logged.

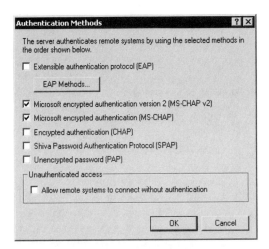

FIGURE 6-8   Configuring available authentication methods

The IP tab shown in Figure 6-9 allows you to configure the RRAS server as an IP router by placing a check mark in the box next to Enable IP Routing and/or configuring it to allow IP-based remote access and demand-dial connections. The IP tab is also the area on which the IP address assignment method is configured. The two options, again, are automatic through DHCP or from a static address pool. If the Static Address Pool option is selected, the configuration of the static pool can be performed on the IP tab using the Add, Edit, and Remove buttons.

The Enable IP Routing option is similar to the option in Windows NT 4.0 that allowed remote access clients access to the entire network. If the Enable IP Routing option is not enabled, remote access clients will only be able to access resources on the RRAS server. The Allow IP-Based Remote Access and Demand-Dial Connections option allows you to control whether remote access and demand-dial connections are permitted. Not enabling this option would prevent remote access clients from establishing a connection with the RRAS server.

The IPX tab provides a location to configure the properties relating to the IPX/SPX protocol, as shown in Figure 6-10. Connections using IPX can be enabled on the RRAS server by selecting the option Allow IPX-Based Remote Access and Demand-Dial Connections. The check box immediately beneath this option allows you to control whether a remote access client connecting with IPX is able to connect to only the local computer or whether RRAS will support IPX routing and give access to the rest of the remote network. The IPX tab also provides an area to configure the IPX network number assignment.

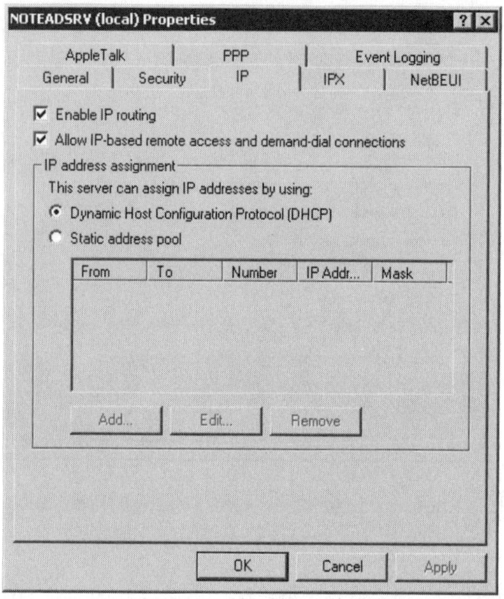

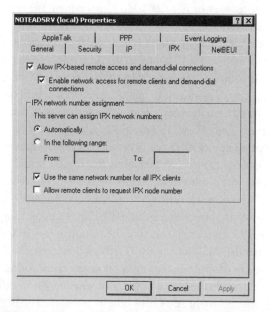

FIGURE 6-9 Configuring the IP properties in RRAS

FIGURE 6-10 Configuring the IPX/SPX properties

As mentioned earlier in this chapter, NetBEUI is not normally a routable network protocol, but RRAS does support the routing on NetBEUI. The configuration options available for NetBEUI are very straightforward and are shown in Figure 6-11. You must first decide whether to permit NetBEUI connections. If you decide to permit them, you must then decide whether you want to limit them to only the RRAS server or allow access to the entire network.

The PPP tab allows you to configure multilink connections, the Bandwidth Allocation Protocol (BAP), Link Control Protocol (LCP) extensions, and software compression, as shown in Figure 6-12.

Exam Tip

The default multilink setting allows a remote access client to connect with two modems simultaneously. In order for multilink connections to work, both the client and the server must be configured to support and use multilink.

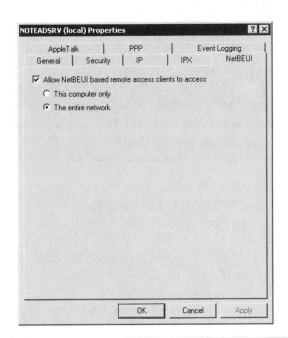

FIGURE 6-11   Configuring NetBEUI properties

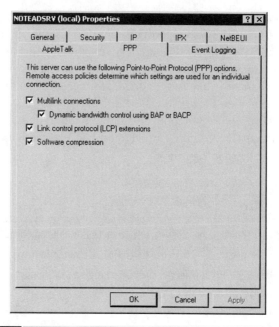

FIGURE 6-12   Configuring the PPP settings

Exam Tip

Each tab representing a dial-in protocol allows you to decide whether you want to limit dial-in connectivity to the RRAS server or permit dial-in connections to access the entire network.

Configuring an RRAS server to accept multilink connections allows remote access users to configure their computers with multiple modems, each with a different phone number, and connect to the RRAS server using more than one device. This allows more than one physical connection to be combined into a single logical connection. If you decide to enable multilink, you might also want to consider enabling the Bandwidth Allocation Protocol (BAP), which allows the RRAS server to monitor multilink connections and drop one of the physical connections if its utilization drops below a defined percentage for a defined period of time.

<table>
<tr><td>

Exam Tip

</td><td></td></tr>
</table>

For multilink to work, it must be configured on both the client and the server.

Link Control Protocol (LCP) extensions can also be enabled on the PPP tab of the RRAS server's Properties dialog box. The Link Control Protocol allows RRAS to send time-remaining and identification messages and request callback during LCP negotiations.

The last of the configurable options on the PPP tab is software compression. Enabling software compression allows the RRAS server to use Microsoft Point-to-Point Encryption (MPPE) to compress data sent by the remote access server.

The Event Logging tab, shown in Figure 6-13, allows you to choose from one of the available logging options. The Event Logging tab is also where you can enable Point-to-Point Protocol (PPP) logging.

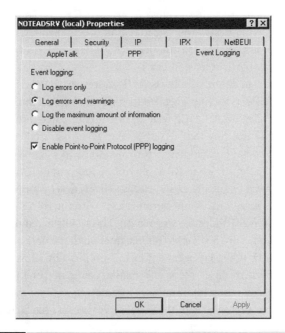

FIGURE 6-13   Configuring the event logging properties

Configure Routing and Remote Access for DHCP Integration

The RRAS service is tightly integrated with the DHCP service to allow it to lease out IP addresses to remote access clients. When configuring your remote access server, you will be asked how you want dial-in clients to obtain an IP address. The two options are dynamically through a DHCP server and from an IP address pool that you configure the RRAS server to use.

Choosing to automatically assign IP addresses from a DHCP server does not require that the DHCP service be installed and configured on the network. If the DHCP service is not available on the network, RRAS will use its own built-in DHCP Allocator service to lease out IP addresses in the Automatic Private IP Addressing network ID of 169.254.0.0/16. For information about the installation and configuration of DHCP, see Chapter 1.

When the RRAS service is configured to automatically assign IP addresses from a DHCP server, and a DHCP server exists on the network, the RRAS service obtains a block of ten IP addresses plus one for itself, for a total of 11, and it makes the block of ten IP addresses available to remote access clients. Once the block of ten IP addresses has been leased out, the RRAS server contacts the DHCP server to obtain another block of ten addresses.

If you choose to automatically assign IP addresses from a DHCP server and you have a DHCP service running on your network, it is recommended that you install a DHCP relay agent. DHCP relay agents are configured through RRAS. The reason for recommending that a DHCP relay agent be installed on the RRAS server is that, by default, IP addresses provided to remote access clients through the DHCP Allocator service in RRAS do not include any WINS or DNS server information. This is because the remote access clients never communicate directly with the DHCP server; they only communicate with the RRAS server that provides them with their IP address information. This results in remote access clients not being able to resolve host or NetBIOS names on the remote network they are dialing in to. A DHCP relay agent solves this problem by allowing the remote access clients to receive all the scope information configured on the DHCP server, including name resolution information. This, too, is a result of the remote access clients only communicating with the RRAS server because the DHCP relay agent is configured through RRAS and located on the RRAS server.

The remote access clients themselves never communicate directly with the DHCP service on the remote network; rather, all communication with the DHCP

service is handled by RRAS. RRAS clients also automatically drop their IP lease when they disconnect, making the IP address they were using available to other remote access clients. This released IP address is still retained, however, by the RRAS server and simply goes back into the block of available IP addresses that RRAS obtained from DHCP. The blocks of ten IP addresses requested by RRAS from DHCP appear in DHCP as leased out and therefore unavailable IP addresses in the DHCP scope.

Objective 6.05
Configure Remote Access Security

The remote access authentication process has changed dramatically in Windows 2000 from how it worked in Windows NT 4.0. In Windows 2000, two areas potentially require configuration in order for a remote user to authenticate to an RRAS server. As in Windows NT 4.0, users have dial-in access properties in their individual user account properties. In an Active Directory domain environment, this user attribute information can be configured using Active Directory Users and Computers. The Dial-In tab of a user's Properties dialog box, like the one shown in Figure 6-14, displays the three different dial-in access permissions that can be assigned.

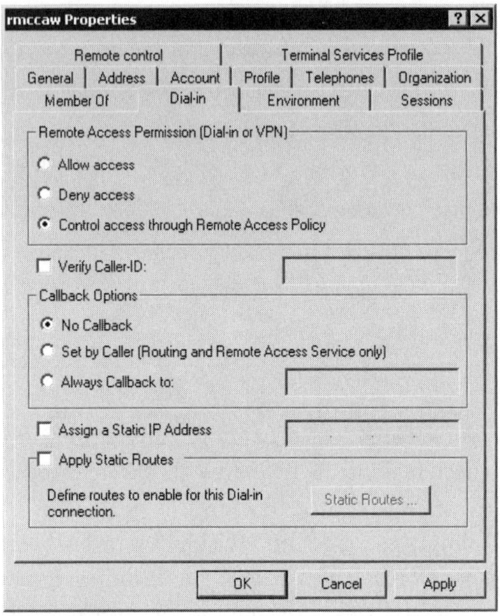

FIGURE 6-14 Configuring user dial-in permission in Active Directory Users and Computers

In a mixed-mode domain, only two user dial-in permissions are available: Allow Access and Deny Access. The default setting is to deny access for all users. In a native-mode domain, all three dial-in permission options are available, and the default is Control Access Through Remote Access Policy.

Local Lingo

mixed-mode domain A mixed-mode domain is a domain that contains Windows 2000 domain controllers but also supports Windows NT 4.0 Backup Domain Controllers (BDCs). A native-mode domain is a Windows 2000 Active Directory domain that only contains Windows 2000 domain controllers.

Step 1 in the remote authentication process, shown in the next illustration, is for the user to send a hash of his authentication credentials to the RRAS server. The RRAS server then queries a domain controller that contains the Active

Directory database for the dial-in permissions of the remote access user (step 2).
There are three possible outcomes from this query:

- If the user's dial-in permission is set to Deny Access, the user is denied access and no further authentication is required.
- If the user's dial-in permission is set to Allow Access, the RRAS server looks to its remote access policy to verify that the remote access client meets both the conditions and the profile settings in the policy. If the remote access client meets both the conditions and the profile settings, the user is granted access based on the remote access policy profile settings.

Exam Tip

If the user's dial-in permission is set to Allow Access, only the conditions and profile components of the remote access policy are examined; the permissions of the remote access policy are ignored.

- If the user's dial-in permission is set to Control Access Through Remote Access Policy, the RRAS server looks to its remote access policy to verify that the remote access client meets the conditions of the remote access policy. If the conditions are met, RRAS looks at the permission associated with the condition. The permission in the RRAS policy can be set to either Allow Access or Deny Access. If the permission is set to Deny

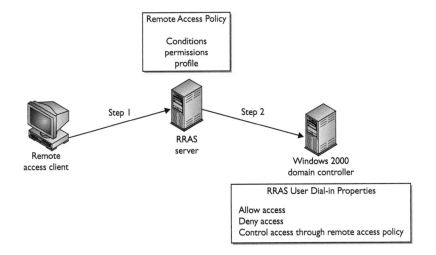

Access, access is denied. If the permission is set to Allow Access, the profile settings of the policy are checked to ensure the client meets them. If the remote access client meets the profile settings, the remote access user is granted access.

Exam Tip

At least one remote access policy must exist in order for users to be able to authenticate to the RRAS server. This is true even when the domain is in mixed mode. One remote access policy must exist on the RRAS server; otherwise, no access will be permitted. The default remote access policy is set to Deny Access but is only effective in a native-mode domain. In a mixed-mode domain, the remote access policy is overridden if the user's dial-in permission is set to Allow Access. By default, the user's dial-in permission is set to Deny Access in a mixed-mode domain.

Because the concept of remote access policy is new to Windows 2000 and you must become very comfortable with how the remote authentication process works, Table 6-1 summarizes the remote authentication process.

Table 6-1 shows the remote authentication process using the combination of user dial-in permissions and remote access policy permissions. The first component to always be evaluated in the authentication process is the user dial-in permission. Based on its configuration, you can see the sequential order in which the components of the remote access policy are evaluated.

The concept of RAS policy evaluation is critical, so let's ensure that you have a solid understanding of it by running through some of the possible scenarios.

TABLE 6.1   The Remote Authentication Process in Sequential Order

User's Dial-in Permission	Conditions	Permissions	Profile
Allow	1	X	2
Deny	X	X	X
Control Access Through Remote Access Policy	1	2	3

Allow Dial-in Permission—Default RAS Policy

In this scenario, your user account has been granted Allow Access on the dial-in tab of your user object's properties dialog box, and only the default RAS policy exists on the RRAS server. The policy evaluation would then consist of the following steps:

1. The RRAS server would query the Active Directory for your user account's dial-in permission and find that it is set to Allow Access.
2. The RRAS server would then examine all of the local RAS policies, starting with the policy at the top of the list. It would look through the first policy to see if you meet all of the conditions of that policy. RRAS would find that you do meet the condition.
3. The RRAS server would then ignore the RAS policy permission because your Active Directory user account's dial-in permission takes precedence.
4. The RRAS server would then look to the profile component of the RAS policy to ensure that you meet all of the criteria defined in the profile. If you hadn't met all of the profile settings, you would have been denied, but because you do meet all of the profile settings, you are granted access.

Deny Dial-in Permission—Default RAS Policy

In this scenario, your user account has been granted Deny Access on the dial-in tab of your user object's properties dialog box, and only the default RAS policy exists on the RRAS server. The policy evaluation would then consist of the following:

1. The RRAS server would query the Active Directory for your user account's dial-in permission and find that it is set to Deny Access.
2. The RRAS server would immediately deny you access.

Control Access through RAS Policy—Default RAS Policy

In this scenario, your user account has been granted Control access through Remote Access Policy on the dial-in tab of your user object's properties dialog box and only the default RAS policy exists on the RRAS server. The policy evaluation would then consist of the following steps:

1. The RRAS server would query the Active Directory for your user account's dial-in permission and find that it is set to Control Access through Remote Access Policy.

2. The RRAS server would then examine all of the local RAS policies, starting with the policy at the top of the list. It would look through the first policy to see if you meet all of the conditions of that policy. RRAS would find that you do meet the condition. If there were multiple conditions, you would be required to meet all of them. If you did not meet all of the conditions, the RRAS server would move on to the next RAS policy in the list and see if you met all of the conditions in that policy. If the RRAS server came to the end of the list of RAS policies and found that you do not meet all of the conditions of any one policy, you would be denied access.

3. The RRAS server would then look at the RAS policy permission, because your Active Directory user account's dial-in permission is set to Control Access through Remote Access Policy. If the RAS policy permission is set to Deny Access, you are denied access. If the RAS policy permission is set to Allow Access, the RRAS server examines the profile settings.

4. The RRAS server then looks to the profile component of the RAS policy to ensure that you meet all of the criteria defined in the profile. If you don't meet all of the profile settings, you will be denied, but if you do meet all of the profile settings, you will be granted access.

As you can see, the RAS policy evaluation process is a multi-step process that provides the opportunity to deny a remote user access at a number of different spots. Install RRAS and play around with RAS policies until you have a good understanding of the process and different settings and options. Now let's spend a minute or two discussing multiple policies.

Multiple RAS Policies

Before moving on from the remote access authentication process, you should know that it is possible to have multiple remote access policies. If multiple remote access policies exist, the order in which they are listed is very significant. The processing order of remote access policies is top-down, meaning that the remote access policy at the top of the list is checked first. The first remote access policy whose conditions the dial-in user meets is the policy that is applied. Let's look at an example to better illustrate this.

As the administrator in your network, you have configured two remote access policies in addition to the default policy that still exists on the RRAS server. The first policy is titled Policy 1 and is configured with a single condition. The condition is that the remote user must be a member of the sales group. The permission assigned to the policy is to allow access, and no profile settings have been modified. The second policy, titled Policy 2, is configured with two conditions. The first condition is that the remote user must be a member of the Domain Users group. The second condition is that access is only permitted between 6 P.M. and 6 A.M.

In the first scenario, the order of the remote access policies from top to bottom are Policy 1, Policy 2, and Default policy, and a user in the accounting group tries to establish a connection at 10 P.M. Policy 1 would be evaluated first, in this case, and because the conditions aren't met, Policy 2 would be evaluated next. The conditions in Policy 2 would both be met, and access to the RRAS server would be granted to the remote user.

In the second scenario, the order of the remote access policies from top to bottom are Policy 2, Policy 1, and Default policy, and a user in the sales group tries to establish a connection at 10 P.M. Policy 2 would be evaluated first, and because the conditions are met, the sales user would be granted access. The problem here is that you probably intended to allow access to the member of the sales group only through the sales policy. However, because of the order of the remote access policies, Policy 1 did not require evaluation because access had already been granted.

Exam Tip

The order in which you configure your remote access policies is very important in the remote access authentication process. The first remote access policy whose conditions the remote access user meets is the policy that will be processed.

Remote access security is comprised of three components in Windows 2000. These three components include the user's dial-in permission, the remote access policy stored on the RRAS server, and the authentication and encryption protocols that are configured on the RRAS server. Each component, in turn, can include subcomponents that can also be configured. In this section, we will examine each of these remote access security components, but before we look at them, it is important that you understand where each component is stored in your network infrastructure.

In an Active Directory domain environment, the user's dial-in permission is stored in the Active Directory as an attribute of the user object. In the case of a workgroup environment, the user's dial-in permission is stored in the local computer account database.

Remote access policies are stored on individual RRAS servers, not in the Active Directory. This means that if your network has multiple RRAS servers, each will have to be configured with their own unique remote access policies. The reason for this is that remote access policies can be configured to be very hardware or media specific, requiring each RRAS server to have its own unique remote access policy.

Authentication and encryption protocols are configured through the RRAS snap-in as well, and this configuration information is also stored on the RRAS server. Individual remote access policies can be created to provide different authentication and encryption configurations to different groups of users, or they can be applied at the server to apply to all connections.

> **Exam Tip**
>
> The MaxDenials value in the registry of the RRAS server can be set to a value greater than 1 to enforce an account lockout policy for remote access connections. This account lockout policy is different from a domain account lockout policy because it locks out the account on the local RRAS server, not in the Active Directory. The default RRAS setting unlocks locked-out accounts every 48 hours, by default.

Authentication Issues in a Mixed-Mode Domain

Here is one additional RRAS authentication scenario you should be aware of. Authentication problems can occur when the RAS service is run on a computer running Windows NT 4.0 as a member server in a mixed- or native-mode domain. In a mixed-mode domain that contains both Windows 2000 Active Directory domain controllers and Windows NT 4.0 BDCs, the remote user will only be able to authenticate if the RAS server queries the NT 4.0 BDC for authentication, because only NT 4.0 domain controllers allow NULL sessions.

> **Local Lingo**
>
> **NULL session**   A NULL session is when a computer is able to establish a communication session with another computer without a password or username. A NULL session allows the NT 4.0 RAS server to query the NT 4.0 BDC without authenticating.

Three options are available to avoid this potential authentication problem. The first option is to allow the down-level Windows NT 4.0 RAS server to query a Windows 2000 Active Directory domain controller through a NULL session. This can be accomplished by adding the Everyone group to the "Pre-Windows 2000 Compatibility Access" group. This will allow authentication to be successful regardless of the domain controller contacted for authentication. A second option to avoid this type of authentication problem is to upgrade the Windows NT 4.0 RAS server to Windows 2000. The third, and most time consuming way to avoid this potential authentication problem is to reinstall the Windows NT 4.0 RAS server as a BDC, which would allow authentication to occur locally.

Exam Tip

Adding the Everyone group to the "Pre-Windows 2000 Compatibility Access" group will avoid authentication problems in a mixed-mode domain when the RAS server is running on a computer running Windows NT 4.0.

Create a Remote Access Policy

Remote access policy is something new to Windows 2000. Remote access policy provides an additional layer of security that can help network administrators to better secure their remote access servers and protect the integrity of their organization's data. A remote access policy is comprised of three components:

- Conditions
- Permissions
- Profile

Let's take a look at each component of a remote access policy.

Remote Access Conditions

The first component of a remote access policy that is used to evaluate whether a user is granted access on an RRAS server is made up of the conditions of the policy. The conditions of a remote access policy are used in the authentication process when the user's dial-in permission is set to either Allow Access or Control Access

Through Remote Access Policy. If the user's dial-in permission is set to Deny Access, the user is explicitly denied access and the remote access policy does not need to be evaluated.

Multiple conditions can be configured for a single remote access policy, but the conditions are processed in a top-down order and the remote user is only required to meet one condition. Once the user has met a single condition in the list, the other two components of the policy are then evaluated. To configure remote access conditions, follow these steps:

1. Open RRAS. Select Remote Access Policies and right-click the default policy named Allow Access If Dial-in Permission Is Enabled.
2. Select Properties from the context menu, and the Properties dialog box shown in Figure 6-15 will appear.
3. Use the Add, Remove, or Edit button to configure the conditions for the remote access policy.

The different types of conditions available for configuration include the following:

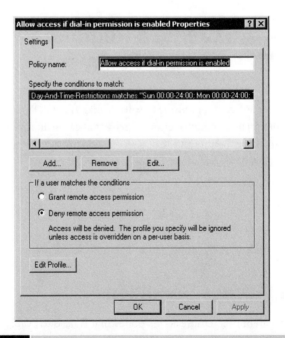

FIGURE 6-15   Configuring remote access policy conditions

- **Called-Station-ID** The phone number dialed by the user
- **Calling-Station-ID** The phone number from which the connection originated
- **Client-Friendly-Name** The name for the RADIUS client (IAS only)
- **Client-IP-Address** The RADIUS client's IP address (IAS)
- **Client-Vendor** The RADIUS proxy or Network Access Server's (NAS) manufacturer (IAS only)
- **Day-and-Time-Restrictions** A schedule for when access is permitted or denied
- **Framed-Protocol** The protocol to be used
- **NAS-Identifier** The string of the NAS on which the request originated (IAS only)
- **NAS-IP-Address** The IP address of the NAS on which the request originated (IAS only)
- **NAS-Port-Type** The physical port type used by the NAS on which the request originated
- **Service-Type** The service type requested by the remote user
- **Tunnel-Type** The tunneling protocol to be used
- **Windows-Groups** Membership that allows you to restrict or permit access to only those members of a specific group or groups

The default condition found in the default remote access policy is a Day-and-Time-Restriction of 24x7 access, which is a bit of an oxymoron because access any time throughout the week is not really a restriction. However, the default permissions of the default remote access policy deny access based on anyone who meets that condition, which again, by default, is every remote access user. Once you have defined the conditions for the remote access policy, you can assign a permission to the policy, which we will explore next.

Remote Access Permissions

Each remote access policy must be configured with a permission. The two permission choices—Grant Remote Access Permission and Deny Remote Access Permission—can be seen in Figure 6-15. The permissions of a remote access policy will only be used in the authentication process if the user's dial-in permission is set to Control Access Through Remote Access Policy. If the permission you configure in the remote access policy is to deny access, access will then be denied and the profile will not be looked at. If you configure the permission in the remote access policy to allow access, the settings in the profile will be evaluated next before access is granted.

Objective 6.07 — Configure a Remote Access Profile

The profile component of a remote access policy allows for the configuration of numerous settings found in the six tabs of the Profile Properties dialog box, displayed in Figure 6-16. The six tabs include Dial-in Constraints, IP, Multilink, Authentication, Encryption, and Advanced.

Dial-in Constraints Settings

The configuration of the Dial-in Constraints tab, shown in Figure 6-16, allows for restrictions to be configured in the profile component of the Remote Access Policy. The available restriction options include the following:

- **Idle disconnect time** Sets the amount of time after which the remote access session will be disconnected

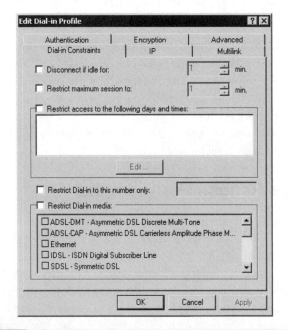

FIGURE 6-16 Configuring the profile settings of a remote access policy

- **Maximum session time**   Sets he maximum time permitted for a remote access session after which the session will be disconnected
- **Day and time restrictions**   Establishes a schedule for when access is permitted
- **Limiting dial-in to a single number**   Forces the remote user to dial in from a single number
- **Media type**   Restricts incoming connections to one or more types of media

IP Settings

The IP tab, shown in Figure 6-17, allows for the configuration of the IP address assignment policy for remote access clients. Here you have three choices:

- Server must supply an IP address
- Client may request an IP address
- Server settings define policy

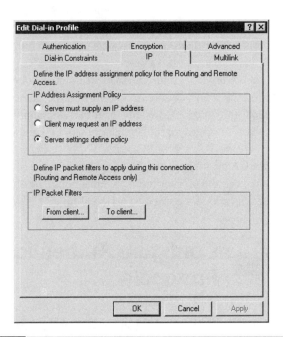

Configuring the IP profile settings of a remote access policy

The Server Settings Define Policy option is the default option and means that remote access clients will get IP addresses based on the IP address assignment settings of the server.

The other configuration option in the IP tab of the profile's Properties dialog box is the ability to configure incoming and outgoing packet filters for all remote access connections. Select the From Client button to configure an incoming packet filter and limit what types of traffic the remote users can send to the RRAS server. Creating an incoming packet filter requires you to define the destination network to which the packet would be headed and then specify that network by network ID and subnet mask. You then select a protocol such as TCP and a source and destination port on which the service operates that you wish to block.

Objective 6.08   Configure Multilink Connections

The Multilink tab, shown in Figure 6-18, allows for the configuration of both multilink and Bandwidth Allocation Protocol (BAP) settings. The default multilink settings default to the RRAS server settings, but that can be changed to disable them completely or enable them and set a maximum number of ports in the profile.

Remember that in order for multilink to function, it must be configured on both the client and the server. Configuring it only on the client or only on the server will not allow it to function. Also remember that without multilink enabled and configured, there is no need for the configuration of the bandwidth allocation protocol.

The Bandwidth Allocation Protocol settings can be set in conjunction with multilink to allow a remote user's multilink connection to be dropped if it falls below a specified utilization for a specified period of time.

Objective 6.09   Configure Authentication Protocols

The remote access profile, which is displayed in Figure 6-19, can also be configured with profile-specific authentication settings. It is on the Authentication

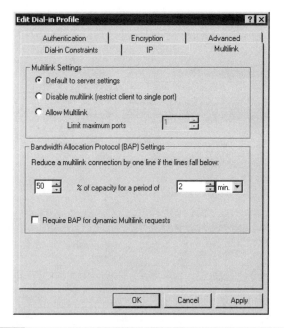

FIGURE 6-18 Configuring multilink profile settings

tab that the Extensible Authentication Protocol (EAP) is enabled. EAP provides support for a number of enhanced authentication methods, including smart cards and certificates. The two authentication methods enabled by default are MS-CHAP versions 1 and 2. Other options include CHAP, PAP, SPAP, and the unauthenticated access option. The unauthenticated access option can be handy when you're trying to troubleshoot RRAS connectivity problems that you believe to be related to the authentication protocols selected.

Exam Tip

EAP-TLS is only supported on a remote access server running Windows 2000 that is a member of a Windows 2000 mixed-mode or native-mode domain. A remote access server running stand-alone Windows 2000 does not support EAP-TLS. EAP-TLS is the most secure authentication protocol.

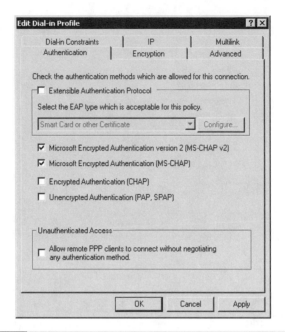

FIGURE 6-19 Configuring authentication profile settings

To help you decide which authentication protocols are best suited for your own environment, we will explore what each of the protocols has to offer.

The Microsoft Encrypted Authentication version 2, known as Microsoft Challenge Handshake Authentication Protocol (MS-CHAP v2), provides mutual authentication and data encryption that uses different keys for sending and receiving. MS-CHAP v2 no longer sends the user's encrypted password during authentication negotiations, making it the strongest authentication protocol in the list.

MS-CHAP is the first version of the authentication protocol and uses a challenge-response authentication process that encrypts the responses. The security weakness in this implementation is that the user's password is sent across the network in an encrypted state during authentication negotiations, allowing users sniffing the network to capture the encrypted password and perform a brute-force attack against it to decode and obtain the password.

CHAP is an authentication protocol that allows non-Microsoft clients to communicate using encryption with a Windows 2000 Server or for a Windows 2000 client to communicate using encryption with a server running a non-Microsoft operating system. CHAP uses a challenge-response authentication process that encrypts the response using Message Digest 5 (MD5), but it does not support mutual authentication.

Local Lingo

MD5 MD5 is an industry-standard hashing algorithm. A hashing algorithm is used to encrypt and decrypt data transferred on a network.

Password Authentication Protocol (PAP) is the least restrictive authentication protocol and should only be used when you are not worried about the security of passwords being sent across the network.

Shiva Password Authentication Password (SPAP) should be used to allow dial-in access from Shiva clients. Like PAP, SPAP is not a secure authentication protocol.

Configure Encryption Protocols

There are four different encryption settings that can be configured individually or in combination with one another. The four different settings, as shown in Figure 6-20, are No Encryption, Basic, Strong, and Strongest. By default, all four setting are enabled.

No Encryption is just as it sounds; it does not require the remote user to use any encryption when sending data to the RRAS server. In order for the No Encryption setting to be effective, it must be the only encryption setting enabled.

Basic encryption is the least secure of the encryption settings after No Encryption. When enabled, it requires the use of IPSec 56-bit DES or Microsoft Point-to-Point Encryption (MPPE) 40-bit encryption.

Strong encryption is the second-most secure encryption setting available. When enabled, it requires the use of IPSec 56-bit DES or MPPE 56-bit encryption.

The most secure encryption setting is the Strongest setting, which when enabled requires the use of IPSec Triple DES (3DES) or MPPE 128-bit encryption.

Each of the encryption settings can be used by themselves or in combination with one another. When multiple settings are selected, the RRAS server tries to negotiate the most secure encryption settings first with the remote computer and moves down the list to the least secure setting until it finds one that both computers support and agree to.

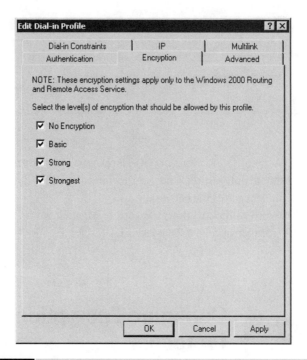

FIGURE 6-20 Configuring encryption profile settings

Advanced Settings

The advanced profile options allow for the configuration of specific connection attributes—which there are too many to list. The two default connection attributes shown in Figure 6-21 indicate that Framed-Protocol must be PPP and Service-Type must be Framed.

Objective 6.11

Manage and Monitor Remote Access

A number of tools and utilities are available to manage your remote access server. Let's start by looking at what you can do in the RRAS snap-in.

The RRAS snap-in can be used to manage and monitor individual user connections and check the status of modems and ports. To look at the users who are currently connected to the server, follow these simple steps:

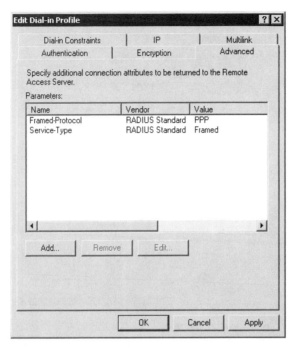

FIGURE 6-21 Configuring connection attributes in the Advanced tab of the profile

1. Open RRAS.
2. Select Remote Access Clients.

This will give you a really quick look at the number of remote users connected to the server and will let you know the name of each user connected, how long they have been connected, and the number of ports they are using.

Also, in RRAS you can check the status of modems and ports by right-clicking the modem or port that is of interest to you and selecting Status from the context menu. This will quickly allow you to see the speed of the connection, bytes sent and received, any errors, and network registration information. Remote access logging can also be configured through RRAS by selecting Remote Access Logging and right-clicking the Local file and selecting Properties. This will bring up the Local File Properties dialog box, shown in Figure 6-22, which allows you to configure one or more of three logging options: logging accounting requests, logging authentication requests, and logging of periodic status.

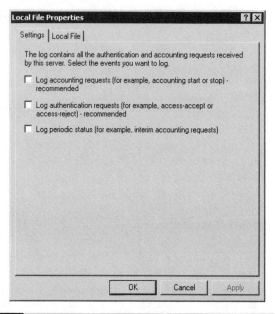

FIGURE 6-22 Configuring logging in RRAS

Exam Tip

The logging options in Remote Access Logging record only accounting and authentication events related to remote access clients. If you are using a RADIUS server, the logs are maintained on the RADIUS server, not the RRAS server.

Like with all other services, the Event logs can be a good starting point for troubleshooting problems with RRAS. Common RRAS events include information about users establishing connections with the server.

RADIUS

The Remote Authentication Dial-in User Service (RADIUS) allows multiple RRAS servers to be administered from a single location and for all accounting and authentication to be maintained in the same central location. RADIUS has two components: a client side, known as a *RADIUS client*, and a server side, known as a *RADIUS server*. A Windows 2000 RRAS server can be configured as a RADIUS client, and a Windows 2000 Server running Internet Information Services (IIS) and the Internet Authentication Service (IAS) can be configured as a RADIUS server. The IAS service is not installed by default and must be installed through the Add/Remove Windows Components section of Add/Remove Programs in Control Panel through the following steps:

Exam Tip
IAS can be used to provide authentication for RRAS, IIS, and other services, including non-Microsoft dial-up servers.

1. Configuring your RRAS servers to use RADIUS authentication and accounting can be done through the RRAS snap-in by right-clicking the name of your server and selecting Properties from the context menu.
2. On the Security tab of the Server Properties dialog box, select RADIUS Authentication and RADIUS Accounting from the two drop-down menus.
3. Click the Configure button next to each drop-down box and click Add on the RADIUS Authentication dialog box.
4. Add in the name or preferably the IP address of the RADIUS server to redirect authentication requests to.
5. Configure a shared secret up to 255 characters in length to be used to authenticate access to the RADIUS server. Then click OK.

Exam Tip
Configuring RRAS to use RADIUS authentication allows all remote access policies to be configured on the RADIUS server and prevents them from being edited on the RRAS server.

CHECKPOINT

✔ **Objective 6.01: Configure and Troubleshoot Remote Access** RRAS is automatically installed with the installation of Windows 2000 Server and is enabled and configured using the RRAS snap-in. You must be a member of the Administrators group to enable RRAS.

✔ **Objective 6.02: Configure Inbound Connections**   The RRAS Setup Wizard provides you with five server configuration options: Internet Connection Server, Remote Access Server, Virtual Private Network Server, Network Router, and Manually Configured Server. RRAS supports all five network protocols for dial-in access to an RRAS server. These protocols include TCP/IP, IPX/SPX (NWLink), NetBEUI, AppleTalk, and DLC. Windows 2000 Server only supports incoming PPP connections, not SLIP connections.

✔ **Objective 6.03: Configure a Virtual Private Network (VPN)**   Windows 2000 supports two VPN protocols: PPTP and L2TP. PPTP is the default and provides support for down-level operating systems. L2TP uses IPSec for encryption and is therefore limited to only computers running Windows 2000. L2TP can work over any intertransit network, whereas PPTP is limited to IP intertransit networks. L2TP cannot be used when access to the Internet is configured through a NAT server. When you configure RRAS as a VPN server, five default PPTP and L2TP ports are configured.

✔ **Objective 6.04: Configure Routing and Remote Access for DHCP Integration**   RRAS can be configured to assign IP addresses automatically through a DHCP server or from a static address pool. If IP addresses are to be assigned by DHCP, RRAS obtains a block of 11 addresses from the DHCP server upon configuration, one IP address for itself and ten for dial-in VPN clients. If RRAS is configured to automatically assign IP addresses from a DHCP server and a DHCP server isn't available, RRAS will assign addresses on the 169.254.0.0 network. A DHCP relay agent must be installed on the RRAS server to allow remote access clients to receive additional scope information such as WINS and DNS server information. Remote access clients never communicate directly with the DHCP server; rather, all communication is done through RRAS.

✔ **Objective 6.05: Configure Remote Access Security**   The user dial-in permission Control Access Through Remote Access Policy is the default dial-in permission in native-mode domains and is only available in a native-mode domain. The default user dial-in permission in mixed mode is Deny Access. If the user's dial-in permission is set to Allow Access, only the conditions and profile components of the remote access policy are examined. A minimum of one remote access policy must exist to allow dial-in permission, regardless of the user dial-in permission configured. Multiple remote access policies are processed from the top down until the conditions of one of the policies is met by a remote access user.

✔ **Objective 6.06:** **Create a Remote Access Policy**   Remote access policies include three components—conditions, permissions, and profile settings— and are stored locally on the RRAS server, as opposed to in the Active Directory.

✔ **Objective 6.07:** **Configure a Remote Access Profile**   A remote access profile allows specific restrictions to be configured for users who meet the conditions of a remote access policy. If the remote access user does not meet the profile settings, their connection is terminated. The profile settings are not analyzed if the user's dial-in permission is set to Deny Access.

✔ **Objective 6.08:** **Configure Multilink Connections**   RRAS can be configured to support multilink connections, allowing two or more physical connections to be merged into a single logical connection. By default, a remote access client is able to connect to RRAS with two modems. Both the server and the client must be configured to support multilink. Bandwidth Allocation Protocol (BAP) can be configured to drop a multilink connection if it drops below a specified utilization rate for a specified period of time.

✔ **Objective 6.09:** **Configure Authentication Protocols**   The two default authentication protocols configured in RRAS are MS-CHAP v1 and v2. EAP-TLS is the most secure authentication protocol and is only supported on a remote access server running Windows 2000 that is a member of a Windows 2000 mixed-mode or native-mode domain.

✔ **Objective 6.10:** **Configure Encryption Protocols**   There are four encryption settings to choose from: No Encryption, Basic, Strong, and Strongest. Basic uses MPPE with a 40-bit key. Strong uses MPPE with a 56-bit key for dial-up and PPTP connections and 56-bit DES for L2TP connections. Strongest uses MPPE with a 128-bit key for dial-up and PPTP connections and triple DES for L2TP connections.

✔ **Objective 6.11:** **Manage and Monitor Remote Access**   Disabling the RRAS service causes all configuration information to be lost. The Netsh tool is a command-line utility that can be used to save and later reapply the configuration of an RRAS server. RADIUS authentication and logging allow authentication and logging requests to be sent to an IAS server and allow administration to be performed centrally on a RADIUS server.

REVIEW QUESTIONS

1. You have configured your RRAS server to automatically assign IP addresses to remote access clients. Your network is configured with a DHCP server, and a block of ten IP addresses have been obtained by the RRAS server. Name resolution is working fine internally, but the remote access clients that are connecting successfully are unable to resolve the names of servers on the network. What can you do to correct the problem?

   A. Install a WINS server on the local network and configure the DHCP scope with the IP address and node type of the WINS server.

   B. Install a DNS server on the local network and configure the DHCP scope with the IP address of the DNS server.

   C. Install a DHCP relay agent on the RRAS server.

   D. On the remote access clients, enter the ipconfig /flushdns command followed by the ipconfig /renew command.

2. You are the administrator of your Active Directory domain. You have just completed the configuration of an RRAS server on your network. You are trying to configure the user dial-in permission Control Access Through Remote Access Policy but the option is not available. What is the cause of the permission not being available?

   A. The Control Access Through Remote Access Policy option is only available on member servers.

   B. The domain is in native mode.

   C. The domain is in mixed mode.

   D. The Control Access Through Remote Access Policy option must be enabled on the RRAS server before being available in Active Directory Users and Computers.

3. You have configured Skline, a remote access user in your domain, with the Allow Access dial-in permission. You have configured a new remote access policy with two conditions. The first condition is that the remote access user must be a member of the Domain Users group. The second condition is that dial-in access is only permitted between 6 a.m. and 6 p.m. The permission of the policy is set to Deny Access. The default remote access policy is still configured on the remote access server. What will the outcome be for Skline when she attempts to connect to the RRAS server at 7 p.m.? (Choose all that apply.)

    A. Skline will be allowed access based on her user dial-in permission.

    B. Skline will be allowed access based on the default remote access policy.

    C. Skline will be denied access based on the new remote access policy.

    D. Skline will be denied access based on the default remote access policy.

4. As the administrator of your domain, you would like to force all remote users to use certificates to authenticate. Which of the following will you choose to configure?

    A. EAP-TLS

    B. MS-CHAP v1

    C. MS-CHAP v2

    D. IPSec

5. You have configured three RRAS servers on your network to use RADIUS for authentication: RSrv1, Rsrv2, and RSrv3. Prior to the configuration of RADIUS, authentication was managed through four remote access policies on each of the RRAS servers. Your organization has undergone some restructuring lately and you need to change one of the policies on RSrv1 and RSrv3. Which of the following will allow you to accomplish this goal? (Choose all that apply.)

    A. Open RRAS on RSrv1 and change the remote access policy.

    B. Open RRAS on RSrv3 and change the remote access policy.

    C. Open IAS on the RADIUS server and change the remote access policies.

    D. Open RADIUS on the RADIUS server and change the remote access policies.

6. As the administrator of your network, you are planning the configuration of one of your RRAS servers. You would like to configure it to use MPPE 56-bit encryption. Which of the following will allow you to accomplish that?

    A. MS-CHAP

    B. Strong

    C. Strongest

    D. CHAP

7. As the administrator of your Windows 2000 network, you are responsible for setting up a single server with RRAS to support both a VPN server and NAT. During the enabling and configuring process, you chose to configure a NAT

server and now must configure the VPN server manually in RRAS. Which of the following actions must you take on the General tab of the RRAS server's Properties dialog box to allow both NAT and VPN functionality?

A. Enable the computer as a router for local area network routing only.

B. Enable the computer as a router for LAN and demand-dial routing.

C. Enable the computer as a remote access server.

D. Enable access to the entire network.

8. Which of the following is the default dial-in user permission for all users in a mixed-mode domain?

A. Allow Access

B. Deny Access

C. Control Access Through Remote Access Policy

D. Grant Access

9. You are the administrator of a Windows 2000 native-mode domain. You have configured three remote access policies on a single RRAS server in your domain. You have configured each of the three remote access policies with two conditions that grant access and have configured each policy with specific profile settings. In the Active Directory, you have configured all users with the Control Access Through Remote Access Policy permission. Place the following steps in the correct sequence in which they will occur during remote access authentication. (Choose only those that apply.)

A. The permission of the remote access policy is evaluated.

B. The remote user's dial-in permission is checked in the Active Directory.

C. The remote access policy conditions are evaluated in the remote access policies from the bottom up until the conditions of one of the policies are met.

D. The profile of the remote access policy is evaluated.

E. The remote access policy conditions are evaluated in the remote access policies from the top down until the conditions of one of the policies are met.

F. The remote user's dial-in permission is checked in the local RRAS server's account database.

10. You are the administrator of a Windows 2000 mixed-mode domain. You have configured three remote access policies on a single RRAS server in your domain. You have configured each of the three remote access policies with two conditions that grant access and have configured each policy with

specific profile settings. In the Active Directory, you have configured all users with the Allow Access permission. Place the following steps in the correct sequence in which they will occur during remote access authentication. (Choose only those that apply.)

A. The permission of the remote access policy is evaluated.

B. The remote user's dial-in permission is checked in the Active Directory.

C. The remote access policy conditions are evaluated in the remote access policies from the bottom up until the conditions of one of the policies are met.

D. The profile of the remote access policy is evaluated.

E. The remote access policy conditions are evaluated in the remote access policies from the top down until the conditions of one of the policies are met.

F. The remote user's dial-in permission is checked in the local RRAS server's account database.

REVIEW ANSWERS

1. **C** Installing a DHCP relay agent will allow WINS and DNS information configured in the scope properties on the DHCP server to be provided to the remote access clients.

2. **C** The option is not available in a mixed-mode domain. The user dial-in permission Control Access Through Remote Access Policy is only available in native-mode domains.

3. **A** **B** Skline will be allowed access based on her user dial-in permission and the default remote access policy. Skline's user dial-in permission and the conditions of the default remote access policy allow her access to the remote access server.

4. **A** EAP-TLS is the authentication protocol that must be enabled if you wish to require certificates for the purpose of authenticating your remote access users.

5. **C** IAS will allow you to change the policies on the RADIUS server because all policies will have been removed from the RRAS servers and moved to the RADIUS server where authentication takes place.

6. **B** Strong encryption can be configured on the RRAS server to allow it to use MPPE 56-bit encryption.

7. **B** To enable an RRAS server as both a NAT and VPN server, the Enable This Computer As a Router for LAN and Demand-Dial Routing option must be selected on the General tab of the RRAS server's Properties dialog box.

8. **B** The default user dial-in permission in a mixed-mode domain is set to deny access to all users.

9. **B** **E** **C** **D** The sequence of the remote authentication process when a user's dial-in permission is set to Control Access Through Remote Access Policy is to verify the user's dial-in permission and then evaluate the remote access policies from the top down until the conditions of a policy are met. Next, the permissions of the policy whose conditions were met are evaluated and then the profile settings are evaluated.

10. **B** **E** **D** The sequence of the remote authentication process when a user's dial-in permission is set to Allow Access is to verify the user's dial-in permission and then evaluate the remote access policies from the top down until the conditions of a policy are met. 1. Next, the profile of the policy whose conditions were met is evaluated.

IP Routing Network Infrastructure

	NEWBIE	SOME EXPERIENCE	EXPERT
ETA	7–10 hours	4–7 hours	2–4 hours

The configuration of network communications is fundamental to the successful deployment and support of Windows 2000 or any operating system in your network. Understanding the fundamentals of the available routing protocols supported in Windows 2000 is the first step in this process. This first step includes having a familiarity with IP addressing, subnetting, and Classless Interdomain Routing (CIDR) notation. Knowing how to divide a network into different segments (or *subnets*) must be understood before any discussion on effective configuration can take place. Once you have a solid understanding of the fundamentals, we will explore the installation and configuration options.

Our journey into routing will begin with the two routing protocols supported in Windows 2000: Routing Information Protocol (RIP) and Open Shortest Path First (OSPF). Once the routing protocols have been installed and configured, we will look at how to troubleshoot communication problems that can arise. Success on the Implementing and Administering a Microsoft Windows 2000 Network Infrastructure exam requires that you have a very good understanding of all the components involved in the routing process—from the initial subnetting of the network, to troubleshooting communication problems and adding static routes. This chapter will cover the ins and outs of routing in a Windows 2000 network.

Objective 7.01

Install, Configure, and Troubleshoot IP Routing Protocols

The first step in this journey toward a better understanding of routing in a Windows 2000 network environment begins with a look at the basic elements that lead up to the need for implementing and configuring routing—multiple network segments. Multiple network segments are used to isolate traffic to a single network and reduce overall network congestion. Subnet masks are used in TCP/IP network environments to break networks into multiple segments. Let's begin our journey into routing with a look at subnetting fundamentals.

Subnetting Fundamentals

Before we can talk about routing, configuring routing interfaces, adding static routes, and the different routing protocols, we must explore the fundamentals of subnetting. Networks can grow to be very large in size. As they grow, the number of hosts on each subnet increases the amount of traffic on the subnet. At some point, depending on the number of clients and the types of traffic they are sending, the performance of the network will begin to degrade. To improve performance, a network can be divided into segments, also known as *subnets*. This will help to improve network performance in a number of ways, one of which is limiting broadcast traffic to the local subnet from which it originated.

An IP address is comprised of two parts: a network ID and a host ID. The network ID allows intermediary devices such as routers or switches to determine the destination network of the IP datagram. The host ID is used to identify the host on that network. A subnet mask, or what is sometimes referred to in routers as a *netmask*, is used to break an IP address into its two parts. A subnet mask, like an IP address, is a 32-bit value that can be expressed in a couple ways but is most commonly shown as four octets separated by periods. There are five network classes: Class A through Class E. You should be familiar with the first three classes (Class A, Class B, and Class C). The three standard IP address classes and their associated subnet masks are displayed in Table 7-1.

TABLE 7.1 The Different Network Classes and Their Associated Subnet Masks

Class	Subnet Mask	Binary Value
A	255.0.0.0	11111111.00000000.00000000.00000000
B	255.255.0.0	11111111. 11111111. 00000000. 00000000
C	255.255.255.0	11111111. 11111111. 11111111.00000000

Each class of IP address allows for networks of various sizes. In TCP/IP networks, size is measured by two factors: the number of possible subnets and the number of hosts per subnet. All three classes of networks can be identified quickly by looking at the decimal value in the first octet of an IP address. The first octet of Class A networks will have a decimal value between 1 and 126. Class B networks will begin with a decimal value between 128 and 191, and Class C networks will begin with a decimal value between 192 and 223. This means that binary notation is very important to your understanding of subnetting. If the first octet of a Class A network must have a decimal value between 1 and 126, it can therefore only use the last 7 bits of the binary value. Look to the decimal equivalents of the each binary bit to see that the first (left most) bit has a value of 128 and therefore cannot be used in Class A networks (it must be a 0 bit as opposed to a 1 bit):

- Binary: 1   1   1   1   1   1   1   1
- Decimal: 128 64 32 16   8   4   2   1

This leaves multiple combinations of the remaining seven 1 bits available to make up the value of the first octet and brings us to the formula that can be used to determine the number of available network segments that each class of network can support. The formula to calculate this is $2^n - 2$, where n is the number of 1 bits that can be used to make up the value in the first octet (note that two networks are subtracted to account for the 0.0.0.0 and 127.0.0.0 networks, which are not available for use). The 0.0.0.0 network is reserved for the default route, and the 127.0.0.0 network is reserved for the loopback address. In the case of a Class A network, n would be represented by the number 7 (seven available 1 bits), and when it's plugged into the formula ($2^7 - 2$), you can see that a total of 126 network segments are available in a Class A network.

Look to Table 7-2 to identify the number of available networks and the number of available hosts per network that each of the classes will support. What you will notice from Table 7-2 is that Class A networks allow for the highest number of host addresses, and Class C networks allow for the lowest number of hosts. The formula for determining the number of available hosts is the same as that used to determine the number of available network segments, $2^n - 2$, where n is now the number of bits available to make up the host portion of the IP address. Using a Class A network again as an example, think of this network class in binary format nnnnnnnn.hhhhhhhh.hhhhhhhh.hhhhhhhh, where the instances of n in the address represent the bits of the network ID and the instances of h represent bits of the host ID. There are three octets, each 8 bits in size, for a total of 24 bits in the host ID. Using the formula $2^{24} - 2$, you find that a maximum of 16,777,214 hosts can exist on a Class A network.

Note that no address range begins with 127 and that there are no addresses above 223. The 127.0.0.0 network is reserved for testing and troubleshooting purposes and is referred to as the *loopback address*. Addresses that begin with 224 and higher are reserved for special protocols such as IP multicasting and are therefore not available for use as host addresses. Additionally, host addresses that begin with 0 and 255 are used as broadcast addresses and also cannot be assigned to hosts on a network.

Based on Table 7-2, you can see that the number of available addresses in a given address class is fixed, with Class A networks supporting a maximum of

TABLE 7.2   Breaking the Network Classes into Network
Segments and Hosts Per Segment

Class	Decimal Range in First Octet	Number of Available Network Segments	Number of Hosts Per Network	Subnet Mask
A	1–126	126	16,777,214	255.0.0.0
B	128–191	16,384	65,534	255.255.0.0
C	192–223	2,097,151	254	255.255.255.0

16,777,214 hosts and Class C networks supporting a maximum of 254. The class of network you choose for your organization will depend on a number of factors, including the current number of hosts, expected growth, existing Internet connectivity, and network architecture. Four network IDs have been reserved as private network IDs for organizations to use internally for the hosts on their networks. These four private network IDs are as follows:

- 10.0.0.0/8
- 169.254.0.0/16
- 172.16.0.0/12
- 192.168.0.0/16

If your network is not connected to the Internet and you do not plan to connect it to the Internet, you are free to use any IP addressing scheme you like. However, if you do decided to connect to the Internet in the future, your entire network will have to be re-addressed to use one of the private network IDs.

The preceding network address ranges are listed in Classless Interdomain Routing (CIDR) notation. CIDR notation uses the convention of listing the network address followed by a slash character (/) and then the number of bits in the subnet mask used to mask off the network. In other words, the CIDR notation of 10.0.0.0/8 refers to the network ID 10.0.0.0 with an 8-bit subnet mask (or 255.0.0.0), which in binary is represented as 11111111.00000000.00000000.00000000. The reason for discussing CIDR will become more clear when we begin to look at routing table configuration later in the chapter.

The Internet authorities adopted this new notation for two reasons. The first is that with the growth of the Internet, assigning Class B network IDs (which allow for a maximum of 65,534 hosts per network) to companies that only require 2,000 host IPs on their networks was wasteful—the number of available IP addresses would soon be depleted if that continued. One solution to this was to assign multiple Class C addresses to such organizations. With each Class C address supporting a maximum of 254 hosts, a company requiring 2,000 host IPs would need eight Class C network IDs, which would allow for 2,032 host IDs.

However, a second problem arose from this, which is more of a routing and administrative problem. Each of the Class C network IDs assigned would require its own route on the routing tables of routers on the Internet. CIDR was designed to allow for multiple Class C address spaces to be assigned in order to preserve IP addresses and to deal with the problem of increased administration and complexity generated by the need for multiple routes. CIDR solves the problem of multiple routes by collapsing multiple network ID entries into a single entry that corresponds to all the Class C network IDs assigned to a company. In this example, the eight Class C network IDs are allocated to the company beginning with the 220.78.168.0 network ID, which results in a starting network ID of 220.78.168.0 and an ending network ID of 220.78.175.0. The CIDR entry that would be added to the routing table is 220.78.168.0/21, meaning that hosts in this network would use the subnet mask 255.255.248.0.

Exam Tip

In order for routers to support CIDR, they must be able to support the exchange of routing information in the form or network ID/network mask pairs. The routing protocols RIP v2, OSPF, and Border Gateway Protocol (BGP) v4 support the exchange of paired routing information. RIP v1 does not; therefore, it does not support CIDR.

You will be required to know how to subnet a network into multiple logical segments on the exam. Therefore, to ensure that you are comfortable with this, let's take a look at a couple of subnetting examples.

Subnetting Example 1

As the network architect in your organization, your local ISP has assigned your company a portion of a Class C network. The ISP uses a 27-bit subnet mask to divide the 205.219.129.0 network. First, determine how many subnets and how many hosts per subnet the ISP can support. Then, determine what the available host ranges are for the ISP to use.

To solve this problem, the first step is to use the formula $2^n - 2$ to determine the number of hosts per subnet. To do this, you need to break the subnet mask into binary format. A 27-bit subnet mask is equivalent to 11111111.11111111.11111111. 11100000. This means that the subnet mask used by the ISP would be 255.255.255.224. There are 5 bits available in the fourth octet for the network ID. Using the formula $2^n - 2$, where n equals 5, the maximum number of IP addresses per subnet is 30. To determine the number of subnets, use the formula 2^n, where n equals 3 (the first three bits in the fourth octet that represent the network ID) and you'll find that eight subnets are available.

The last question then becomes how to determine the host ranges. To do this, look at the last octet of the subnet mask in binary, 11100000, and you'll see that the first three bits represent the network ID. These three bits are then used to increment the values between the host ranges. Each host range will contain 30 IP addresses. The first available host range in this example is 205.219.129.1 plus 30 IP addresses, which is 205.219.129.30. The three network bits are added to the last IP in the first host range, giving you the starting point of the second host range, 205.219.129.33, onto which another 30 IP addresses are added. This produces the following eight host ranges:

- 205.219.129.1–205.219.129.30
- 205.219.129.33–205.219.129.62
- 205.219.129.65–205.219.129.94
- 205.219.129.97–205.219.129.126
- 205.219.129.129–205.219.129.158
- 205.219.129.161–205.219.129.190
- 205.219.129.193–205.219.129.222
- 205.219.129.225–205.219.129.254

Subnetting Example 2

Given the subnet mask 255.255.255.192 and the network 221.41.6.0, which of the following IP addresses are on the same subnet?

- 221.41.6.17
- 221.41.6.32
- 221.41.6.45
- 221.41.6.61

- 221.41.6.64
- 221.41.6.73
- 221.41.6.121
- 221.41.6.127
- 221.41.6.135
- 221.41.6.208

In order to solve this problem, you must figure out all the valid host ranges and then analyze whether each of the IP addresses fall within those valid ranges. To accomplish this, you must first determine the number of hosts per subnet. To identify the number of host bits that n will be equal to, write the subnet mask out in binary, as follows:

11111111.11111111.11111111.11000000

This tells you that n is equal to six host bits. Using the formula $2^n - 2$, where n equals 6, you find that each subnet will have 62 IP addresses. The number of available network segments will be 2^2, which is 4. Knowing this you can begin to draw out the valid host ranges, knowing that you will increment the end IP address of each valid host range by 2, thus making the following your valid host ranges:

- 221.41.6.1–221.41.6.62
- 221.41.6.65–221.41.6.126
- 221.41.6.129–221.41.6.190
- 221.41.6.193–221.41.6.254

Knowing the valid IP ranges, you are now able to see which of the preceding IP address fall into the valid ranges. The first four IP addresses, the sixth and seventh and the last two IP addresses in the list are all valid IP addresses.

Exam Tip

Practicing your subnetting skills should be done prior to taking the exam because they will have to be sharp in order for you to be successful on the exam. To assist you in your practicing endeavors, I highly recommend downloading a subnetting tool from http://www.tucows.com. Execute a search on the site for *subnetting* and a number of freeware and shareware tools will result.

Routing Fundamentals

Routing allows networks to scale and maintain bandwidth by segmenting network traffic into manageable pieces. As we have just discussed, subnetting allows networks to be broken into manageable pieces. Routing is required to allow a host on one subnet to communicate with a host on another subnet. Windows 2000 can be configured with the Routing and Remote Access Service to provide both local and remote routing through a variety of connections. These connections include dial-up, Frame Relay, integrated services connections (ISDN), X.25, direct LAN connections, and point-to-point connections through Virtual Private Networks (VPNs). For a router to route IP datagrams, it must be connected to two or more network segments and be configured with a valid IP address for the network segment to which the interface is connected.

A router must be configured to know where to send an IP datagram once it is received. Routing tables are what routers use to figure this out. Routing tables are like air traffic controllers. Air traffic controllers manage and direct traffic in their immediate airspace and make decisions about where to send traffic based on the traffic's destination. Routers are very similar, in the sense that they manage the flow of IP datagram traffic in their immediate "airspace" (the networks they are connected to) by reading the destination IP address in the IP datagram header and forwarding the packet on, based on the rules in its routing table.

Routers also help to improve the efficiency of packet delivery as well through the use of metrics assigned to different routes. A *metric* is a cost that is assigned to a specific route. The lower the cost, the more efficient the route. When it comes to costs and metrics, think of planning a vacation from Toronto to Maui, Hawaii. There are a number of ways in which you can get from Toronto to Maui, but the one with the lowest metric would be a direct flight. A flight that originated in Toronto and took you to Chicago, then Los Angeles, then Honolulu, and finally on to Maui would accomplish the same goal, but because it is much less efficient, it would be assigned a higher metric. (Sounds like the kind of flight you might get when you try to use your air miles to fly—not speaking from experience at all!)

So, you know now that *routing* is the process of forwarding packets between connected networks, and it is part of the Internet Protocol (IP) and uses other network protocol services to forward network traffic and information about routes. There are some terms that I will be using in this chapter that you need to understand to ensure that you grasp all the concepts in this chapter for the exam.

The first term that is used on a regular basis throughout this chapter is *IP datagram* or *packet*. This is the term used to describe each incoming or outgoing packet. IP datagrams contain two IP addresses: the source address of the host sending the pack and the destination address of the host that is to receive the packet.

A second term that is used in routing discussions is *end system*. An end system is a network device that is not able to forward IP datagrams between different network segments. End systems are also referred to as *hosts*.

Intermediate systems is another term used to describe network devices such as bridges, switches, and routers. Intermediate devices are devices that are capable of forwarding IP datagrams on an internetwork.

The term *internetwork* is used to define a environment where two or more networks are connected by an intermediate device.

Lastly, the term *router* will be used. A router is an intermediary device that is designed and optimized for routing traffic on an internetwork. Routers come in two forms: hardware and software. Hardware routers are dedicated intermediate systems designed and optimized for routing. Software routers are nondedicated intermediate systems capable of performing routing, but routing is not generally their sole function, as in the case of a multihomed computer running Windows 2000 Server configured with the Routing and Remote Access Service. This type of software router will be focused on in this chapter and is designed to allow IP datagrams to be routed from one segment to another.

Travel Advisory

Check out the video *Warriors of the Net* at http://www. warriorsofthe.net/movie.html to watch a really well done short video on TCP/IP.

Routing Tables

Routers forward IP datagrams between network segments based on rules that allow for more efficient IP datagram delivery. The rules that are used are stored in a table known as a *routing table*. A routing table contains IP information about all the network segments to which the router is connected and information on how to forward IP datagrams that are destined for networks the router is not directly connected to. Routing tables are built automatically on all computers running the TCP/IP protocol and can be displayed by entering the following command at the command prompt:

```
Route print
```

The results of this command are shown in Figure 7-1.

So that you better understand how the routing table is used to generate the rules for forwarding information, let's explore the composition of the routing table. We will start this exploration by looking at each of the individual columns.

The information in each row of the Network Destination column is used with information in the same row of the Netmask column to find a match for the destination IP address in the IP datagram. The addresses available for use in the Network Destination column range from 0.0.0.0 to 255.255.255.255. If the destination IP address in the IP datagram matches that of the Network Destination column when the netmask is applied, the packet is forwarded to the IP address found on the same row in the Gateway column. If no other network route matches the destination IP address in the IP datagram, the default route is used to forward the IP datagram. The default route is the first listed and has a network destination of 0.0.0.0. The default route is used for destination IP addresses that have no other routes defined.

The netmask is also known as the *subnet mask*. When it's applied to the network destination address, it distinguishes the network ID from the host ID.

The Gateway column identifies the IP address that the local host uses to forward IP datagrams to other IP networks and is defined for each interface.

The Interface column indicates the IP address of the network adapter. This is useful on a multihomed computer that has more than one network adapter to identify which routing information is associated with which interface.

The Metric column specifies the cost of a route. If multiple routes exist to the same destination, the route with the lowest cost is selected over other routes

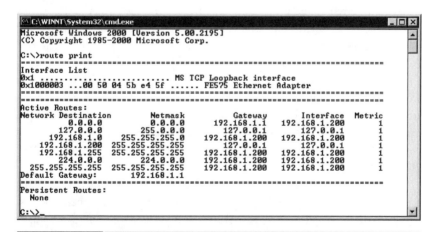

FIGURE 7-1 Displaying the local routing table

because a lower cost generally indicates that the IP datagram will get to its final destination faster or through a shorter number of intermediary devices (known as *hops*). As an IP datagram passes through a router, the IP datagram's time-to-live (TTL) value is decremented by 1. IP datagrams are usually configured with a hop limit of 30, meaning that once an IP datagram passes through 30 routers, the packet expires. This is a safeguard designed to prevent packets from traveling eternally around a large network, never getting to their end destination but consuming bandwidth.

- A Windows 2000 computer running TCP/IP contains four default routing table entries:0.0.0.0 is the default route.
- 127.0.0.1 is the local loopback address.
- 224.0.0.0 is the IP multicast address.
- 255.255.255.255 is the IP broadcast address, which is received by all computers on the network segment.

We will examine the routing table shown in Figure 7-1, line by line, to ensure that you understand its contents and where the rules for forwarding IP packets come from.

The first row represents the default route. The default route is the route that the router uses when no other routes apply to the destination IP address of an IP datagram. In other words, if a user at a computer with an IP address of 192.168.1.2 on your local area network, as shown in the following illustration, wanted to communicate with a remote computer with an IP address of 207.164.59.100 on the Internet, the computer sending the information, known as the *source computer*, would look to its local routing table. This would indicate that the IP datagram is destined for a remote network and, therefore, to send the packet to the client's default gateway for further forwarding. This would result in the IP datagram being sent to the 192.168.1.1 address of the Windows 2000 Server configured as a Network Address Translation (NAT) server. A NAT server, as discussed in detail in Chapter 8, allows for internal private IP addresses to be used on the internal network and hidden from the Internet. NAT then translates the IP header information and changes the original source IP address of the internal client to be the external IP address of the NAT server. In this case, the source IP address would be changed from 192.168.1.2 to 24.164.59.39 and sent out to the destination IP of 207.164.59.100.

The second row in the routing table is used to determine where to route IP datagrams with a destination IP of 127.0.0.1, which is the local loopback address. The local loopback address is a reserved address space used for troubleshooting IP connectivity. If you are experiencing TCP/IP communication problems and want

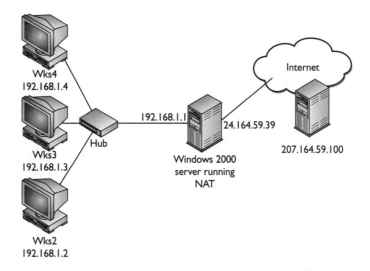

to rule out the network adapter as the problem, you simply ping the loopback address, 127.0.0.1. If you receive a response, you have confirmed that your network adapter is functioning correctly and can continue to troubleshoot the problem.

The third row contains the network ID for the network that the local computer is connected to—in this case, 192.168.1.0/24. The network ID here is shown in CIDR notation, with the network ID separated by a slash character (/) from the number of bits in the subnet mask for the network. In this case, the local client is on the 192.168.1.0 network, which uses a 24-bit subnet mask (or a subnet mask of 255.255.255.0).

As you can see, a strong understanding of subnetting is required to allow you to read a routing table and determine where an IP datagram will be forwarded to.

Manage and Monitor IP Routing Protocols

Now that you know that a router uses its routing table to determine where to forward IP datagrams based on the destination IP address in the header of the IP datagram, the next question arises. Where do routers learn about and obtain the routes in their routing tables? The answer is that there are a number of ways for a router to learn about and obtain routes.

One way is through manual configuration, where an administrator adds static routes to a router. Another way is through dynamic configuration, where routers exchange route information among themselves. In order for routers to dynamically exchange information, they must support a common way of communicating or a common network routing protocol.

The two most common routing protocols for Internet Protocol routing are the Routing Information Protocol (RIP) and Open Shortest Path First (OSPF). Windows 2000 Server supports both routing protocols, which we will look at in more detail in the next sections.

Objective 7.03   Manage and Monitor Internal Routing

RIP is a routing protocol designed to be implemented in small and mid-size organizations and is relatively easy to configure. RIP is limited to smaller organizations because it has a maximum hop count of 15, meaning that it considers any IP address more than 15 hops away to be unreachable.

Windows 2000 supports both versions of RIP: version 1 and version 2. Version 2, the more recent version, includes the following additional features:

- Peer security
- Route filtering
- Multicasting (version 1 uses broadcasting for its announcements)

Routers that use RIP only contain route information in their routing tables for the networks that they are physically connected to when they are initialized. RIP, however, is designed to periodically broadcast announcements of its routing table entries, and other routers configured to use RIP on the same segments receive these broadcasts and use the information in them to update their own routing tables. One downside to RIP version 1 is that the announcements are distributed through a broadcast, which increases the amount of traffic on the local segment. RIP is typically limited to networks with fewer than 50 servers.

RIP also uses a process known as *triggered updates*, which are immediate broadcasts used to update network changes detected by a RIP router, such as an interface becoming available or unavailable on the network.

The following illustration shows how RIP routers are configured at initialization, and the second illustration shows the router configuration after the routers broadcast their route table information.

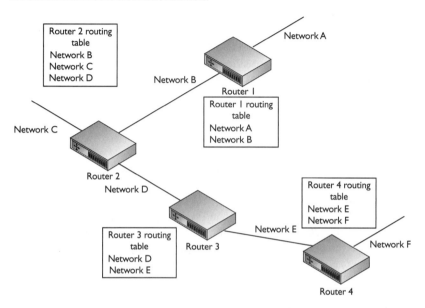

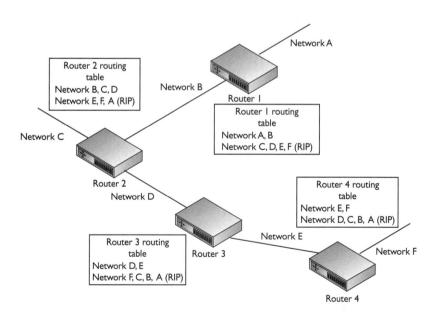

As you can see in the first illustration, at initialization the routers are only aware of the network segments they are directly connected to. For example, Router 2 only knows of networks B, C, and D, and Router 1 only knows of networks A and B. After the RIP announcements, however, you can see in the second illustration that the routers are now aware of all other network segments in the internetwork, and their individual routing tables have been updated to reflect this. This can be seen by looking at Router 2. Notice that it is still aware of network segments B, C, and D but is also aware, through RIP announcements, of network segments E, F, and A.

Installing RIP

RIP is installed using the RRAS snap-in. Simply follow these steps:

1. Open RRAS.
2. Expand the name of the server and then expand IP Routing. Right-click General and select New Routing Protocol from the context menu.
3. In the New Routing Protocol dialog box, shown in Figure 7-2, select RIP Version 2 for Internet Protocol and then click OK.

Configuring RIP

Once RIP is installed, it must be configured to use one or more interfaces. To configure an interface for RIP, follow these steps:

FIGURE 7-2   Installing RIP

1. Open RRAS.
2. Expand the name of the server and then expand IP Routing. Right-click RIP and select New Interface from the context menu.
3. Select an interface from the list in the New Interface for RIP Version 2 for Internet Protocol dialog box and click OK.
4. The RIP Properties dialog box will appear, as shown in Figure 7-3. Click OK to accept the default configuration settings or proceed to configure the settings to meet your requirements.

On the General tab of the RIP Properties dialog box shown in Figure 7-3 are a number of configuration choices that we will look at. The first section in the dialog box is titled Operation Mode. This section allows you to specify how RIP announcements are handled. There are two options to choose from in the drop-down dialog box under Operations Mode: Periodic Update Mode and Auto-Static Update Mode.

Periodic Update Mode configures RIP to send announcements periodically. If Periodic Update Mode is selected, the announcement interval can be configured on the Advanced tab. The setting is the default for a LAN interface.

Auto-Static Update Mode configures the RIP server to send RIP announcements only when other routers request an update. In Auto-Static Update Mode, all routes learned through RIP announcements are marked as static in the routing

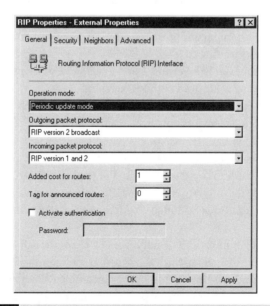

FIGURE 7-3 Adding and configuring a RIP interface

table and will remain there until automatically deleted. The Auto-Static Update Mode setting is the default for demand-dial interfaces.

Outgoing RIP announcements can be configured through the drop-down box under Outgoing Packet Protocol on the General tab of the RIP Properties dialog box. Here, you have four options to choose from: RIP Version 1 Broadcast, RIP Version 2 Broadcast, RIP Version 2 Multicast, and Silent RIP.

The RIP Version 1 Broadcast option should be used in networks that contain only RIP version 1 routers. As the option name suggests, the RIP announcement is sent out via broadcasts.

Use the RIP Version 2 Broadcast option if your network contains both RIP version 1 and RIP version 2 routers. Again, as the option name suggests, the RIP announcement is sent out via broadcasts. This is the default for a LAN interface.

Use the RIP Version 2 Multicast option only if the other routers on the network are RIP version 2 routers also. This option will send the RIP announcements out as multicasts, which helps to minimize the amount of routing protocol traffic on the network. This is the default setting for demand-dial interfaces.

The last option is Silent RIP, which configures the RIP server so that it does not send out RIP announcements but rather listens for other RIP server announcements and updates its routing table accordingly.

How a RIP server handles incoming RIP announcements is configured from the drop-down menu under Incoming Packet Protocol. Here, four options are available: Ignore Incoming Packets, RIP Version 1 and 2, RIP Version 1 Only, and RIP Version 2 Only.

Choose the Ignore Incoming Packets option when you don't want the RIP router to update its routing table.

The second option, RIP Version 1 and 2, is the default option and accepts incoming announcements from both RIP versions.

The last two options are self-explanatory. RIP Version 1 Only and RIP Version 2 Only except announcements only from routers running the respective version of RIP selected.

A cost can also be added in the Added Cost for Routes box. The cost specified will be added to the hop count as advertised in the RIP message. The higher the cost, the less likely the interface will be used if an interface with a lower cost exists. The cost value is limited to 1 through 15. After 15 hops, RIP will discard of the IP datagram.

The last configuration option on the General tab of the RIP Properties dialog box is Activate Authentication, which allows you to configure the RIP interface with a password. If authentication is activated, any incoming RIP version 2 announcements will have to include the same password. The use of RIP authentication is not highly secure because the passwords are transmitted in clear text.

The Security tab on the RIP Properties dialog box, shown in Figure 7-4, is where we will turn our attention to next.

The Security tab is used to define how a router accepts and announces routes. The security settings can also be used to block RIP announcement information from unauthorized routers. The drop-down box under Action allows you to select one of two choices: For Incoming Routes or For Outgoing Routes. The default is set to accept all routes. This can be changed to one of the other two options:

- Accept All Routes in the Ranges Listed
- Ignore All Routes in the Ranges Listed

Selecting one of these two options requires that beginning and ending IP addresses be entered in the section underneath these options in the RIP Properties dialog box.

The Neighbors tab, shown in Figure 7-5 (which, incidentally, is spelled incorrectly in the Canadian version of the operating system) is used to list RIP routers that you wish to send announcements to that are located on different network segments. You have three options to choose from that allow you to control how the router interacts with the listed neighboring routers.

The Use Broadcast or Multicast Only option sends RIP announcements using the outgoing packet protocol specified on the General tab. This is the default setting.

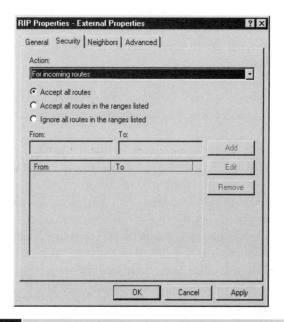

FIGURE 7-4   Configuring the security options on a RIP interface

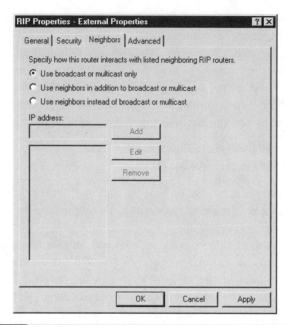

FIGURE 7-5   Configuring the Neighbors tab on the RIP Properties dialog box

The Use Neighbors in Addition to Broadcast or Multicast option sends RIP announcements using unicast messages in addition to using the outgoing packet protocol specified on the General tab.

The Use Neighbors Instead of Broadcast or Multicast option sends RIP announcements by unicast only to the neighboring routers that are specified. This option should be used if you are working with non-broadcast networks such as Frame Relay.

The Advanced tab, shown in Figure 7-6, allows for the configuration of a number of options. The first option allows you to configure the periodic announcement interval. This is set to 30 seconds by default and only needs to be configured if Periodic Update Mode has been selected for the operation mode on the General tab.

The second setting on the Advanced tab is Time Before Routes Expire (in seconds). This has a default setting of 180 seconds (or 3 minutes) and is used to expire records that were added through RIP announcements that are not updated.

The Enable Split-Horizon Processing option is enabled by default and prevents routes learned through RIP announcements from being announced again on the network.

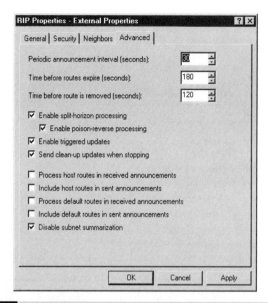

The Enable Poison-Reverse Processing option is only available after split horizon is enabled. This option allows routes learned on a network to be announced with an unreachable metric of 16 in RIP announcements sent out of the network.

The Enable Triggered Updates option allows new routes and metric changes to initiate immediate updates of only the changes that have occurred. The maximum delay of triggered updates is 5 seconds by default but can be configured on the global RIP Properties dialog box, shown in Figure 7-7, by right-clicking RIP in RRAS and selecting Properties.

The Send Clean-up Updates when Stopping option instructs RIP to send an announcement with all routes that are marked with a metric of 15 if RIP is stopped on that interface. This allows all neighboring routers to immediately update their routing tables to specify that the routes available on the router taken offline are no longer available. This box is enabled by default.

The Process Host Routes in Received Announcements option is not enabled by default, which means that host routes received through RIP announcements are ignored. When this option is enabled, host routes received by RIP announcements are accepted.

The Include Host Routes in Sent Announcements option indicates whether host routes are included in RIP announcements. The default setting is that host routes are not included in RIP announcements.

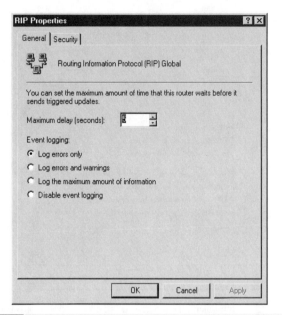

FIGURE 7-7   Configuring the maximum delay of triggered updates

The Process Default Routes in Received Announcements option indicates whether default routes in received RIP announcements are accepted. The default is that default routes are ignored.

The Include Default Routes in Sent Announcements option indicates whether default routes are included in RIP announcements. The default is that default routes are not included.

The Disable Subnet Summarization option indicates that subnet routes should not be summarized by class-based network ID for outgoing announcements on networks that are not part of a class-based network. Subnet summarization is disabled by default and requires RIP Version 2 Broadcast or RIP Version 2 Multicast be selected for the outgoing packet protocol on the General tab of the RIP Properties dialog box.

Manage and Monitor Border Routing

The second routing protocol supported in Windows 2000 is Open Shortest Path First (OSPF). OSPF is designed to be used in larger network environments and uses an algorithm to calculate the shortest path between the router and adjacent networks. OSPF routers maintain a link state database, which is a dynamic map of the internetwork that changes as modifications to the network topology are made. OSPF routers synchronize their link state database and recalculate their routing tables with other OSPF routers on the same network segment. Thanks to the scalability provided by the link state database, OSPF is geared toward larger networks but is more complex to configure than RIP.

Exam Tip

OSPF sends its router information using either multicast or unicast messages but never broadcasts.

Installing OSPF

Installing OSPF is very similar to installing RIP. Follow these steps:

1. Open RRAS.
2. Expand the name of the server and then expand IP Routing. Right-click General and select New Routing Protocol from the context menu.
3. In the New Routing Protocol dialog box, shown earlier in Figure 7-2, select Open Shortest Path First (OSPF) and click OK.

Configuring OSPF

The first task in the configuration process of OSPF is to add a new interface. Here are the steps to follow:

1. Open RRAS.
2. Expand the name of the server and then expand IP Routing. Right-click OSPF and select New Interface from the context menu.
3. Select an interface from the list in the New Interface for Open Shortest Path First (OSPF) dialog box and then click OK.
4. The OSPF Properties dialog box for the interface selected will appear, as shown in Figure 7-8. Click OK to accept the default configuration settings or proceed to configure the settings to meet your requirements.

The General tab of the OSPF Properties dialog box has a number of configuration options that we will look at.

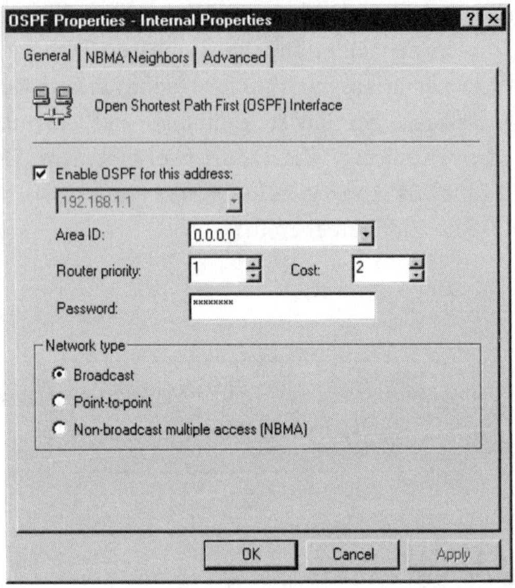

FIGURE 7-8   Configuring an interface for OSPF

The option Enable OSPF for this address is used to enable OSPF for a specific interface if more than one IP address is bound to the interface. OSPF options must be enabled or disabled for each IP address bound to a single interface. The Area ID, Router Priority, Cost, and Password properties apply to only the IP address specified, allowing different values to be defined for different IP addresses on the same interface, if required.

One area ID must be associated with each IP address you are configuring. The 0.0.0.0 area ID is the default area ID and is the only one automatically created. Different IP addresses can be assigned to different area IDs, or they can all be in the same area ID.

The Router Priority property is used to specify which router is the designated router when multiple routers exist on the network. The router with the highest router priority becomes the designated router.

The Cost property is used to define the efficiency and priority of the router in relation to other routers. The router with the lowest cost is used over those with higher costs.

The Password property allows you to specify a password for router authentication with other routers in the area. The default password is set to 12345678. The password property is grayed out if plain-text passwords are disabled for the area.

The three network types that can be configured are broadcast, point-to-point, and non-broadcast multiple access (NBMA). Choose the Broadcast option to identify that the interface is connected to a broadcast-based network type, such as Ethernet. Select the Point-to-Point option if the interface is connected to a point-to-point network, such as a T1 or ISDN connection, and choose the Non-Broadcast Multiple Access (NBMA) option when the interface is connected to an NBMA network such as Frame Relay.

The NBMA Neighbors tab, shown in Figure 7-9, only requires configuration when the NBMA option is selected in the Network Types section on the General tab, described previously. This tab allows you to configure the neighboring routers and specify an IP address and routing priority for each.

The Advanced tab, shown in Figure 7-10, allows you to configure timings for various options.

The Transit Delay setting is your estimate of how long (in seconds) it will take to transmit a link state update packet over the specified interface.

The Retransmit Interval setting is the expected time between retransmission of the link state advertisements. This value should be double the Transit Delay value and should be increased when you're transmitting over slow connections.

The Hello Interval setting is the period of time between hello broadcasts. Hello broadcasts are used to discover changes to the network structure, such as new routers. The Hello Interval value must be the same for all routers on the same network.

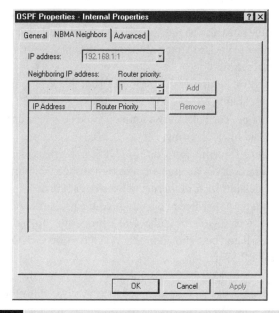

FIGURE 7-9   Configuring the NBMA properties for an OSPF interface

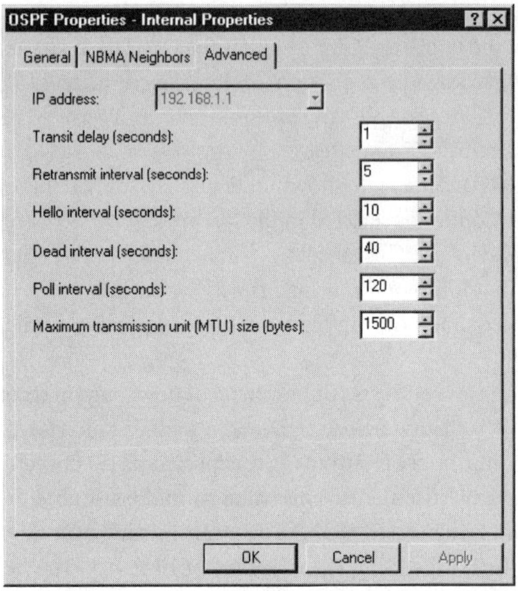

FIGURE 7-10   Configuring the advanced properties for an OSPF interface

The Dead Interval setting is the period of time after which routers on the same network consider a router offline if they haven't received a response to their hello packets. This value must also be the same for all routers on the same network. It is common to configure the Dead Interval setting with a time four times greater than the Hello Interval setting.

The Poll Interval setting is the period of time between network polls on NBMA interfaces. Polling is the way routers determine whether an offline router has come back online. The Poll Interval setting should be at least double the length of time of the Dead Interval setting.

The Maximum Transmission Unit (MTU) Size setting is used to specify the maximum size in which IP datagrams can be transmitted without requiring fragmentation. The default size for Ethernet networks is 1500.

Now that you have specified and configured the properties of a router interface, you must also configure the global OSPF properties. To open up the global OSPF Properties dialog box, shown in Figure 7-11, right-click OSPF and select Properties in the RRAS snap-in.

The first tab in the global OSPF Properties dialog box is the General tab. On this tab, the IP address of the computer used to uniquely identify the router is displayed by default and can be edited on a multihomed computer.

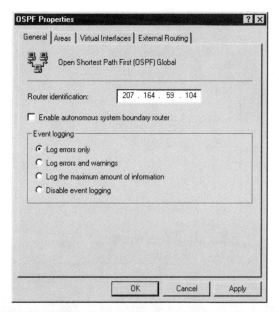

FIGURE 7-11   Configuring the OSPF global properties

The Enable Autonomous System Boundary Routing option can be enabled to allow the router to advertise routing information from a source other than simply the link state database, which might include static addresses and routes received through RIP announcements.

The Event Logging section can also be configured with one of these four self-explanatory options:

- Log errors only
- Log errors and warnings
- Log the maximum amount of information
- Disable event logging

The Areas tab, shown in Figure 7-12, can be used to add, remove, and edit additional network areas. An *area* is a 32-bit number in dotted decimal notation, much like an IP address, but it does not have to correlate to any IP address or network ID on the network. An area is used to identify specific network ranges in order to summarize routes within those defined IP networks. All OSPF routers must belong to a single area.

The Virtual Interfaces tab can only be configured if one or more additional areas have been created in the Areas tab. Virtual links create a connection to the

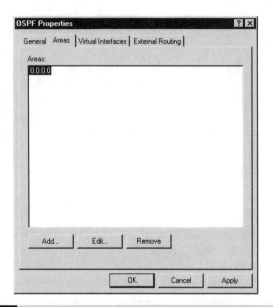

FIGURE 7-12   Configuring the Areas tab of the global OSPF Properties dialog box

backbone area router (0.0.0.0) from an area border router that isn't physically connected to the backbone area. The virtual link is used to send routing data between the two areas and has configurable properties such as a transit delay, retransmit interval, hello internal, dead interval, and plain-text password.

The External Routing tab is only configurable if the Enable Autonomous System Boundary Router option is enabled on the General tab. If this option is enabled, the External Routing tab can be configured to list the route sources from which the router will accept incoming route information. A list of route filters can also be defined and configured to accept or ignore the list of routes based on their destination addresses or network masks.

Exam Tip

Both RIP and OSPF can be used on the same network, but an order of preference must be set. When the same routing protocol finds two different routes for the same destination, the metric is used to choose the best route. When two different routing protocols find two different routes to the same destination, the route found by the preferred protocol is used.

Internet Group Message Protocol Multicast Forwarding

There are two types of IP traffic: unicast and multicast. Unicast traffic is sent to a single location—the destination IP address in the IP datagram header. Multicast traffic is sent to a multicast IP address, and all clients configured to listen for multicast traffic receive the same IP datagram, thus allowing for more than one client to receive the same IP datagram instead of requiring individual IP datagrams to be sent out to all clients. Multicasting is most often used in audio or videoconferencing applications.

Exam Tip

Windows 2000 does not include any multicast routing protocols but does include limited multicast routing functionality through multicast forwarding.

Windows 2000 supports multicast forwarding through the IGMP routing protocol, which allows a computer running Windows 2000 Server to listen for multicast traffic on all configured interfaces and to forward that traffic on to networks that have multicast clients. The IGMP protocol listens for IGMP membership report packets that are used by multicast clients to identify themselves to a multicast router or forwarder. When the Windows 2000 Server receives a membership report packet, it updates its multicast forwarding table, allowing it to forward multicast traffic to clients on the networks configured in the forwarding table.

Interfaces on your Windows 2000 router can be configured to function in one of two modes: IGMP router mode or IGMP proxy mode.

IGMP Router Mode

In IGMP router mode, the interface on which you configure IGMP sets the network adapter to multicast-promiscuous mode. Multicast-promiscuous mode passes all multicast packets received on the interface up the protocol stack for further processing.

Travel Advisory
Not all network adapters support multicast-promiscuous mode. Verify support for this mode in the documentation for the network adapter. 

The interface on which you configure IGMP also listens for multicast membership report messages and updates its forwarding table.

Exam Tip
When multiple routers in a network are configured with the IGMP routing protocol, one router is elected to query and update all membership queries. 

IGMP Proxy Mode

A Windows 2000 Server configured in IGMP proxy mode allows IGMP traffic to be passed through it to and from multicast clients on the Internet. This is referred to as a *multicast backbone* or *Mbone*. The IGMP proxy also listens for IGMP membership report packets and forwards them on all interfaces running in IGMP router mode, thus allowing multicast groups connected to the proxy mode router to pass their membership report packets to IGMP routers.

Update a Windows 2000–Based Routing Table by Means of Static Routes

The third option for configuring routers is to manually configure static routes. In a small environment with few network segments that are static for long periods of time, the use of static routes can allow routing to function properly and reduce the amount of traffic consumed through unnecessary broadcasts of routing information, which is done regularly by routing protocols such as RIP.

There are two ways to add static routes. The first method uses the RRAS snap-in. You simply expand the server name, expand IP Routing, right-click Static Routes, and select New Static Route from the context menu. This will bring up the Static Route dialog box, shown in Figure 7-13.

To create a static route, you must first specify the interface for which you want to associate the route. Next, you must enter a destination network ID, followed by a network mask (subnet mask) and the IP address of the gateway you want IP datagrams that fall within this route to use. You can also set a metric for the route if there are other routes available and you want to indicate the efficiency of this route over the others. Routes with lower metrics will always be chosen first over routes with higher metrics.

The second method for configuring static routes involves entering **route** at the command prompt. The command syntax for the **route** command when adding a route is as follows:

```
Route add <destination network ID> mask <network mask> <gateway>
metric <number> if <number>
```

In the preceding **route** command, **add** is used to indicate the addition of a route and is followed by the destination network ID. The word **mask** follows. Then the network mask is entered followed by the gateway IP address where you want traffic to be routed to if it meets the criteria of the route. This is followed by

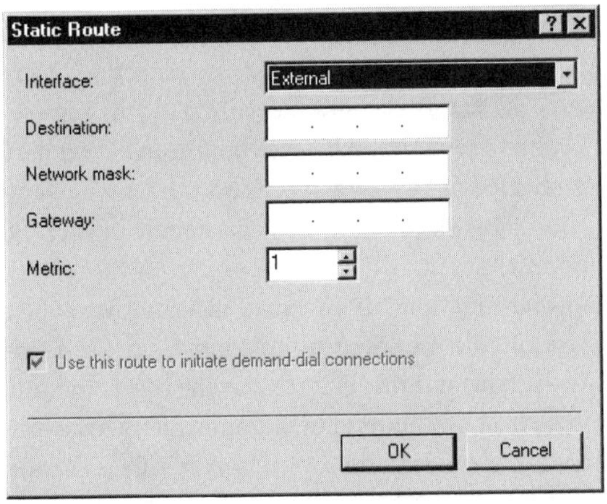

FIGURE 7-13   Configuring a static route in RRAS

metric and a number for the metric, followed by **if**, representing the interface and the number of the interface for which you are adding the route.

By default, routes added through the **route** command are not persistent, meaning that when the computer is rebooted, all static routes are lost. To ensure that static routes persist after a reboot, the **–p** switch can be used when adding the root to mark it persistent. Here's an example:

```
Route -p add <destination network ID> mask <network mask> <gateway>

metric <number> if <number>
```

The **route** command includes a number of other commands as well that you should be familiar with. The **route delete** command followed by the route information that you wish to delete can be used to delete static routes from a routing table. The **route print** command, as you have seen earlier in this chapter, is used to display the routing table. The **route –f** command can be used to clear the routing table of all gateway addresses, which may be required if the IP addresses of all your routers are changed.

Objective 7.06   Implement Demand-Dial Routing

Windows 2000 can be configured to use demand-dial connections, which allow a Windows 2000 router to initiate a connection to a remote network when the router receives an IP datagram destined for the remote network. This allows the connection to be active only when communication needs to take place and remain disconnected but waiting to connect the remainder of the time. This is one way that your network configuration can significantly reduce your organization's connection costs.

The demand-dial functionality included in Windows 2000 also allows for demand-dial filters and dial-out hours to be configured. Demand-dial filters can be used to specify the type of traffic that triggers the router to initiate the dial-on-demand connection. Dial-out hours allow administrators to govern when a router is allowed to make a dial-on demand connection, ideally preventing connectivity during times of the day when telecommunication costs are more expensive.

Exam Tip

If you enable demand-dial routing on a computer that is a member of an Active Directory domain, the computer account must be added to the RAS and IAS Servers security group before demand-dial routing will work. When a member of the Domain Admins group enables RRAS, the computer is automatically added to the group.

The next illustration shows a geographically dispersed network where the head office of the company is located in Calgary and two of the company's many branch offices, Branch 1 and Branch 2, are located more than 6 hours away in small mining towns, with cost-effective connectivity only available through dial-up connections. Instead of maintaining expensive costly connections, the use of demand-dial connections can be implemented, thus taking advantage of demand-dial filters that will govern what routes trigger the initiation of a demand-dial connection. Two demand-dial filters will have to be configured for Demand Dial Interface 1 in the Calgary head office.

The first connection will allow the head office to create a connection with Branch 1. We will give this connection the name Branch Office 1 and set the user credential to Calgary. We will then create a static route that consists of an IP address 192.168.2.1 with a mask of 255.255.0.0 for the Demand Dial Interface 1. This allows any IP datagrams sent to the network ID 192.168.2.0/16 to be routed to the Branch Office 1 network by initiating a demand-dial connection using Demand Dial Interface 1 and having it connect to Demand Dial Interface 2.

The second connection on Call Router will be named Branch Office 2. Again, we'll set the user credential to Calgary and define a static route with an IP address of 192.168.3.1, a mask of 255.255.0.0 and use the Demand Dial Interface 1. This allows any IP datagrams sent to the network ID 192.168.3.0/16 to be routed to the Branch Office 2 network by initiating a demand-dial connection using Demand Dial Interface 1 and having it connect to Demand Dial Interface 3. Additional steps could also be taken to configure each of the branch offices with a demand-dial connection to the head office in Calgary to allow users in the branch offices to send information to the head office through a demand-dial connection.

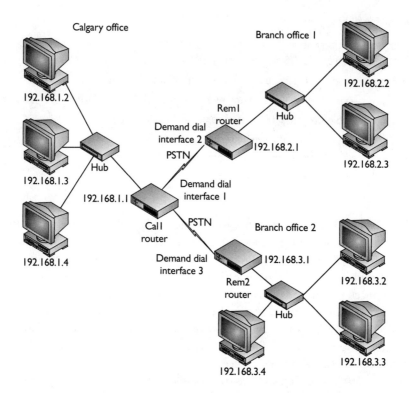

The first step in creating and allowing demand-dial connections is to ensure that each of the devices you are going to use has demand-dial routing enabled. Demand-dial routing is enabled by following these steps:

1. Open RRAS.
2. Expand the name of the server. Right-click Ports and then select Properties.
3. In the Ports Properties dialog box, select the device that you wish to configure for demand-dial routing and click the Configure button.
4. In the Configure Device dialog box, shown in Figure 7-14, place a check mark in the box next to Demand-Dial Routing Connections (Inbound and Outbound).

Exam Tip

Remote access policies configured in RRAS can be used with demand-dial routing to define and control conditions and settings on the answering router.

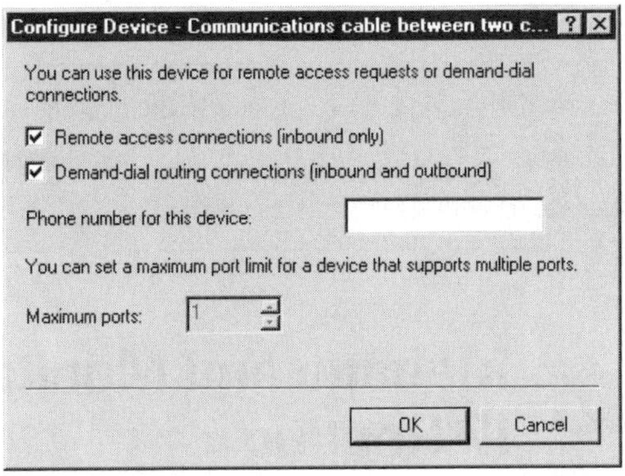

FIGURE 7-14   Configuring ports to allow demand-dial connections

If the demand-dial option does not show up, you must first enable the demand-dial connection in the RRAS server's Properties dialog box.

The next step in the demand-dial process is the creation of a demand-dial interface, which is described in the following steps:

1. Open RRAS.
2. Expand the name of the server. Right-click Routing Interfaces and select New Demand Dial Interface from the context menu.
3. Click Next on the Demand Dial Interface Wizard and enter a name for the interface. Select Next.
4. Select the type of demand-dial interface you want to create. You have two choices here. The first is to use a modem, ISDN adapter, or another physical device, and the second is to use a VPN. Once you have selected one of the two choices, click Next.
5. Select the Transports and Security options to use for this connection and click Next. You have multiple options to choose from:

   - Route IP packets on this interface.
   - Route IPX packets on this interface.
   - Add a user account so a remote router can dial in.
   - Send a plain-text password if that is the only way to connect.
   - Use scripting to complete the connection with the router.

6. In the Dial Out Credentials dialog box, enter the username, domain, and password for the interface to use when connecting to the remote router. These credentials must match the dial-in credentials configured on the remote router. Click Next and then Finish.

Exam Tip

For two-way demand-dial routing to work properly, the dial-out credentials of the calling router must match the interface name of the demand-dial interface on both sides of the connection.

Manage and Monitor IP Routing

The management and monitoring of your IP routers has a significant impact on the security within your network. There is always a tradeoff to be made between security and functionality. By default, when a Windows 2000 server is configured as a router, it is optimized for functionality as opposed to security, allowing all traffic to pass through the router. Once the router is functioning correctly, the next step, depending on the requirements of your network, is to configure it from a security perspective. One of the features available to allow you to accomplish this is packet filtering.

Packet Filtering

An IP router can be configured to allow or deny the forwarding of specific types of IP traffic. The ability to allow and deny different IP traffic types can be an extremely value component in your security strategy. To better understand the IP filtering process, let's use the example shown on the next page.

This example shows three networks—networks A, B and C—all connected to the same router using three different interfaces, all bound with IP addresses for their respective network. IP filters are set up for the interfaces on networks A and B. If a user on network A tries to ping a computer on network B or C, the ping request will not be permitted thanks to the input filter configured on the interface connected to network A that blocks the passing of all Internet Control Message Protocol (ICMP) traffic. The same user, however, could open an Internet browser and browse to an intranet server on either network B or C and connect without any problem because the input filter has been created to block ICMP traffic only—not HTTP traffic or any other types of traffic.

Input filters preprocess IP datagrams coming into a network interface and subject the IP datagrams to the rules configured within them. If any of the rules

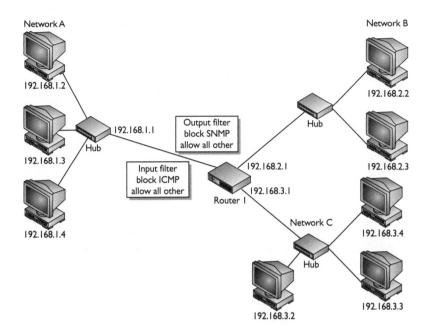

of a filter match, the filter looks for how to handle a match. It has two choices: Deny the IP datagram to be routed or allow the IP datagram to be routed.

Another example of packet filtering using the preceding example can be seen if a user on network A tries to manage a computer using the Simple Network Management Protocol on network C. The SNMP packet will be successfully routed through interface 192.168.1.1 but will be blocked on interface 192.168.2.1 due to the output filter on that interface.

Like input filters, output filters are capable of denying or allowing specific IP traffic to leave the interface. An output filter postprocesses the IP datagram before it is released onto the physical network that the interface is connected to. In this example, SNMP traffic is denied through an output filter configured on interface 192.168.2.1 but all other traffic is allowed through.

Configuring IP Filters

IP filters can be configured by following these steps:

1. Open RRAS.
2. Expand the name of the server and then expand IP Routing and select General.

3. Right-click the interface on which you wish to configure an IP filter and select Properties.

4. On the General tab of the Interface Properties dialog box, select either the Input Filters or Output Filters button.

5. Selecting the Input Filters button will open the Input Filters dialog box, where you must click Add.

6. This will display the Add IP Filter dialog box, shown in Figure 7-15.

7. You can place a check mark in the box next to Source Network and specify the IP address and subnet mask of the source network. If you do not choose a specific source network, it will be set to Any.

8. Alternatively, you can place a check mark in the box next to Destination Network and specify the IP address and subnet mask of the destination network. If you do not choose a specific destination network, it will be set to Any.

9. Leave the Protocol field set to Any or select an alternative protocol. Selecting an alternative protocol may require you to specify a source and destination port on which the service protocol you wish to block operates.

10. Click OK. Back on the Input Filters dialog box, select how you want to filter the specified protocols and click OK. Here are the two choices:

- Receive all packets except those that meet the criteria below.
- Drop all packets except those that meet the criteria below.

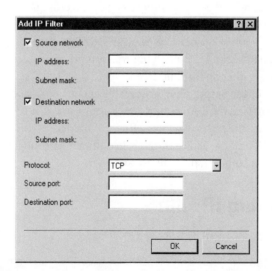

FIGURE 7-15   Adding an input filter

Exam Tip

You should be very familiar with how to configure input and output filters for popular protocols such as **PPTP, DNS, L2TP,** and so on.

To ensure you have a solid understanding of the common types of filtering scenarios, the following subsections review how to implement HTTP, FTP, PPTP, and L2TP filters as well as how to deny spoofed packets from private IP addresses.

Filtering Web Traffic

The use of the Internet is commonplace throughout most organizations in North America, Europe, and parts of Asia and Australia. Because of the rapid adoption of the Internet in most organizations, there can be a need to filter out Web-based traffic, such as HTTP, on certain internal network segments. IP filtering can also be a major component of your Web server security plan and used to block traffic on all ports but TCP port 80, on which the HTTP protocol operates by default. This will help to protect the Web server from malicious attackers on the Internet or the company intranet.

To configure a Web server to accept only HTTP and secure HTTP traffic, use the Drop All Packets Except Those That Meet the Criteria Below filter action and configure the following IP filters:

- Create an input filter for the destination IP address of the Web server, select TCP from the protocol list, and add port 80 as the destination port.
- Create an input filter for the destination IP address of the Web server, select TCP from the protocol list, and add port 443 as the destination port. This will allow Secure Sockets Layer (SSL) connections to the server.
- Create an output filter for the source IP address of the Web server, select TCP from the protocol list, and add port 80 as the source port.
- Create an output filter for the source IP address of the Web server, select TCP from the protocol list, and add port 443 as the source port.

Filtering FTP Traffic

IP filters can also be created to permit or deny FTP traffic. To configure an FTP server to only allow FTP traffic, use the Drop All Packets Except Those That Meet the Criteria Below filter action and configure the following IP filters:

- Create an input filter with the destination IP address of the FTP server, select TCP from the protocol list, and add port 21 as the destination port. Port 21 is the FTP control port that negotiates the initial connection.
- Create an input filter with the destination IP address of the FTP server, select TCP from the protocol list, and add port 20 as the destination port. Port 20 is the FTP data port used in the transmission of data.
- Create an output filter for the source IP address of the FTP server, select TCP from the protocol list, and add port 21 as the source port.
- Create an output filter for the source IP address of the FTP server, select TCP from the protocol list, and add port 20 as the source port.

Filtering PPTP Traffic

To filter Point-to-Point Tunneling Protocol (PPTP) traffic on computers configured as PPTP servers to allow only PPTP traffic in and out of these servers, use the Drop All Packets Except Those That Meet the Criteria Below filter action and configure the following IP filters:

- Create an input filter with the destination IP address of the PPTP server, select TCP from the protocol list, and add port 1723 as the destination port.
- Create an input filter with the destination IP address of the PPTP server, select Other from the protocol list, and add the protocol number 47. Protocol number 47 represents the Generic Routing Encapsulation (GRE) protocol, which PPTP uses to encapsulate PPP frames.
- Create an output filter for the source IP address of the PPTP server, select TCP from the protocol list, and add port 1723 as the source port.
- Create an output filter for the source IP address of the PPTP server, select Other from the protocol list, and add the protocol number 47.

If the PPTP server is also used as a PPTP client to initiate PPTP connections to remote PPTP servers, the following additional IP filters will be required:

- Create an input filter with the destination IP address of the PPTP server, select TCP (established) from the protocol list, and add port 1723 as the source port.
- Create an output filter with the source IP address of the PPTP server, select TCP (established) from the protocol list, and add port 1723 as the destination port.

The TCP (established) filter is used to allow traffic on the TCP connection established by the PPTP client. This prevents other outside users for sending IP datagrams from applications configured to use port 1723.

Filtering L2TP Traffic

To filter Layer 2 Tunneling Protocol (L2TP) traffic on computers configured as L2TP servers to allow only L2TP traffic in and out of these servers, use the Drop All Packets Except Those That Meet the Criteria Below filter action and configure the following IP filters:

- Create an input filter with the destination IP address of the L2TP server, select UDP from the protocol list, and add port 1701 as the destination port.
- Create an input filter with the destination IP address of the L2TP server, select UDP from the protocol list, and add port 500 as the destination port.
- Create an output filter for the source IP address of the L2TP server, select UDP from the protocol list, and add port 1701 as the source port.
- Create an output filter for the source IP address of the L2TP server, select UDP from the protocol list, and add port 500 as the source port.

L2TP uses UDP port 1701 and UDP port 500 for the Internet Key Exchange (IKE). It is IKE that creates the IPSec security association. IPSec itself uses the Encapsulation Security Payload (ESP) header, which has a protocol ID of 50, but because IPSec first processes the incoming and outgoing packets and removes the ESP header, IP filters for protocol ID 50 are not required.

Filtering Spoofed IP Packets from Private IP Addresses

To filter spoofed IP packets from specific private IP addresses of computers configured as Windows 2000 routers, use the Accept All Packets Except Those That Meet the Criteria Below filter action and configure the following IP filters:

- Create an input filter on the Internet interface with the source IP address of 10.0.0.0 and a subnet mask 255.0.0.0.
- Create an input filter on the Internet interface with the source IP address of 172.16.0.0 and a subnet mask 255.240.0.0.

- Create an input filter on the Internet interface with the source IP address of 192.168.0.0 and a subnet mask 255.255.0.0.

Configuring your router connected to the Internet with these packet filters will prevent denial-of-service attacks from flooding your router. A denial-of-service attack occurs when a TCP connection requests packets from addresses that cannot accept a reply. An IP address sent to a private network address on the Internet receives an ICMP Destination Unreachable message.

CHECKPOINT

✔ **Objective 7.01:** Install, Configure, and Troubleshoot IP Routing Protocols   There are three classes of networks that you can use to assign IP addresses from: Class A, B and C. The first octet of Class A, B, and C networks will have values ranging from 1–126, 128–191, and 192–223, respectively. The maximum number of available hosts on a network segment can be calculated using the formula $2^n - 2$, where n is the number of bits in the subnet used for the host ID. Four network IDs have been assigned for use in private networks: 10.0.0.0/8, 169.254.0.0/16, 172.16.0.0/12 and 192.168.0.0/16. Classless Interdomain Routing (CIDR) notation lists network IDs using the format

```
IP address/number of network ID bits in the subnet mask
```

For example, 192.168.1.0/24 indicates a 24-bit subnet mask. The 127/8 network is reserved for the localhost also known as the loopback address, which is used in troubleshooting network communications related to the network adapter.

✔ **Objective 7.02:** Manage and Monitor IP Routing Protocols   Windows 2000 supports two routing protocols: RIP versions 1 and 2 and OSPF. RIP version 1 does not support CIDR notation and is limited to a maximum of 15 hops.

✔ **Objective 7.03:** Manage and Monitor Internal Routing   RIP version 2 offers peer security, route filtering, and the use of multicasts for RIP announcements. RIP can be configured for triggered updates, which immediately send out announcements containing all changes to the network's configuration. When an RIP router initializes, its routing table only knows of the networks that its interfaces are directly connected to. All other routing information is added through RIP announcements. RIP version 2 routers support Silent RIP, which allows them to listen only for RIP announcements and not broadcast their own changes.

✔ **Objective 7.04: Manage and Monitor Border Routing**   OSPF is designed for larger networks and uses an algorithm to calculate the shortest path between the router and adjacent networks. OSPF uses a link state database, which is a dynamically updated map of the network topology, as opposed to a routing table. Windows 2000 supports multicast forwarding and can operate in two modes: IGMP router mode and IGMP proxy mode. IGMP routers maintain a forwarding table compiled by reading IGMP membership report messages. IGMP proxies forward IGMP membership report messages to IGMP routers.

✔ **Objective 7.05: Update a Windows 2000–Based Routing Table by Means of Static Routes**   Routing tables provide routers with a set of rules that instructs them where to forward IP datagrams to ensure that they get to their end destination. If no route exists in the routing table that matches the destination network of the IP datagram, the default route (0.0.0.0) is used. Configuring a static route requires that you specify a destination network ID, a netmask, and a gateway address. Static routes can be configured through RRAS or by using the **route add** command at the command prompt. The **route print** command will display the routing table, **route add** will allow you to add a route, **route delete** will allow you to delete a route, and **route change** will allow a route to be edited. The **–p** switch with the **route add** command makes a route persistent, and the route **–f** switch deletes all default gateways.

✔ **Objective 7.06: Implement Demand-Dial Routing**   If you enable demand-dial routing on a computer that is a member of an Active Directory domain, the computer account must be added to the RAS and IAS Servers security group before demand-dial routing will work. When a member of the Domain Admins group enables RRAS, the computer is automatically added to the group.

✔ **Objective 7.07: Manage and Monitor IP Routing**   IP filtering can be set up to block or allow specific IP traffic. There are two types of IP filters:

input filters and output filters. To filter out all traffic except PPTP, use the Drop All Packets Except Those That Meet the Criteria Below filter action and create input filters with a destination IP address of the PPTP server for destination TCP port 1723 and another for protocol ID 47. Create output filters with a source IP address of the PPTP server for source port 1723 and another for protocol ID 47. To filter out all traffic except L2TP, use the Drop All Packets Except Those That Meet the Criteria Below filter action and create input filters with a destination IP address of the L2TP server for destination UDP port 1701 and another for UDP destination port 500. Create output filters with a source IP address of the L2TP server for UDP source port 1701 and another for UDP source port 500.

REVIEW QUESTIONS

1. As the administrator of your organization's Windows 2000 network, you have just changed the IP address of the router that all internal clients use as their default gateway. The network router is configured with RIP version 2. All the client computers on your network are dynamically configured and are shut down on the weekends when you perform the changes. You want all clients to change their default gateway configuration when they reboot. Which of the following will allow you to achieve that goal?

   A. Write a script that uses the **route –f** command to delete the gateway address on the local client computer. RIP will update the gateway information on reboot.

   B. Change the scope information on your DHCP server to include the new gateway address.

   C. Write a script that uses the **route –p** command to delete the gateway address on the local client computer. RIP will update the gateway information on reboot.

   D. Manually change the default gateway address on all client computers on the network.

2. As the administrator of a Windows 2000 Active Directory network, you need to configure one of your routers with a static route to allow all traffic sent to 192.168.1.0/25 to be directed to IP address 192.168.1.1 on the newly configured router. The router has a total of three network interface adapters. Network interface adapter 2 is configured with the IP address 192.168.1.1. Which of the following commands will create the desired static route for you?

   A. Route add 192.168.1.0 mask 255.255.255.128 192.168.1.1 metric 1 if 2

   B. Route add 192.168.1.1 mask 255.255.255.192 192.168.1.0 metric 1 if 2

   C. Route add 192.168.1.0 mask 255.255.255.128 192.168.1.0 metric 1 if 2

   D. Route add 192.168.1.0 mask 255.255.255.192 192.168.1.1 metric 1 if 2

3. Which of the following IP routing protocols are supported in Windows 2000? (Choose all that apply.)

   A. RIP

   B. IGMP

   C. OSPF

   D. BGP

4. You have been asked to design the new IP network architecture for your organization as they plan their move into a new office space. Your network must allow for 30 subnets with at least 500 hosts per subnet. You have decided to use the 10.10.1.0 network. What IP address will you use to best meet your requirements, assuming your need for additional hosts per subnet will not grow but your need for subnets may?

   A. 255.255.254.0

   B. 255.255.248.0

   C. 255.255.240.0

   D. 255.255.252.0

   E. 255.255.224.0

5. As the network administrator for a Windows 2000 Active Directory network, you are responsible for securing a newly installed and configured RRAS server running PPTP. You want to ensure that only PPTP traffic is allowed to come in and out of the server. What two input filters will you configure as part of the configuration process?

   A. Create an input filter with the destination IP address of the PPTP server, select TCP from the protocol list, and add port 1723 as the destination port.

   B. Create an input filter with the destination IP address of the PPTP server, select Other from the protocol list, and add the protocol number 50.

   C. Create an input filter with the source IP address of the PPTP server, select TCP from the protocol list, and add port 1723 as the source port.

   D. Create an input filter with the destination IP address of the PPTP server, select Other from the protocol list, and add the protocol number 47.

6. As the network administrator for a Windows 2000 Active Directory network, you are responsible for securing a newly installed and configured RRAS server running L2TP. You want to ensure that only L2TP traffic is allowed to come in and out of the server. What two output filters will you configure as part of the configuration process?

   A. Create an output filter for the destination IP address of the L2TP server, select UDP from the protocol list, and add port 1701 as the destination port.

   B. Create an output filter for the source IP address of the L2TP server, select UDP from the protocol list, and add port 1701 as the source port.

   C. Create an output filter for the destination IP address of the L2TP server, select UDP from the protocol list, and add port 500 as the destination port.

   D. Create an output filter for the source IP address of the L2TP server, select UDP from the protocol list, and add port 500 as the source port.

7. As the network administrator for a Windows 2000 Active Directory network, you are responsible for securing a newly installed and configured RRAS server running PPTP. You have configured the server to allow only PPTP traffic to come in and out of the server. What two additional IP filters do you need to configure to allow the PPTP server to act as a PPTP client and initiate PPTP connections with other PPTP servers?

   A. Create an input filter with the destination IP address of the PPTP server, select TCP (established) from the protocol list, and add port 1723 as the source port.

   B. Create an output filter with the source IP address of the PPTP server, select TCP (established) from the protocol list, and add port 1723 as the destination port.

   C. Create an output filter with the destination IP address of the PPTP server, select TCP (established) from the protocol list, and add port 1723 as the source port.

   D. Create an input filter with the source IP address of the PPTP server, select TCP (established) from the protocol list, and add port 1723 as the destination port.

8. As a member of the Domain Admins group, you have configured and enabled RRAS on a server named Galaxy. Which group is Galaxy automatically added to?

   A. RAS and IAS servers distribution group
   B. Pre-Windows 2000 Compatible access distribution group
   C. RAS and IAS servers security group
   D. Pre-Windows 2000 Compatible access security group
   E. Domain Servers security group

9. As the network architect in your organization, you are responsible for designing the IP architecture. Your organization is a large ISP, and you have been assigned a single Class A network ID of 24.0.0.0. You want to break the Class A network into manageable pieces, each to be used by different geographical locations that your company operates in to provide access to your organization's customers. You want to design a scale architecture that allows for growth but limits the number of host IP addresses per network segment to around 950. Which subnet mask will you use to accomplish this?

   A. 255.255.248.0
   B. 255.255.254.0
   C. 255.255.252.0
   D. 255.255.240.0

10. You have just been hired as the administrator for a company. You are immediately asked to set up and configure a new server with a static IP address. The company's network uses the network ID 192.168.1.0/26. You have been given a list of available IP addresses but are skeptical as to whether the network host ranges have be calculated correctly. Which of the following IP addresses could you use to properly configure the new server and allow it to communicate on the network? (Choose all that apply.)

   A. 192.168.1.62
   B. 192.168.1.64
   C. 192.168.1.12110
   D. 192.168.1.127
   E. 192.168.1.128

REVIEW ANSWERS

1. **B** Changing the DHCP scope information and configuring the new address of the default gateway will allow all dynamically configured clients to obtain the new gateway information when they boot up and obtain their IP address. RIP is not used to update client computers but rather only servers configured with the RIP protocol.

2. **A** The correct **route** command to add the static route is Route add 192.168.1.0 mask 255.255.255.128 192.168.1.1 metric 1 if 2.

3. **A C** The two IP routing protocols supported in Windows 2000 are RIP (versions 1 and 2) and OSPF.

4. **A** A subnet of 255.255.254.0 would allow for 32,768 subnets and a maximum of 510 hosts per subnet.

5. **A D** To allow only PPTP traffic in and out of the PPTP server, two input filters for the destination IP address of the PPTP server will have to be created. The first will use TCP port 1723 as the destination port and the second will use the Other protocol choice with the protocol number 47 specified.

6. **B D** To allow only L2TP traffic in and out of the L2TP server, two output filters are required. The first output filter will use the source IP address of the L2TP server, the UDP protocol, and the source port 1701. The second output filter will use the source IP address of the L2TP server, the UDP protocol, and the source port 500.

7. **A B** To allow a PPTP server to initiate PPTP connections with remote PPTP servers and use IP filters to only allow PPTP traffic in and out of these servers, the two additional IP filters required would be one input and one output filter. The input filter would be configured with a destination IP address of the PPTP server, the TCP (established) protocol would be selected from the protocol list, and port 1723 would be added as the source port. The output filter would be configured with a source IP address of the PPTP server, the TCP (established) protocol would be selected from the protocol list, and port 1723 would be added as the destination port.

8. **C** When an RRAS server is configured and enabled by a member of the Domain Admins group, the server is automatically made a member of the RAS and IAS servers security group.

9. **C** The subnet 255.255.252.0 would allow for a maximum of 1,022 hosts per network segment and a maximum of 16,384 network segments.

10. **A** **C** A network with a network ID of 192.168.1.0/26 can have a total of four subnets with valid host ranges of 192.168.1.1–192.168.1.62, 192.168.1.65–192.168.1.126, 192.168.1.129–192.168.1.190, and 192.168.1.193–192.168.1.254.

Network
Address
Translation

	NEWBIE	SOME EXPERIENCE	EXPERT
ETA	3–4 hours	2–3 hours	1–2 hours

Knowledge about the configuration of shared Internet connections in both large and small networks is required of most network administrators. This chapter will discuss the installation and configuration of the two available options in Windows 2000 for sharing Internet access: Internet Connection Sharing (ICS) and Network Address Translation (NAT). We will also examine the configuration requirements for each of these two Internet sharing options and discuss scenarios in which each of the options would be recommended. Once you have a clear understanding of the two options, we will explore how each option works and manages multiple requests from computers on the network, retrieves the requested information on behalf of the internal client, and returns the appropriate response back to the correct client. Both NAT and ICS are new features included in Windows 2000 that were not found in Windows NT 4.0. A thorough understanding of both ICS and NAT is required for success on the Implementing and Administering a Microsoft Windows 2000 Network Infrastructure exam (70-216). This chapter will cover all the key points you will need to know to prepare for the exam as well as cover material you will require in your daily administration of NAT and ICS.

Objective 8.01 Install Internet Connection Sharing

Internet Connection Sharing (ICS) is the simplest of the available options for configuring shared Internet access in a small organization. ICS is designed to allow multiple computers on the same network segment to access the Internet through a shared connection. ICS is designed for smaller networks and provides address translation, address assignment, and name resolution to internal computers on the network.

Computers running both Windows 2000 Professional and Windows 2000 Server can be configured to use ICS. For a computer running Windows 2000 to be configured with ICS, the computer must have a minimum of two adapters—one to the local area network and the other to the Internet, as shown in Figure 8-1. The external adapter does not, however, have to be a network interface card; it could be a modem or wireless device used to establish a connection with the Internet. Also, the computers on the local area network must be configured to obtain IP addresses automatically, and they must be on a single IP segment. ICS has a built-in DHCP Allocator service used to lease IP addresses to internal clients on the 192.168.0.1/24 network.

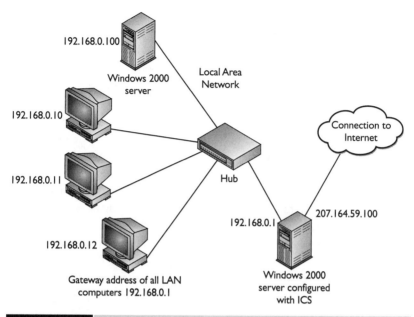

FIGURE 8-1   A network configured with ICS

If the computer you decide to configure with ICS has a static IP address, you will receive the information dialog box shown in Figure 8-2, which indicates that choosing to configure ICS will change the static IP address to a dynamic IP address on the 192.168.0.1 network. The dialog box gives you the option to accept this configuration change by selecting Yes or to continue to use a static IP address and forgo the use of ICS by selecting No.

It is the external adapter's address of the computer running ICS that uses a valid Internet IP address, as shown in Figure 8-1. The internal clients must then be configured with a gateway address that is the internal IP address of the computer running ICS.

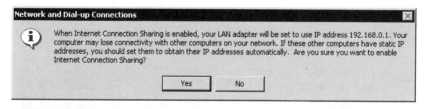

FIGURE 8-2   ICS Information dialog box indicating the computer's static IP address will be changed to dynamic

ICS uses address translation as opposed to routed connections to provide access to multiple computers in small networked environments. The use of address translation, as opposed to routing, allows the IP addresses of internal client computers to be hidden from the view of external users and computers, thus increasing the level of security on the network. It also allows for private internal IP addresses to be assigned to all internal clients, reducing the number of valid Internet IP addresses required for a single organization. Only computers like those configured with ICS that are connected directly to the Internet require a valid Internet IP address. ICS converts the source and destination addresses of the internal client computers into its own valid external Internet address, thus ensuring that the addresses of internal clients are not revealed on the Internet. Let's look at the steps involved in this translation process in more detail using the network in Figure 8-1.

In our example, we will make the assumption that a user is logged on to a computer running Windows 2000 Professional with the IP address of 192.168.0.10. This user would like to connect to a Web site located on the Internet with an IP address of 207.165.21.10 and an associated URL of www.mccaw.ca.

1. The process begins with the user opening their Web browser and entering the URL to the Web site that they wish to connect with. This leads to the behind-the-scenes DNS name resolution process.

2. The client computer sends a name resolution request to the ICS server, which is configured statically with the IP address of one or more DNS Servers. The ICS server acts as a DNS proxy and forwards the internal clients name resolution request on to the DNS server configured as its preferred DNS server.

3. Upon receiving a name resolution response from the DNS server, the DNS proxy returns the response to the client.

4. The client computer running Windows 2000 Professional with an IP address of 192.168.0.10 now has an IP address for the Web site it wishes to establish a connection with and sends its HTTP GET request to 207.165.21.10:80 through its default gateway of 192.168.0.1.

5. The Windows 2000 Server configured with the internal IP address of 192.168.0.1 is the computer running ICS on the network. It receives the outgoing request but changes the TCP/IP packet information. The original source IP address of 192.168.0.10 is changed to the external IP address of the server running ICS 207.164.59.100. This serves two purposes. First, the TCP/IP packets are provided with a valid Internet IP address, and second, the internal IP addresses are hidden from hosts on the Internet.

6. The ICS Service then creates a mapping in its translation table that maps the internal client's IP address of 192.168.0.10 to the external destination IP address and port that the internal client is trying to establish a connection on. In this case, that information is the destination IP address 207.165.21.10 and the TCP port 80 for the HTTP service. This way, when the Web server with IP address 207.165.21.10 replies to the ICS server's external IP address of 207.164.59.100, ICS knows (thanks to its mapping) to forward the reply on to the internal computer with an IP address of 192.168.0.10.

ICS also includes an implementation of Dynamic Host Configuration Protocol (DHCP), known as a DHCP Allocator service, and a DNS proxy service. The purpose of the DHCP Allocator service is to lease out IP addresses, subnet masks, and gateway information to clients on the local segment. The DHCP Allocator service is not a full implementation of DHCP but does allow ICS to lease IP addresses from the default address pool the protocol is configured to use (192.168.0.0–192.168.0.254). The DNS proxy service is also included in order to allow name resolution to occur by letting the server running ICS forward the name resolution request to the DNS servers that it is configured to use in the TCP/IP properties.

Exam Tip

ICS should not be used in a network with Windows 2000 domain controllers, DNS servers, routers, and DHCP servers or with computers configured to use static IP addresses; Network Address Translation should be used instead.

Installing ICS is as simple as modifying the properties of your Internet connection. Using the example of the network shown in Figure 8-1, you would open the properties of the external connection on the Windows 2000 Server to configure ICS and then follow these steps:

1. Open Network and Dial-up Connections and right-click the external connection to the Internet and then select Properties.
2. Select the Sharing tab and place a check mark in the box next to Enable Internet Connection Sharing for This Connection, as shown in Figure 8-3.

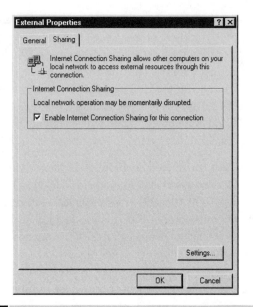

FIGURE 8-3   Installing ICS

Exam Tip

When ICS is installed, it automatically defaults to the private address range 192.168.0.0 with a subnet of 255.255.255.0, and it assigns the internal interface on the computer being configured with ICS an IP address of 192.168.0.1. You must be an Administrator to configure ICS.

The use of ICS is primarily intended to allow internal users on the same network segment to share a single connection to the Internet. ICS can also be configured to allow access to applications running on a computer on the internal (private) network from computers on the Internet through the computer running Windows 2000 that is configured with ICS. This is accomplished by clicking the Settings button at the bottom of the properties dialog box shown in Figure 8-1 and selecting the Applications tab.

To allow access to an internal application from the Internet through ICS, select the Application tab, click Add, and then enter the required information for the application into the Internet Connection Sharing Application dialog box, shown in Figure 8-4.

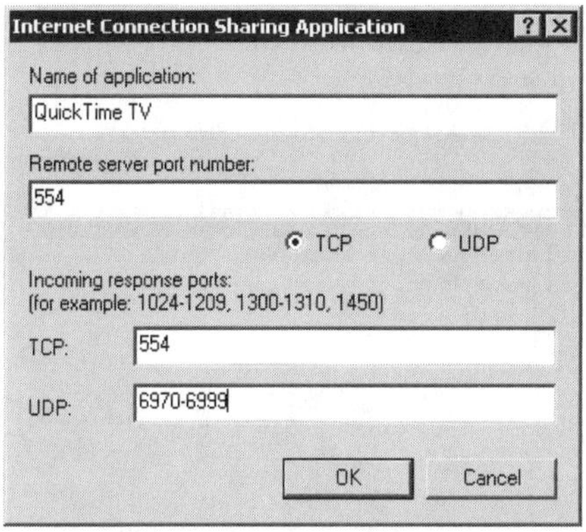

FIGURE 8-4   Configuring access to an internal application through ICS

Here's the information required:

- The name of the application
- A remote server port number
- The choice of TCP or UDP
- Incoming TCP or UDP response ports

Let's use the example of the QuickTime TV application running on an internal computer with an IP address of 192.168.0.50. As shown in Figure 8-4, enter **QuickTime TV** as the name of the application and enter **554** as the Remote server port number. TCP Port 554 is the port that the QuickTime Real Time Streaming Protocol uses to establish connectivity. The name of the application that you enter can be any user-friendly name that best identifies the application to you, the administrator. This name will not be seen by any external users. The remote server port number is the port number on the internal server that is associated with the application. The TCP and UDP options allow you to choose the type of connection the application requires. The incoming response ports allow you to specify ports for the internal remote application to listen on. In the example shown in Figure 8-4, the QuickTime TV application will require both TCP port 554 and UDP ports 6970 through 6999 to be added in the ICS Application dialog box. Another example could be an internal LDAP application that uses TCP port 389. In that case, TCP would be selected and port number 389 would be entered in the Remote Server Port Number box as well as the incoming response port for TCP.

To provide access for specific services running on computers on the internal network, select the Services tab, shown in Figure 8-5. On the Services tab, you can

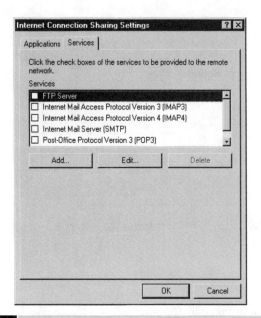

FIGURE 8-5   Configuring ICS to resolve internal services

select from one of the predefined services or add one of your own. Selecting one of the predefined services, such as FTP, provides all the appropriate port information and requires only that you enter the hostname or IP address of the internal computer hosting the service.

Let's assume that you want to provide access to the FTP service running on an internal computer that has an IP address of 192.168.1.100. To accomplish this, follow the steps below:

1. On the Services tab, shown in Figure 8-5, select the FTP Server option. This will automatically open the Internet Connection Sharing Service dialog box, shown in Figure 8-6.
2. Enter the name (or, preferably, the IP address 192.168.0.100) for the computer on your internal network that is configured with the FTP service.
3. Click OK until all dialog boxes are closed.

ICS is not the solution for all networks because it does have the following limitations:

- The DHCP Allocator server cannot be disabled. Clients on the LAN must be configured to obtain an IP address through DHCP.

FIGURE 8-6   Configuring ICS to resolve an internal FTP Server

- Only a single external connection is supported. ICS does not support multiple external connections.
- ICS cannot be used in a network that contains a DHCP server, DHCP relay agent, or router.
- ICS only works for single-segment networks on the network 192.168.0.0/24.
- ICS and NAT are mutually exclusive. ICS cannot be installed on a computer configured with NAT.

Exam Tip	
Only a single external adapter can be configured to use ICS.	

I don't want to confuse the issue, but I would like to clarify one small point that has to do with the configuration of ICS. All of the documentation supplied with ICS states that all internal clients must be configured to obtain their IP addresses dynamically, and this is the configuration you should remember when taking the exam. In reality, however, there is another configuration scenario. The internal clients can be configured with a static IP address as long as it is on the 192.168.0.1 network and their gateway addresses are configured as 192.168.0.1, which is the IP address of the internal interface on the computer running ICS.

Objective 8.02

Install Network Address Translation

L ike ICS, Network Address Translation (NAT) uses translated connections instead of routed connections. The benefit of NAT over ICS is that it is more scalable and offers you more configuration options.

NAT can be installed only on a computer running Windows 2000 Server. The advantage of NAT over routing is that, like ICS, it allows the IP addresses of internal client computers to be hidden from the view of external users and computers, thus increasing the level of security on the network.

NAT has many advantages over ICS, such as:

- NAT can be configured with multiple external network adapters to increase network throughput.
- NAT can operate in a routed network that contains DHCP servers and DHCP relay agents, thus making it the recommended alternative for larger corporate networks.
- NAT can be configured to use packet filtering on the external adapter to increase the security on your Internet sharing configuration.
- NAT is more scalable.
- NAT offers more configuration options.
- The NAT table is viewable through the RRAS snap-in, which can be helpful in troubleshooting efforts.
- It requires you to have less-valid Internet IP addresses, as does ICS, which helps keep your costs down.

Exam Tip

NAT cannot be used for access scenarios that require the use of Layer Two Tunneling Protocol (L2TP) Virtual Private Network (VPN) support.

NAT does have some limitations, though, and these limitations will be the focus of some of the questions you come across on the exam. These limitations include

- If your shared Internet connection scenario requires the ability to cache Web pages, restrict users' Internet access, or support the IPX protocol, using a proxy server would be the recommended approach to meeting these needs, because NAT will not handle them.
- NAT is not compatible with IPSec. This incompatibility is due to the translation of the computer's IP address in the packet header to that of the NAT server's external interface, which is transparent to the user.
- NAT cannot be installed on a computer that uses ICS, as the two Shared Internet Connection options are mutually exclusive.
- NAT can be installed only on computers running a Windows 2000 Server operating system, increasing the costs of a NAT solution.
- The computer to be configured with NAT must have a minimum of two adapters, both with statically configured IP addresses and subnet information. Only the external adapters should be configured with DNS and gateway information.

Exam Tip

Become familiar with what NAT can and cannot do, because the exam will require you to have a solid understanding of both its uses and its limitations.

Prior to installing NAT, you need to understand how the TCP/IP information should be configured on the server that is to act as your NAT server. The NAT server must have two network adapters. One or both of these adapters will be configured as external adapters with valid Internet IP addresses, subnet masks, and gateway and DNS information. The internal network adapter's TCP/IP information should include only an internal IP address and subnet mask. Do not configure the internal network adapter with gateway or DNS server information. An example of this configuration is shown in Figure 8-7.

Exam Tip

Do not configure DNS or gateway information in the TCP/IP properties of the internal network adapter on the NAT server.

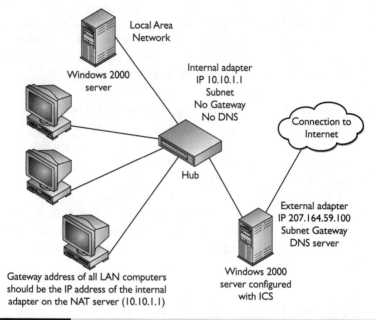

Local Area
Network

Windows 2000
server

Internal adapter
IP 10.10.1.1
Subnet
No Gateway
No DNS

Connection to
Internet

Hub

External adapter
IP 207.164.59.100
Subnet Gateway
DNS server

Gateway address of all LAN computers
should be the IP address of the internal
adapter on the NAT server (10.10.1.1)

Windows 2000
server configured
with ICS

FIGURE 8-7   Recommended NAT configuration

NAT is installed through the Routing and Remote Access snap-in, hence the RRAS service must be enabled and configured on the computer in order for NAT to be installed. Membership in the Administrators group is also required to install and administer NAT and other RRAS components. To install NAT on a computer that does not already have the Routing and Remote Access service enabled, follow these steps:

1. Open Routing and Remote Access and double-click the name of the server that you want to configure.
2. Right-click on the server name and select Configure and Enable Routing and Remote Access.
3. Click Next on the first screen of the Routing and Remote Access Server Setup Wizard.
4. Select the Internet connection server option on the Common Configurations page and click Next.
5. Select "Set up a router with the Network Address Translation (NAT) routing protocol" and click Next.
6. Select Use the selected Internet connection option, select the external connection from the list of available connections , click Next, and then click Finish.

7. Expand the IP Routing section and then right-click General and select New
   Routing Protocol. Select NAT from the list of routing protocols in the New
   Routing Protocol dialog box and click OK.

Objective 8.03   Configure NAT Properties

The configuration of the NAT properties is done by right-clicking NAT under
IP Routing in the RRAS snap-in, then selecting Properties. This will bring up
the NAT Properties dialog box, shown in Figure 8-8. The General tab of the NAT
Properties dialog box allows for the logging option to be enabled, with the default
set to log only errors.

Exam Tip
When you're configuring NAT or ICS, the internal adapter should not be configured with a gateway or DNS server address.

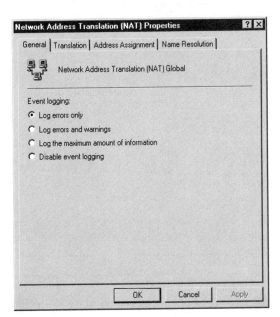

FIGURE 8-8   Configuring the General Tab of the NAT properties

The Translation tab, shown in Figure 8-9, allows you to configure the time period in minutes after which a TCP mapping is removed. The default is 24 hours. This is the amount of time that a dynamic mapping for a TCP session remains in the Network Address Translation table. The same type of setting is available for the removal of UDP mappings, with a default of one minute. UDP mappings are kept for a very short period of time due to the "un-guaranteed" nature of the protocol.

Like ICS, NAT can be used to allow external users access to specific applications on the internal network. To do this, click the Applications button on the Translation tab and click Add to configure the name of the application and the remote server port number as well as to specify whether the communication will be TCP or UDP. The dialog box used to configure an application for access from the Internet through the NAT is the same as that used in ICS, as shown earlier in Figure 8-4. As in ICS, enter the name of the application and the remote server port number, choose from either TCP or UDP, and specify the TCP and UDP incoming response ports. Doing this will allow access from the Internet to applications running on internal computers on your network through the NAT

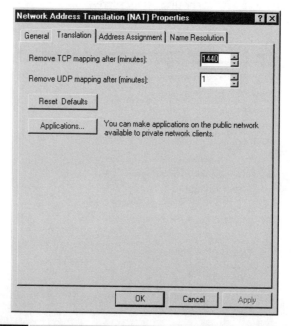

FIGURE 8-9 Configuring the Translation Tab of the NAT properties

service. The implementation of NAT in Windows 2000 is a two-way NAT implementation allowing for internal clients to access the Internet through the NAT server and for clients on the Internet to access applications running on internal computers when they are configured on the NAT server. The Address Assignment tab, shown in Figure 8-10, allows you to configure the use of DHCP to lease out IP addresses. The default setting does not enable the use of DHCP to allow all the internal clients to have a static configuration or to obtain their IP addresses from another DHCP server already configured on the network. If RRAS detects the presence of a DHCP server on the network, NAT will disable the DHCP Allocator service on the RRAS server, allowing the existing DHCP server to continue to lease out IP addresses.

If you choose to use the DHCP implementation included with RRAS, the default network ID is set to 192.168.0.0, with a subnet mask of 255.255.255.0, similar to ICS. Unlike ICS, an exclusion range can also be configured. Using the DHCP implementation included with NAT in RRAS does not require that a DHCP server be available on the network.

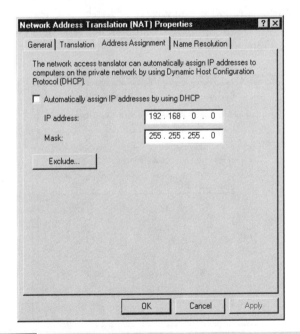

FIGURE 8-10   Configuring the Address Assignment properties of NAT

Exam Tip

Do not be confused by the default network ID of 192.168.0.0/24 used when you assign IP addresses using DHCP. NAT allows this network ID to be changed to any network ID that suites you; only ICS restricts you to using the 192.168.0.0/24 network ID.

The last tab used in the configuration of NAT is Name Resolution, shown in Figure 8-11. The Name Resolution tab is used to configure the NAT server to act as a DNS proxy and provide DNS name resolution for clients on the internal network, allowing those internal clients to use friendly DNS names as opposed to IP addresses. Again, like the DHCP service, this is not a full implementation of DNS, nor does it require that a DNS server be on the local network. If a DNS server is not located on the local internal network, the NAT server forwards DNS name resolution requests to the preferred DNS server configured in the TCP/IP properties of the external network interface. The NAT protocol offers name resolution capabilities for clients using DNS and forwards the requests to an external DNS server for resolution when the options "Resolve IP addresses for Clients using Domain Name System (DNS)" and "Connect to the public network when a name needs to be resolved" are both enabled.

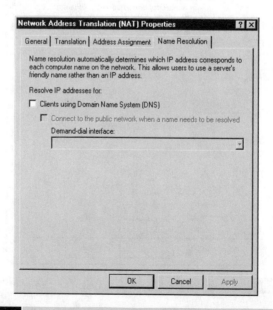

FIGURE 8-11   Configuring the Name Resolution tab of the NAT properties

Objective 8.04 Configure NAT Interfaces

Configuration of individual NAT interfaces can be accomplished by right-clicking each interface listed in the NAT section of the RRAS snap-in and selecting Properties. Both the internal and external NAT interface properties should be configured. The Properties dialog box for the external NAT interface—that is, the interface connected to the Internet with the IP address of 207.164.59.100, as shown in Figure 8-7—consists of three tabs, with the first being the General tab. On the General tab, shown in Figure 8-12, you are able to specify whether the interface is connected to a public or private network. In the case of the external interface, you want to select the radio button next to "Public interface connected to the Internet." Selecting the radio button to the left of the "Private interface connected to the network" radio button removes the two additional tabs from the dialog box because that's all the configuration required for the private interface.

In the case of the external interface that is connected to a public network, place a check mark in the box next to Translate TCP/UDP headers, which will allow for translation through this interface to occur.

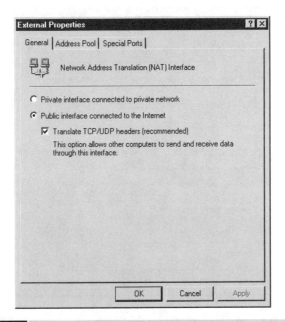

FIGURE 8-12 Configuring the external NAT interface

Exam Tip

Enable translation only on external interfaces that are connected to the Internet, not on any internal interfaces.

The second tab in the dialog box, assuming you are configuring a public interface, is the Address Pool tab, shown in Figure 8-13. Here, you are able to assign multiple external IP addresses to the NAT server to increase network throughput. This is useful if your ISP has assigned you a block of valid IP addresses for connecting to the Internet (as opposed to a single valid Internet IP address) and your NAT server is configured with more than one external adapter. Clicking the Add button on the Address Pool tab allows you to enter the start IP address, subnet mask, and end IP address.

NAT also provides the ability to make internal computers accessible to users on the Internet by allowing you to map one of the external IP addresses on the NAT server to an internal IP address. This allows you to keep your internal IP addresses hidden from Internet users, but allows Internet users to access the internal server thinking that the internal server has a valid Internet IP address.

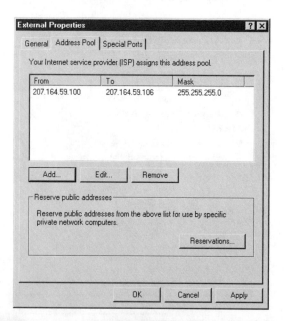

FIGURE 8-13   Configuring the NAT address pool for multiple external interfaces

Once you have configured an address pool, you can select the Reservations button on the Address Pool tab and specify a public IP address that you wish to map to a specific internal computer's IP address. Clicking the Reservations button will bring up the Reserve Addresses dialog box, on which you will click the Add button to access the Edit Reservation dialog box, shown in Figure 8-14. The Edit Reservation dialog box allows you to enter the public IP address that you wish to map to the internal address, which you also enter. Placing a check mark in the box next to "Allow incoming sessions to this address" will configure the mapping to allow incoming sessions from the Internet to access the specified internal server through the mapping IP address.

To allow incoming sessions on the valid Internet IP address 207.164.59.106 to the internal IP address 192.168.1.100, configure the Add Reservation dialog box as shown in Figure 8-14. Enter the external IP address of 207.164.59.106 in the top box and the internal IP address of 192.168.1.100 in the lower box. Then place a check mark in the box next to "Allow incoming sessions to this address." This will provide users on the Internet with the ability to establish a session with an internal computer using the external IP address on the NAT server.

On the third tab, Special Ports, shown in Figure 8-15, you are able to configure specific service ports that incoming requests come in on and map those port-specific requests to a specific internal server as well as specify an outgoing port. An example of this might be a Microsoft Exchange mail server configured on the internal network with an IP address of 192.168.1.200 that receives mail on TCP port 110 using the POP3 protocol and sends mail out on TCP port 25 using the SMTP protocol. NAT allows you to map the incoming and outgoing service ports from an external IP address on the NAT server to the internal IP address of your mail server to enable mail to be sent and received externally without requiring the mail server to have an external connection.

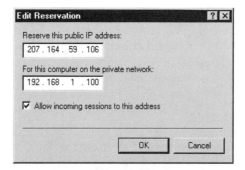

FIGURE 8-14   Mapping external IP addresses to internal IP addresses

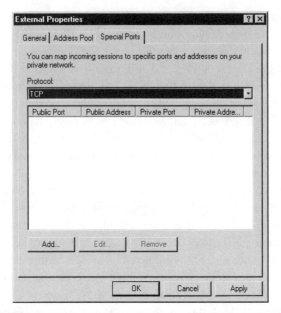

FIGURE 8-15   Configuring the Special Ports of the external NAT interface

To configure this, click the Add button on the Special Ports tab of the External Properties dialog box, shown in Figure 8-15. Assuming the internal IP address of your mail server is 192.168.1.200 and the external IP address you want to allow incoming mail requests on is 207.164.59.100, you would configure the information in the Add Special Port dialog box as shown in Figure 8-16.

Multiple NAT interfaces can also be configured when a computer has multiple adapters that you wish to use in the NAT configuration. To add an additional interface, follow these steps:

1. Open RRAS.
2. Expand IP Routing and right-click Network Address Translation. Select New Interface from the context menu.

Travel Assistance

More information can be found on NAT at http://rfc.net in RFC 1631.

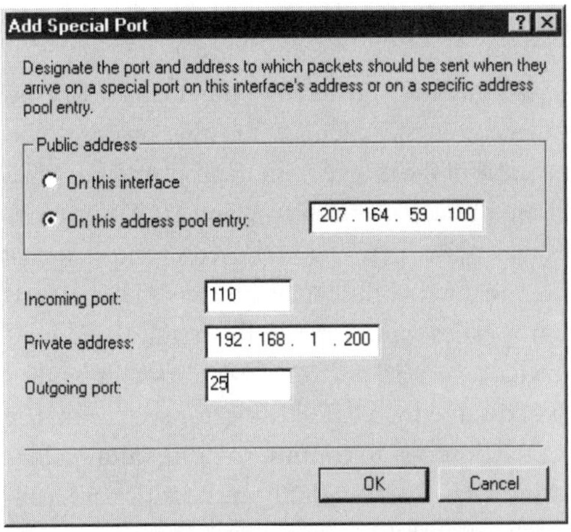

FIGURE 8-16   Configuring incoming mail requests in the Add Special Port dialog box

3. Select the new interface you wish to add from the list of available interfaces and click OK.
4. On the General tab of the interfaces properties dialog box select whether the new interface is to be a public or private interface and click OK.

Packet Filters

Each individual interface used by the NAT protocol can be configured to use IP packet filters. The configuration of IP packet filters in RRAS is discussed in Chapter 6. Packet filters come in two forms: input filters and output filters. An input filter is used to control the types of packets that are received and forwarded on a specific network interface. Output filters are used to control the types of packets that are allowed to be sent from a specific interface.

As an example of where a packet filter could help to control the types of applications users on the internal network are using, you could use an output filter that blocks all IRC chat traffic. This would prevent any internal user from sending IRC chat messages to another individual through the NAT interface. The output filter would be configured on the internal interface of the NAT server to block all outgoing IRC chat packets. This, by itself, would not prevent anyone on the Internet from sending IRC chat packets through the NAT interface. To block incoming IRC traffic, you could create an input filter on the external interface(s) on the NAT server.

Troubleshooting NAT and ICS

Troubleshooting NAT and ICS generally comes down to basic network troubleshooting. If you encounter problems with either protocol, check the Event logs for error messages. Some of the most common problems you will encounter include DHCP-related issues, connectivity problems, and TCP/IP configuration problems.

DHCP issues may arise if you have chosen to implement NAT to share an Internet connection on a network that already has a DHCP server and have configured the NAT properties to Automatically Assign IP Addresses Using DHCP. When the NAT service detects that another DHCP server is attempting to lease IP addresses, NAT will disable the DHCP Allocator service on the RRAS server to allow the existing DHCP server to continue to lease out IP addresses. Prior to the detection of the other DHCP server, duplicate IP addresses may have been leased out, thus causing network communication problems.

DHCP issues may also arise if ICS is installed on a computer that is connected to a network with an existing DHCP server or DHCP relay agent. ICS is not as sophisticated a service as NAT, and conflicts may arise from both ICS and the DHCP server leasing out IP addresses to clients.

Basic connectivity issues may also arise but are not generally caused by the implementation of either ICS or NAT. With an ICS implementation, ensure that all internal clients are on the same segment and are configured to obtain an IP address through DHCP. If any clients need to be statically configured, ensure that their IP addresses are in the default range of 192.168.0.2 through 192.168.0.254 and that they don't not conflict with IP addresses leased out by ICS. Statically configured clients will also need to have a gateway address that is the ICS server's internal IP address.

TCP/IP configuration problems may also arise and lead to network communication problems. Utilities such as Ping, Tracert, and Pathping, which are discussed in Chapter 5, can be used to help troubleshoot communication problems. To verify that a specific internal client has a NAT mapping in the translation table, you can use RRAS to view the translation table by following these steps:

1. Open RRAS and expand IP Routing.
2. Click Network Address Translation. Right-click the external interface and select Show Mappings.

The Network Address Translation Session Mapping Table will appear and list all the internal clients by IP address that have a mapping on the NAT server, as shown in Figure 8-17. The table displays the client's internal IP address and the external IP address that it is mapped to as well as the internal and external ports used to send and receive information.

Protocol	Direction	Private address	Private port	Public Address	Public Port
UDP	Outbound	192.168.1.200	2,361	207.164.59.100	2,361

LEXUS - Network Address Translation Session Mapping Table

FIGURE 8-17   Displaying the name mappings

CHECKPOINT

✔ **Objective 8.01: Install Internet Connection Sharing**   ICS can be installed on computers running both Windows 2000 Server and Windows 2000 Professional. ICS changes the IP address of the internal adapter to 192.168.0.1 and works only on a single-segment network that does not use DHCP, DHCP relay agents, and routers. ICS supports only the use of a single external network adapter. ICS uses address translation (as opposed to routed connections), allowing the internal IP addresses to remain hidden from the view of external users. ICS includes a DHCP Allocator service capable of leasing out IP addresses to clients on a single network segment and a DNS proxy capable of providing DNS name resolution to internal clients. You must be a member of the Administrators group to enable ICS. ICS and NAT are mutually exclusive and cannot be installed on the same computer.

✔ **Objective 8.02: Install Network Address Translation**   NAT can be installed only on computers running Windows 2000 Server. NAT is much more scalable than ICS and supports multiple adapters for increased network throughput. NAT is installed and configured through the RRAS snap-in and, like ICS, uses network translation as opposed to routed connections to share access to the Internet.

✔ **Objective 8.03: Configure NAT Properties**   The NAT protocol includes implementations of both DHCP and DNS. Both NAT and ICS allow for internal applications and services to be accessed through the translation service from the external network. NAT can operate in a routed environment and with the presence of a DHCP server or DHCP relay agents. NAT will disable the DHCP Allocator service on the RRAS server, allowing the existing DHCP server to continue to lease out IP addresses if it detects the presence of a DHCP server on the network. NAT will allow for the use of any internal addressing scheme, whereas ICS limits you to the 192.168.0.1/24 network. NAT can also be configured to use packet filters on the external adapter for increased security. NAT's translation table is also viewable through the RRAS snap-in, which is helpful in troubleshooting. NAT cannot be used in Internet sharing configurations that require the use of L2TP or IPSec.

✔ **Objective 8.04: Configure NAT Interfaces**   Translation should be enabled only on interfaces connected to the Internet. When you're configuring both NAT and ICS, the internal adapter should not have a gateway address. NAT uses a unique private port number to manage the translation session between it and the internal client.

REVIEW QUESTIONS

1. You are the administrator of a small network that consists of only a single network segment with 15 client computers. You have decided to install and configure ICS to allow all client computers access to the Internet. Which of the following will be the default IP address assigned to the internal adapter on the Windows 2000 computer running ICS?

   A. 172.16.0.1
   B. 192.168.0.1
   C. 10.10.0.1
   D. 224.240.0.1

2. Which of the following network services can run on the same network running ICS without causing any network problems? (Choose two.)

   A. DHCP
   B. NAT
   C. WINS
   D. IIS

3. You have just received a new server that was ordered for the purpose of configuring shared Internet access to the 15 users in your department. The clients in your department's domain are configured to use APIPA. Your departmental network is connected to other departmental networks, but only your department requires Internet access. Which of the following would you recommend implementing?

   A. Install NAT and configure the internal adapter with an IP address of 169.254.25.1.

   B. Install ICS and configure the internal adapter with an IP address of 192.168.0.1.

   C. Install NAT and configure the external adapter with an IP address of 169.254.25.1.

   D. Install ICS and configure the external adapter with an IP address of 192.168.0.1.

4. Implementations of what two network services are included with the NAT protocol?

   A. DHCP

   B. WINS

   C. DNS

   D. QoS

5. You have configured a computer running Windows 2000 Server with RRAS and NAT. You now want to set up a VPN on the same server. Which two of the following statements are true with respect to a VPN server in this environment? (Choose two.)

   A. The VPN can be established only from the RRAS server.

   B. The external connection must be either persistent or demand-dial.

   C. L2TP must be chosen as the default server type.

   D. PPTP must be chosen as the default server type.

   E. IPSec should be chosen as the encryption protocol.

6. You have installed and configured NAT to automatically assign IP addresses to the computers sharing the Internet connection. Which of the following is a true statement with respect to what will happen when NAT discovers another DHCP server on the network that is leasing out IP addresses?

A. NAT will disable the other DHCP server.

B. NAT will change the IP addressing pool it is using to avoid duplicate IP addresses from being leased out.

C. The DHCP server is stopped from leasing out IP addresses and is shut down once it detects the NAT DHCP implementation.

D. NAT will disable the DHCP Allocator service on the RRAS server, allowing the existing DHCP server to continue to lease out IP addresses.

7. You have installed NAT on a computer running Windows 2000 Server, and on the Address Assignment tab in the NAT Properties dialog box you have enabled the option "Automatically assign IP addresses using DHCP." Which of the following statements is correct regarding IP addresses allocated to the client computers?

A. The NAT server determines whether to lease out IP addresses itself or to use the DHCP server.

B. Client computers will obtain their IP addresses from the DHCP server.

C. The first server to receive the request will respond.

D. The client computers will obtain their IP addresses from the NAT server.

8. As the administrator of your network, you have just completed the installation of the NAT protocol on a computer running Windows 2000 Server. The IP address you wish to use for the external adapter is 207.164.59.98, and the network ID for the internal adapter is 10.10.1.0/24. The gateway address that your ISP told you to use is 207.164.59.1. Which of the following represents a correct IP configuration for an internal client on the network?

A. IP 10.10.1.10, subnet 255.255.255.0, gateway 207.164.59.1

B. IP 10.10.2.10, subnet 255.255.252.0, gateway 10.10.1.1

C. IP 10.10.1.5, subnet 255.255.255.0, gateway 10.10.1.1

D. IP 10.10.1.1, subnet 255.255.252.0, gateway 207.164.59.1

9. What does NAT use to uniquely identify each client on the network?

A. NetBIOS name

B. IP address

C. Port number

D. Hostname

10. Which of the following would be the recommended tool to use if you wanted to monitor the activities of the DHCP Allocator service?

A. System Monitor

B. Right-clicking the Network Address Translation protocol in RRAS

C. Network Monitor

D. Right-clicking the internal interface in the Network Address Translation Protocol section in RRAS

REVIEW ANSWERS

1. **B** The internal adapter's IP address on the Windows 2000 computer running ICS will be configured as 192.168.0.1. ICS always configures the IP address of the internal network adapter with the IP address 192.168.0.1. All other internal clients must then be configured to obtain IP addresses dynamically from a DHCP server and will receive an IP address on the 192.168.0.1/24 network from the computer running ICS.

2. **C** **D** Both IIS and WINS are able to run on the same network on which a computer running ICS is active without causing any network communication problems. DHCP and NAT should not be configured to run on the same network. The DHCP service, if configured, will conflict with the DHCP Allocator service running on the computer configured with ICS. NAT is intended for larger, routed environments and could also cause problems and conflicts with ICS.

3. **A** The use of NAT would be recommended in this case because ICS should not be installed in a routed environment. The internal IP address of the NAT adapter should be set to an IP address on the 169.254.0.0 network because that is the network used by APIPA.

4. **A** **C** Implementations of both DHCP and DNS are included with the NAT protocol. NAT includes an implementation of DHCP via the DHCP Allocator service and a DNS proxy that is capable of forwarding DNS name resolution requests on to DNS servers.

5. **B** **D** The external connection must be either persistent or demand-dial, and the default server type must be set to PPTP. NAT does not support L2TP or IPSec, and a VPN connection that uses PPTP can be established from any internal computer on the network, not just the RRAS server.

6. **D** If NAT detects another DHCP server on the network, it will disable the DHCP Allocator service and let the other DHCP server continue to lease out IP addresses.

7. **D** If you have enabled the "Automatically assign IP addresses using DHCP" feature, the client computers will obtain their IP addresses from the NAT server.

8. **C** A possible configuration for an internal client would be an IP address of 10.10.1.5, with a subnet mask of 255.255.255.0 and a gateway address of 10.10.1.1.

9. **C** NAT assigns each client mapping a unique, private port number. This allows it to manage the translation session between itself and the client.

10. **B** Right-clicking the Network Address Translation Protocol in RRAS will allow you to view the DHCP Allocator service information. Network Monitor could also be used to monitor the DHCP Allocator service by capturing and filtering all of the DHCP-related traffic, but this would not be the recommended tool to use.

About the CD-ROM

Mike Meyers' Certification Passport CD-ROM Instructions

To install the *Passport* Practice Exam software, perform these steps:

1. Insert the CD-ROM into your CD-ROM drive. An auto-run program will initiate, and a dialog box will appear indicating that you are installing the Passport setup program. If the auto-run program does not launch on your system, select Run from the Start menu and type **d:\setup.exe** (where **d** is the "name" of your CD-ROM drive).
2. Follow the installation wizard's instructions to complete the installation of the software.
3. You can start the program by going to your desktop and double-clicking the Passport Exam Review icon or by going to Start | Program Files | ExamWeb | MCSE.

System Requirements

- **Operating systems supported**   Windows 98, Windows NT 4.0, Windows 2000, and Windows Me
- **CPU**   400 MHz or faster recommended
- **Memory**   64MB of RAM
- **CD-ROM**   4X or greater
- **Internet connection**   Required for optional exam upgrade

Technical Support

For basic *Passport* CD-ROM technical support, contact Hudson Technical Support:

- Phone: 800-217-0059
- E-mail: mcgraw-hill@hudsonsoft.com

For content/subject matter questions concerning the book or the CD-ROM, contact MH Customer Service:

- Phone: 800-722-4726
- E-mail: customer.service@mcgraw-hill.com

For inquiries about the available upgrade, CD-ROM, or online technology, or for in-depth technical support, contact ExamWeb Technical Support:

- Phone: 949-566-9375
- E-mail: support@examweb.com

Career Flight Path

Microsoft's ever popular Microsoft Certified Systems Engineer (MCSE) holds a lot of clout for those looking to work in the networking field. Microsoft's NT, 2000, and XP operating systems control a huge portion of all the installed networks out there and those networks need qualified support people to make them run. The Windows 2000 MCSE requires the successful completion of seven exams: four core exams, one design elective, and two additional electives. For details, check out Microsoft's training Web site at www.microsoft.com/trainingandservices.

Most techs following the Windows 2000 track will take the four core exams in the following order. First, the Microsoft 70-210, Installing, Configuring, and Administering Microsoft Windows 2000 Professional, followed by the 70-215, Installing, Configuring, and Administering Microsoft Windows 2000 Server. Next, the 70-217, Implementing and Administering a Microsoft Windows 2000 Directory Services Infrastructure, and then the last of the four core exams is usually the 70-216, Implementing and Administering a Microsoft Windows 2000 Network Infrastructure. The exams taken may vary based on the user's experience, but this is a typical progression.

The next step towards certification is the successful completion of one of the core design exams. Here you can choose from 70-219, Designing a Microsoft Windows 2000 Directory Services Infrastructure (I recommend this exam, particularly if it fits your planned career path because in my opinion, it is one of the easier exams); the 70-220, Designing Security for a Microsoft Windows 2000 Network; or the 70-221, Designing a Microsoft Windows 2000 Network Infrastructure. The latter of these two exams, the 70-221, correlates nicely with the fundamental implementation and administration concepts that are covered in this book, but it too is considered to be one of the tougher of the design exams. The last choice currently—and I say "currently" because, as you know, Microsoft continually releases new exams—is the 70-226, Designing Highly Available Web Solutions with Microsoft Windows 2000 Server Technologies.

The last component of your journey towards the Windows 2000 MCSE is to write two elective exams. If you are already MCSE certified on Windows NT 4.0, you may be able to count some of those exams as your elective exams. The number of elective exams you have to choose from is high and is comprised of exams for all of the other enterprise applications that Microsoft develops, such as SMS, SQL Server, Exchange Server, ISA Server, Site Server, and SNA Server. Each of these enterprise applications generally has multiple exams associated with it that can be used toward the attainment of your two required electives.

Each of the exams that Microsoft releases has a Microsoft Official Curriculum (MOC) course associated with it that is designed not only to help you pass the exam, but also to help you understand the fundamentals behind the application or operating system. The MOC curriculum is a great starting point to help you understand the concepts and provides you with hands-on experience working with the product.

One additional consideration is that Microsoft has announced that Windows 2000 MCSEs will not be required to re-certify for the pending Windows XP exams. This means that the life of your certification has been extended significantly at this point.

Windows 2000 MCSE Certification

	Core Exams	Associated MOC Courses
1	**70-210** Installing, Configuring, and Administering Microsoft Windows 2000 Professional	2151, 2152
2	**70-215** Installing, Configuring, and Administering Microsoft Windows 2000 Server	2151, 2152
3	**70-217** Implementing and Administering Microsoft Windows 2000 Directory Services Infrastructure	2154
4	**70-216** Implementing and Administering a Microsoft Windows 2000 Network Infrastructure	2153

Choose one of the following Designing "Elective" Exams

	70-219 Designing a Microsoft Windows 2000 Directory Services Infrastructure	1561
	70-220 Designing Security for a Microsoft Windows 2000 Network	2150
+1	**70-221** Designing a Microsoft Windows 2000 Network Infrastructure	1562
	70-226 Designing Highly Available Web Solutions with Microsoft Windows 2000 Server Technologies	2088

Choose two of the following "Elective" Exams

	70-222 Migrating from Microsoft Windows NT 4.0 to Microsoft Windows 2000	2010
+2	**70-223** Installing, Configuring, and Administering Microsoft Clustering Services by Using Microsoft Windows 2000 Advanced Server	2087
	70-224 Installing, Configuring, and Administering Microsoft Exchange Server 2000	1572
	70-228 Installing, Configuring, and Administering Microsoft SQL Server 2000 Enterprise Edition	2072

Index

INTERNATIONAL CONTACT INFORMATION

AUSTRALIA
McGraw-Hill Book Company Australia Pty. Ltd.
TEL +61-2-9417-9899
FAX +61-2-9417-5687
http://www.mcgraw-hill.com.au
books-it_sydney@mcgraw-hill.com

CANADA
McGraw-Hill Ryerson Ltd.
TEL +905-430-5000
FAX +905-430-5020
http://www.mcgrawhill.ca

GREECE, MIDDLE EAST,
NORTHERN AFRICA
McGraw-Hill Hellas
TEL +30-1-656-0990-3-4
FAX +30-1-654-5525

MEXICO (Also serving Latin America)
McGraw-Hill Interamericana Editores S.A. de C.V.
TEL +525-117-1583
FAX +525-117-1589
http://www.mcgraw-hill.com.mx
fernando_castellanos@mcgraw-hill.com

SINGAPORE (Serving Asia)
McGraw-Hill Book Company
TEL +65-863-1580
FAX +65-862-3354
http://www.mcgraw-hill.com.sg
mghasia@mcgraw-hill.com

SOUTH AFRICA
McGraw-Hill South Africa
TEL +27-11-622-7512
FAX +27-11-622-9045
robyn_swanepoel@mcgraw-hill.com

UNITED KINGDOM & EUROPE
(Excluding Southern Europe)
McGraw-Hill Education Europe
TEL +44-1-628-502500
FAX +44-1-628-770224
http://www.mcgraw-hill.co.uk
computing_neurope@mcgraw-hill.com

ALL OTHER INQUIRIES Contact:
Osborne/McGraw-Hill
TEL +1-510-549-6600
FAX +1-510-883-7600
http://www.osborne.com
omg_international@mcgraw-hill.com

ExamWeb is a leader in assessment technology. We use this technology to deliver customized online testing programs, corporate training, pre-packaged exam preparation courses, and licensed technology. ExamWeb has partnered with Osborne - McGraw-Hill to develop the CD contained in this book and its corresponding online exam simulators. Please read about our services below and contact us to see how we can help you with your own assessment needs.

www.examweb.com

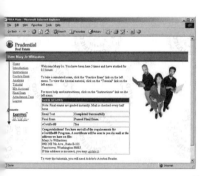

Corporate Assessment

ExamWeb can customize its course and testing engines to meet your training and assessment needs as a trainer. We can provide you with stand-alone assessments and courses or can easily integrate our assessment engines with your existing courses or learning management system. Features may include:

✓ Corporate-level access and reporting

✓ Multiple question types

✓ Detailed strength and weakness reports by key subject area and topic

✓ Performance comparisons amongst groups

Technology Licenses and Partnerships

Publishers, exam preparation companies and schools use ExamWeb technology to offer online testing or exam preparation branded in their own style and delivered via their websites. Improve your assessment offerings by using our technology!

Check www.examweb.com for an updated list of course offerings.

Coming soon:

CNA™ Passport / A+™ Passport / Server+™ Passport / Network+™ Passport / Java™ 2 Passport
MCSE Windows 2000™ Professional Passport / MCSE Windows 2000™ Server Passport
MCSE Windows 2000™ Directory Services Passport
MCSE Windows 2000™ Network Infrastructure Passport

For more infomation, please contact corpsales@examweb.com or call 949.566.9375